TAX Cafe®

Taxcafe.co.uk Tax Guides

Salary versus Dividends

& Other Tax Efficient Profit Extraction Strategies

By Carl Bayley BSc FCA

and

Nick Braun PhD

Important Legal Notices:

Published by:
Taxcafe UK Limited
2.4 West Bridge Mill
Kirkcaldy KY1 1TE

Email: team@taxcafe.co.uk

ISBN 978-1-917392-10-5

Twenty-seventh edition, September 2026

Disclaimer
Before reading or relying on the content of this tax guide please read the disclaimer.

Disclaimer

1. This guide is intended as **general guidance** only and does NOT constitute accountancy, tax, investment or other professional advice.

2. The authors and Taxcafe UK Limited make no representations or warranties with respect to the accuracy or completeness of this publication and cannot accept any responsibility or liability for any loss or risk, personal or otherwise, which may arise, directly or indirectly, from reliance on information contained in this publication.

3. Please note that tax legislation, the law and practices of Government and regulatory authorities (e.g. HM Revenue & Customs) are constantly changing. We therefore recommend that for accountancy, tax, investment or other professional advice, you consult a suitably qualified accountant, tax adviser, financial adviser, or other professional adviser.

4. Please also note that your personal circumstances may vary from the general examples provided in this guide and your professional adviser will be able to provide specific advice based on your personal circumstances.

5. This guide covers UK taxation only and any references to 'tax' or 'taxation', unless the contrary is expressly stated, refer to UK taxation only. Please note that references to the 'UK' do not include the Channel Islands or the Isle of Man. Foreign tax implications are beyond the scope of this guide.

6. All persons described in the examples in this guide are entirely fictional. Any similarities to actual persons, living or dead, or to fictional characters created by any other author, are entirely coincidental.

About the Authors & Taxcafe

Carl Bayley is the author of over twenty Taxcafe guides designed specifically for the layperson and the non-specialist. Carl's particular speciality is his ability to take the weird, complex, and inexplicable world of taxation and set it out in the kind of clear, straightforward language taxpayers themselves can understand. As he often says himself, "My job is to translate 'tax' into English."

In addition to being a recognised author, Carl has often spoken on taxation on radio and television, including the BBC's It's Your Money programme and the Jeremy Vine Show on Radio 2.

A chartered accountant by training, Carl is a past Chairman of the Tax Faculty of the Institute of Chartered Accountants in England and Wales and was a member of the Institute's governing Council between 2003 and 2023.

Nick Braun founded Taxcafe.co.uk in 1999, along with his partner, Aileen Smith. As the driving force behind the company, their aim is to provide affordable plain-English tax information for private individuals and investors, business owners, accountants and other advisers.

Since then Taxcafe has become one of the best-known tax publishers in the UK and has won several business awards.

Nick has been involved in the tax publishing world since 1989 as a writer, editor and publisher. He holds a doctorate in economics from the University of Glasgow, where he was awarded the prestigious William Glen Scholarship and later became a research fellow. Prior to that, he graduated with distinction from the University of South Africa, the country's oldest university, earning the highest results in economics in the university's history.

Contents

Introduction

This guide answers one of the most common questions asked by company owners: "What's the best way to take money out of my company if I want to pay less tax?"

In Part 1 we kick off with a plain English guide to how *companies* are taxed.

Corporation Tax rates increased on 1st April 2023. Calculating your company's tax bill also became more complicated. As a result, new tax planning opportunities have arisen.

In Part 1 we also explain how *company owners* are taxed. As a director/shareholder you can choose the best **mix** of salary and dividends. We examine the pros and cons of each type of income.

Company owners can also choose the most tax efficient **level** of income. We will see how, by smoothing your income or varying it significantly from year to year, you may be able to cut your tax bill considerably.

Part 1 also includes important information on forthcoming changes to the timing of tax payments for company owners: including how to mitigate the impact of these changes and avoid paying two years' worth of tax in the space of twelve months by taking action now.

Tax-Free Salaries & Dividends

In Part 2 we reveal how much tax-free salary and dividend income you can withdraw from your company this year. You'll discover how to calculate the 'optimal' tax-efficient salary and how couples in business together can receive £26,140 this year without paying any Income Tax.

In Part 3 we explain how much dividend income you can take taxed at just 10.75% and how to avoid paying tax at 35.75% (the new rates applying from 6th April 2026).

This part of the guide also contains important tax saving strategies for parents who want to avoid the Child Benefit Charge. This now kicks in when your income exceeds £60,000 (previously £50,000) but many company owners can avoid it completely or in part.

There is also important tax planning information for high income earners (those with income over £100,000) and for *really big* earners, who may actually benefit from reversing the strategy that usually benefits everyone else.

Income from Other Sources

In Part 4 we turn to company owners who have income from other sources (e.g. pensions, rental income, interest income, income from another business, and stock market dividends).

We explain why you may need to adjust your company salary or dividends to avoid the higher tax rates that kick in when your income reaches certain key thresholds (£50,270, £60,000, and £100,000).

We also examine some tax planning techniques that can be used to reduce or eliminate the tax payable on your income from other sources.

Company owners who are also landlords need to be aware of the restriction to tax relief on mortgage interest. Fortunately, company owners have more flexibility than other landlords when it comes to avoiding some of the worst effects of this additional tax charge.

Company owners can also enjoy much more tax-free interest than most other taxpayers (up to £6,000 per year).

Splitting Income with Family Members

Part 5 explains how company owners can gift shares in the company to their spouses, partners, or children and save over £10,000 in tax this year, with similar savings every year.

We also show how additional savings can be achieved by paying tax-free salaries to family members, including minor children.

There are, however, many traps to avoid when it comes to splitting income with family members and these are fully covered in this part of the guide. For example, we examine the danger of gifting shares that have fewer rights than ordinary shares and the danger of using dividend waivers to divert income to your spouse/partner.

Alternative Profit Extraction Strategies

Part 6 looks at alternative profit extraction strategies:

- **Directors' loans:** How they can be used to reduce or postpone tax.

- **Rent:** Why getting your company to pay you rent is more tax efficient than a dividend in many circumstances.

- **Interest:** How to receive up to £6,000 of tax-free interest from your company.

- **Charity:** Who should donate: you or the company?

- **Pension contributions:** Why they're better than dividends, who should make them (you or the company), plus a chapter on putting property into a pension.

- **Capital gains:** How to pay Capital Gains Tax (CGT) at a reduced rate when you sell or wind up your company.

In Part 7 we turn to some of the practical issues and dangers that may arise when extracting money from your company:

- How to avoid the minimum wage regulations
- How to make sure your salary is a tax-deductible expense
- Making sure your company has sufficient distributable profits to declare dividends
- How to declare dividends properly and avoid an HMRC challenge
- What you need to report to HMRC, and how you do it
- When HMRC might try to tax your dividends as earnings

Finally, in Part 8, we look at some other tax saving strategies for company owners, including how they may be able to reduce the amount of CGT payable when assets like rental properties are sold.

In this part we also explain how you may be able to completely avoid tax by emigrating.

Recent and Future Tax Changes

The rate of employer's National Insurance was increased from 13.8% to 15% on 6th April 2025. From the same date the salary threshold, where this tax becomes payable, fell from £9,100 to £5,000.

On the plus side, the employment allowance went up from £5,000 to £10,500 on 6th April 2025, which means the taxman will cover the first £10,500 of most companies' National Insurance bills.

Of course, these changes also affect the amount of employer's National Insurance payable on directors' own salaries, not just their employees.

A number of announcements that may potentially affect company owners were made in the November 2025 Budget. These are worth looking at but it's worth remembering that, since then, we have had a change of Prime Minister, a change of Chancellor, and what is, in effect, a change of Government (without a single vote cast outside Makerfield).

The November 2025 Budget Announcements

- **Income Tax threshold freeze** – the £12,570 personal allowance and £50,270 higher-rate threshold were to remain frozen until 5th April 2031, bringing the total length of the freeze to an astonishing ten years! As a result, we would expect company owners to pay higher-rate tax on more and more of their income.

- **Employer's National Insurance freeze** – The £5,000 salary threshold was also to remain frozen until 5th April 2031. This would mean more National Insurance will be payable (at 15%) even if salaries simply increase with inflation.

- **Dividend tax rates <u>from 6th April 2026</u>** – Increase of 2% from 8.75% to 10.75% (basic-rate taxpayers) and 33.75% to 35.75% (higher-rate taxpayers). The 39.35% paid by additional-rate taxpayers has been left unchanged. This, of course, has already happened.

- **Property income <u>from 6th April 2027</u>** – Increase of 2% from 20% to 22% (basic-rate taxpayers), 40% to 42% (higher-rate taxpayers), and 45% to 47% (additional-rate taxpayers). This will affect company owners who get their companies to pay them rental income (see Chapter 38).

- **Interest income <u>from 6th April 2027</u>** – A similar increase of 2% to 22%, 42%, and 47%. This could affect company owners who get their companies to pay them interest (see Chapter 39).

Using the Personal Allowance

At present, your personal allowance should be allocated to your income in whichever way gives you the lowest Income Tax bill. In the vast majority of cases, for a small company owner with both salary and dividend income, it will be most beneficial to allocate the personal allowance to salary income first.

There are some occasional exceptions to this (see Chapter 33) but, throughout the rest of this guide, we will operate on the basis that the personal allowance is allocated to salary first, other income such as rental income, interest, or pensions next, and dividends last: this is usually the best approach.

From 6th April 2027 onwards, it will no longer be possible to allocate your personal allowance in the most beneficial way. The personal allowance, basic rate band, and all other tax bands will be allocated in a strict order, as follows:

- Employment income, self-employment trading income, and pensions
- Property income
- Savings income
- Dividends

This change has, of course, been driven by the increases to Income Tax rates on property, savings, and dividend income.

Other tax changes were announced in the November 2025 Budget that will affect company owners and these are covered in the chapters that follow.

No tax changes of importance were announced in the March 2026 Spring Statement.

What About the New Guys?

Despite the effective change of Government, we would expect most of the November 2025 Budget announcements set out above to remain in place. Furthermore, the dividend tax increase is already with us.

However, Andy Burham has intimated that he will be looking into a possible increase in the Income Tax personal allowance (frozen since 2021). If this happens, it is likely to apply from 6th April 2027, and not affect the current year. Allowing for inflation totalling 31% over the relevant period would produce a figure of around £16,470.

Such a large increase seems unlikely, but something more like £15,000 is perhaps plausible.

That may sound like good news, but it would cost the Government at least £486 each for the vast majority of taxpayers in the UK with income of at least £15,000 (except most company owners, where the cost to the Government might be just £261 each).

There are over 39 million taxpayers in the UK, so we could be looking at a cost of around £19 billion. That will have to be paid for somehow, and we know where a Labour Government is likely to look to get their money back: higher and additional rate taxpayers, landlords, those with investment income and, of course, company owners!

So, while we can't tell you exactly what is going to happen, if there is an increase in the personal allowance, expect trouble.

Using This Guide

This tax guide deals primarily with the 2026/27 tax year, starting on 6th April 2026 and finishing on 5th April 2027. Unless expressly stated to the contrary, all references, examples, etc, are based on the tax rates, thresholds, and allowances applying for 2026/27.

There are some references to other tax years, for example when discussing the advantages and disadvantages of postponing income to a future tax year. In these cases, we will take account of what we know about the future tax regime. In this respect, we will follow the Budget 2025 announcements described in the Introduction and will not speculate further.

However, the tax rules that will apply in future years are not known with any degree of certainty: and the further one strays into the future, the more uncertain the position becomes!

The reader must bear in mind that tax laws (and HMRC's interpretation of them) are continually changing. In particular, it is important to bear in mind the points made in the Introduction regarding a potential increase in the Income Tax personal allowance in 2027/28, and the consequent impact on company owners.

Please note that, although small company owners are this book's main target audience, this is NOT supposed to be a do-it-yourself (DIY) tax planning guide. Our purpose in writing this guide is to explain in plain English how companies and company owners are taxed and provide some tax planning ideas that can be taken to an accountant or other professional adviser for further discussion.

We do not recommend 'going it alone' when it comes to this type of tax planning and there are several reasons for our cautious approach. Firstly, although the guide covers a fair amount of ground, it does not cover every possible scenario: that would be impossible without making the guide much longer and possibly much more difficult to digest.

In other words, in places we have had to sacrifice definitiveness in favour of making the guide a manageable and hopefully enjoyable read for the average small company owner.

Companies come in many different shapes and sizes, as do their owners, so it is possible the information contained in this guide will not be relevant to your circumstances.

In particular, please note this guide is aimed mainly at UK resident director/shareholders who own and work for UK resident companies.

Secondly, the main focus of this tax guide is *Income Tax* planning: helping company owners pay less tax on their salaries, dividends and other income. There are, however, other taxes that often have to be considered, including CGT and Inheritance Tax.

Steps that you take to reduce one type of tax can have an adverse impact on your liability to pay other taxes. While some mention is made of other taxes in this guide, we cannot guarantee that all interactions are covered.

Thirdly, there are potential risks involved when it comes to structuring your affairs to reduce the tax payable on salaries, dividends, and other payments made by your company.

While most of the tax planning ideas contained in this book are widely used by many accountants and other professional advisers, and have been for many years, this does not mean they have the blessing of HM Revenue & Customs!

There are some grey areas when it comes to this area of tax planning and some tax savings may not always be guaranteed. In other words, we cannot be certain that some of the tax planning ideas contained in this book will not be subject to some sort of attack from HMRC, even if only at some point in the future.

For example, in the chapters that follow, we will show that the most tax-efficient mix of income for most company owners is a small salary coupled with a larger dividend. While this is a well-established, reasonable form of tax planning which, if carried out correctly, is generally accepted, even if grudgingly, by HMRC, there are circumstances under which they might seek to tax dividends as earnings.

We'll look at this potential threat further in Chapter 51, but it's also worth pointing out that, *at present*, such attacks are rare and generally only occur where aggressive tax avoidance schemes are involved. For the vast majority of small company owners, the danger is remote and lies firmly in the future.

Fourthly, there are also *non-tax* factors that have to be considered when deciding how much money you withdraw from your company and in what form. In some instances, other considerations will outweigh any potential tax savings.

For all of these reasons, it is vital that you obtain professional advice before taking any action based on information contained in this guide. The authors and Taxcafe UK Ltd cannot accept any responsibility for any loss that may arise as a consequence of any action taken, or any decision to refrain from taking action, as a result of reading this guide

Corporation Tax (CT) Rates

Much of the planning and analysis in this guide is dependent on the company's CT rate. As we will see in Chapter 1, under the current CT regime, a company's overall tax rate could be anything between 19% and 25%.

However, it is generally a company's *marginal* CT rate that matters for the purposes of this guide, rather than its *overall* tax rate. A company's marginal CT rate will be either 19%, 26.5%, or 25%. It is these three rates we will use in our illustrations, examples, etc, throughout most of this guide.

Matching Up Company and Personal Tax Rates

It is *most likely* that a company owner who is a basic rate taxpayer will have a company paying CT at 19%, while higher or additional rate taxpayers will have companies paying CT at higher rates. We will generally follow these principles for our main examples throughout this guide.

However, we will also cater for the possibility that higher or additional rate taxpayers may have companies paying CT at only 19%, while basic rate taxpayers may have a company paying CT at a higher rate as, for various reasons, all these combinations are possible.

Optimal Salaries

An important concept, which you will see us refer to many times in this guide, is that of a director's 'optimal' salary. This is the level of salary that is most tax efficient overall, taking account of both the director's personal position, and the company's position; and varies under different scenarios, depending on a great many factors, as we will see. We will explain the concept of an 'optimal' salary further in Chapter 12 but, throughout the guide, we will also take account of other factors that may be more important than simply paying the most tax efficient salary.

Company Profits

The starting point for calculating a company's taxable profits is the profit shown by the company's accounts. However, there are many adjustments required to arrive at its taxable profit. For most companies, the most significant adjustments relate to fixed assets (buildings, vehicles, equipment, etc). Depreciation and other adjustments to the value of fixed assets shown in the company's accounts are disregarded for tax purposes and a system of reliefs known as capital allowances substituted instead. For details of adjustments that must be made to arrive at a company's taxable profit, see the Taxcafe guides *Putting it Through the Company*, or *Using a Property Company to Save Tax* for property companies.

The end result of the tax adjustments a company must make is that accounting profit and taxable profit can sometimes be quite different. Throughout this guide, unless stated to the contrary, when we refer to a company's profit, we mean its taxable profit, as this is what determines the effect of the profit extraction strategies we will be examining. Often, since we are looking at the best profit extraction method, we will mean the company's taxable profit *before* making any payments to the company's owner.

The company's accounting profits remain important though. As we will see in Chapter 49, a company can only pay dividends out of its distributable profits: and these, broadly speaking, are the cumulative total of its *accounting profits*, after tax, less dividends paid to date.

Hence, while, for the sake of illustration, we will usually take the simplistic approach that a company can pay out all its taxable profits remaining after payment of Corporation Tax as dividends, it is generally only its accounting profits after tax that can actually be paid out in practice.

Our approach is not unreasonable, however, since:

- For many companies, the tax adjustments they must make are simply timing differences and, over the company's lifetime, accounting profits and taxable profits will eventually total the same amount.
- Due to the current, generous capital allowances regime, taxable profits will often be less than accounting profits.
- In addition to current profits, dividends can also be paid out of retained accounting profits from earlier accounting periods.

So, it's a reasonable approach, but please do be aware of the restrictions on dividends covered in Chapter 49.

Scottish Taxpayers

The Scottish Parliament can set the Income Tax rates applying to most types of income received by Scottish taxpayers, but not interest or dividends.

The vast majority of the information contained in this guide is relevant to Scottish taxpayers. However, unless stated to the contrary, all examples, tables and calculations assume the individual concerned is not a Scottish taxpayer.

Despite this general assumption, there is a great deal of information in this guide specific to Scottish taxpayers, as we want to include them as much as we can without making the guide too complicated.

It's also worth pointing out that, where a director needs to be a basic rate taxpayer for a particular strategy to work (see Chapter 15, for example), a Scottish intermediate rate taxpayer can be included. To be a basic or intermediate rate taxpayer for 2026/27, a Scottish taxpayer needs taxable income excluding dividends, interest, and savings income, of no more than £43,662 *and* total taxable income of no more than £50,270.

Spouses and Civil Partners
Under UK tax law, all legally married spouses and registered civil partners are treated the same. Hence, when we refer to a 'spouse' in this guide, it includes a civil partner. For tax purposes, a spouse does not include a common-law partner or co-habitee. Where we are discussing a partner who may either be a legally married spouse or a common-law partner, we will use the term 'spouse/partner'.

Furnished Holiday Letting
Prior to the abolition of the furnished holiday letting tax regime in April 2025, these businesses were treated as trading businesses for the purpose of a number of key tax reliefs, including business asset disposal relief and holdover relief (as discussed in Chapters 35, 36, and 44). This is no longer the case: furnished holiday lets are now treated the same as other residential property letting for all tax purposes (except VAT and Council Tax).

For more information on these changes, see the Taxcafe guide *Furnished Holiday Lets: Big Tax Changes Ahead.*

Personal Service Companies
A personal service company is one where the majority of the profits are derived from services provided by the company owner personally (e.g. an IT consultant). Some of these companies may be subject to the notorious 'IR35' or other 'off payroll working' rules if the role the company owner performs for their clients is, in practical terms, really akin to an employee. These matters are beyond the scope of this guide. Seek professional advice if you think you may be affected.

Some Assumptions
Unless stated to the contrary, we will assume throughout this guide that directors and company owners are:

i) UK resident individuals
ii) Not subject to the 'off payroll working' rules (sometimes known as 'IR35': see above)
iii) Not subject to the Child Benefit Charge (we will look at this in Chapter 22 however)
iv) Not Scottish taxpayers (see above)
v) Not claiming the marriage allowance (see Chapter 5)
vi) Not subject to the minimum wage rules (see Chapter 46)

We will also generally assume, unless stated to the contrary, that directors are aged over 21 but under state pension age. Nonetheless, the position for older (over state pension age) and younger (under 21) directors is covered extensively in the guide where appropriate, and particularly in Chapter 16.

We will also assume, again unless stated to the contrary, that companies:

i) Have no associated companies
ii) Are UK resident
iii) Have a twelve-month accounting period
iv) Are not close investment holding companies

The relevance of these assumptions is explained in Chapters 1, 3, and 4.

Abbreviations
We don't like jargon at Taxcafe, so we try to avoid using too may abbreviations. To save a little space, we'll allow ourselves a few obvious ones though, including CT (Corporation Tax), National Insurance (NI), and CGT (Capital Gains Tax).

Part 1

How Companies & Company Owners Are Taxed

Chapter 1

How Companies Are Taxed

Companies pay Corporation Tax (CT) on their income and capital gains. From 1st April 2023, there are two official tax rates:

- Small profits rate 19%
- Main rate 25%

The practical effect is that companies generally pay tax as follows:

- **Profits £50,000 or less** – Company pays 19% tax on all its profits

- **Profits between £50,000 and £250,000** – Company pays 19% tax on the first £50,000 and 26.5% on the remainder

- **Profits greater than £250,000** – Company pays 25% tax on all its profits

In the November 2025 Budget, former Chancellor Rachel Reeves stated, *"At this Budget, consistent with the commitments in our corporate tax roadmap, I will retain our competitive Corporation Tax rate, the lowest in the G7 and retain our generous full expensing offer for business investment."* If new Chancellor, John Healey also honours the commitments in Labour's 2024 'corporate tax roadmap', the current Corporation Tax rates should apply until at least April 2029. But we'll see.

Under the current regime, a company with profits of £100,000 pays 19% on the first £50,000, and 26.5% on the final £50,000. The total tax bill is £22,750, which means the company has an overall tax rate of 22.75% (£22,750/£100,000).

A company with profits of £150,000 pays 19% on the first £50,000 and 26.5% on the remaining £100,000. The total tax bill is £36,000, which means the company has an overall tax rate of 24% (£36,000/£150,000).

A company with profits of £20,000 (i.e. less than £50,000) will simply pay £3,800 (19%). A company with profits of £300,000 (i.e. more than £250,000) will simply pay £75,000 (25%).

TABLE 1
Overall Corporation Tax Rates

Profits	Corporation Tax	Corporation Tax Rate
£50,000	£9,500	19.00%
£60,000	£12,150	20.25%
£70,000	£14,800	21.14%
£80,000	£17,450	21.81%
£90,000	£20,100	22.33%
£100,000	£22,750	22.75%
£110,000	£25,400	23.09%
£120,000	£28,050	23.38%
£130,000	£30,700	23.62%
£140,000	£33,350	23.82%
£150,000	£36,000	24.00%
£160,000	£38,650	24.16%
£170,000	£41,300	24.29%
£180,000	£43,950	24.42%
£190,000	£46,600	24.53%
£200,000	£49,250	24.63%
£210,000	£51,900	24.71%
£220,000	£54,550	24.80%
£230,000	£57,200	24.87%
£240,000	£59,850	24.94%
£250,000	£62,500	25.00%

Non-Resident Companies

Only UK resident companies are able to benefit from the 19% small profits rate. A non-resident company that earns rental income from UK properties, for example, has to pay 25% CT on all its UK rental profits.

Accounting Periods vs Financial Years

A company's own tax year (also known as its accounting period) can end on any date, for example 31st December, 31st March, etc.

Corporation Tax, on the other hand, is calculated according to financial years. Financial years run from 1st April to 31st March. The 2026 financial year is the year starting on 1st April 2026 and ending on 31st March 2027.

This doesn't matter most of the time, but does when CT rates change. For example, on 1st April 2023, the main rate of CT increased from 19% to 25%.

A company with profits of more than £250,000 whose accounting period ran from 1st January 2023 to 31st December 2023 was liable for CT as follows:

- 3 months to 31st March 2023 19%
- 9 months to 31st December 2023 25%

The company would have paid 19% CT on roughly one quarter of its profits (3/12) and 25% tax on roughly three quarters of its profits (9/12). (It doesn't generally matter at what point during the year the profits are actually made.)

This means the company's overall CT rate that year was 23.5%. (In practice, CT is calculated using days not months and this will result in a small difference.)

Because the CT increase is now in full force, the above calculations are no longer necessary for current accounting periods. For example, the above company will simply pay 25% CT on all its profits for the accounting period running from 1st January 2026 to 31st December 2026.

However, if CT rates change again in the future, these split-year calculations will become relevant once more.

Marginal Tax Rate Planning

The CT increase in 2023 means many companies are now paying more tax on their profits. The good news is many companies are also enjoying more CT relief on their spending.

Before the increase, companies enjoyed 19% CT relief no matter how much profit they made or when they spent their money. A company incurring an additional £1,000 of tax-deductible spending would reduce its profits by £1,000, saving it £190.

The CT increase means the amount of tax relief a company enjoys now depends on its profits.

The position is as follows:

- A company with profits of £50,000 or less has a marginal tax rate of 19% and enjoys 19% tax relief on its spending.
- A company with profits of between £50,000 and £250,000 has a marginal tax rate of 26.5% and enjoys 26.5% tax relief on its spending. (However, if the company's spending reduces its profits below £50,000, it will start to receive just 19% tax relief on any additional spending.)
- A company with profits of more than £250,000 has a marginal tax rate of 25% and enjoys 25% tax relief on its spending. (However, if the company's spending reduces its profits below £250,000, it will start to receive 26.5% tax relief on any additional spending.)

In Table 1 we listed the *overall* tax rates companies face. For example, a company that makes a profit of £100,000 has an overall tax rate of 22.75%.

However, this overall rate is NOT used for most tax planning purposes, for example calculating the amount of tax a company will save if it spends some more money. Instead, it is the company's marginal tax rate.

This makes sense when you consider a simple example. A company that anticipates making a profit of £100,000 and incurs an additional £10,000 of tax-deductible expenditure will reduce its taxable profits by £10,000. This will reduce its tax bill by £2,650 (26.5%). The company's overall tax rate of 22.75% does not tell us how much tax the company will save.

The Marginal Tax Rate Bands

Companies effectively have three marginal tax rate bands:

Profits up to £50,000	19%
Profits between £50,000 and £250,000	26.5%
Profits over £250,000	25%

These bands apply in the majority of cases, but can be affected by factors such as whether the company has any associated companies (see Chapter 3). They are an important concept in tax planning for companies, so watch out for references to the company's 'marginal tax rate band' later in this guide: it is these bands we are referring to.

(A director also has his or her own marginal tax rate band for Income Tax purposes. We'll get onto those later but, for now, it's important to emphasise that the ***director's*** marginal rate band and the ***company's*** marginal rate band are different things: although both of them are critically important.)

Should My Company Postpone or Accelerate Spending?

Where a company's profit level changes from one year to the next, it may be able to save more CT by postponing or accelerating some of its spending. For example, a company with profits not exceeding £50,000 in the current year will be taxed at 19% but, if it expects to make profits between £50,000 and £250,000 next year, its marginal tax rate will increase to 26.5%.

A company expecting this sort of increase in its marginal tax rate would enjoy an additional 7.5 percentage points of tax relief on spending postponed, saving £750 for every £10,000 postponed.

In other cases, where the company expects its marginal tax rate to *decrease* next year, accelerating expenditure could produce similar savings.

But not all types of expenditure are suitable to be postponed or accelerated. Furthermore, in many cases, the timing of the tax relief is not dependent on the date the money is spent. For more information on this type of planning, which can yield almost 40% greater tax savings on deductible expenditure, see the Taxcafe guide *Putting it Through the Company*. Naturally, the commercial implications of postponing or accelerating business expenditure always need to be considered.

As far as most of the issues covered in this guide are concerned, it is generally the *director's* marginal tax rate that is far more important as this can vary by a great deal more.

Nonetheless, there are exceptions where the company's marginal tax rate alone is the key factor in determining the optimal time for it to spend money: pension contributions on the director's behalf are a prime example (see Chapter 41).

Tax Relief on Salaries etc

If your company pays you a salary, rent, interest, or makes pension contributions on your behalf, these are generally tax-deductible expenses for the company. As we shall see in the chapters that follow, when deciding how much salary or other income to pay yourself, the amount of CT relief your company receives on these payments is an important factor.

If your company's marginal CT rate doesn't change, the amount of tax relief it gets is clear.

Assuming the payment does not itself alter the company's marginal CT rate, it will provide relief at 19%, 26.5%, or 25%.

In the vast majority of cases, it's as simple as that, and you can safely ignore the rest of this chapter.

In fact, we're going to ignore it for the majority of the guide ourselves and, unless stated to the contrary, will assume the company obtains CT relief at 19%, 26.5%, or 25% on all its tax-deductible expenses, including payments made to directors.

Example: *Angela takes a salary of £12,570 out of her company, which makes an annual profit of around £80,000 and thus has a marginal CT rate of 26.5%. Her salary produces a CT saving of £3,331 (£12,570 x 26.5%).*

One quirk to watch out for though, is that the expense itself can sometimes lead to the company's profits dropping into a different marginal tax rate band.

Example: *Belinda also takes a salary of £12,570 out of her company, but its annual profit before paying her salary is just £60,000. The CT saving produced by Belinda's salary is thus:*

£10,000 @ 26.5%	*£2,650*
£2,570 @ 19%	*£488*
Total	*£3,138*

For the sake of illustration, we've ignored employer's National Insurance in these simple examples, but we will, of course look at that later in the guide, as well as examining whether £12,570 was the best salary for these directors to take.

Changing Marginal Corporation Tax Rates

Things can get a little more complicated when a company's marginal CT rate changes during the course of the *Income Tax* year.

Where the company's marginal CT rate changes from one accounting period to the next, the exact amount of tax relief it will enjoy in respect of payments made during the *Income Tax* year will depend on its accounting date and profit level. In some cases, it may also depend on whether the payments are made monthly, annually, or as a 'one off', and on how they are recognised in the company's accounts.

Companies must operate the accruals basis of accounting, which means any periodic cost must be spread over the period to which it relates.

For example, a company with a 31st December accounting date may make a single annual rental payment of £20,000 to its owner/director, who owns the company's trading premises personally. Whenever the payment is made, the director will have taxable rental income of £20,000 for 2026/27 (assuming, for the time being, that the director is not using the cash basis in their personal capacity as a landlord).

But the payment that suffers Income Tax in the director's hands in 2026/27 will need to be recognised on a time apportionment basis in the company's accounts. Hence £15,000 (9/12ths) of the rent will fall into the company's accounting period ending 31st December 2026 and attract CT relief at its marginal rate for that year; and £5,000 (3/12ths) will fall into the accounting period ending 31st December 2027 and attract CT relief at its marginal rate for that year.

Let's say the company's profits turn out to be £200,000 for 2026 and £300,000 for 2027. Hence, it will have a marginal CT rate of 26.5% for the year ending 31st December 2026, and 25% for the year ending 31st December 2027. The CT relief for the rent on which the director pays Income Tax in 2026/27 will therefore be:

£15,000 @ 26.5%	£3,975
£5,000 @ 25%	£1,250
Total	£5,225

The overall effective rate of relief is thus 26.125%.

The director will pay Income Tax on £20,000 of rental income in 2026/27; the company will enjoy CT relief of £5,225.

Where something is a periodic cost, it's important to appreciate that, for CT purposes, it is generally spread over the period to which it relates, regardless of when it is actually paid. Hence, the rent payment above would attract the same amount of CT relief, and in the same accounting periods, even if it was not paid until after 5th April 2027.

There are some exceptions to this rule, however. Companies cannot claim CT relief on:

- Salaries or bonuses that are still unpaid nine months after the end of the accounting period
- Interest charged by the company's owner that is still unpaid twelve months after the end of the accounting period

In these cases, relief can only be claimed when payment is actually made: credits to the director's loan account do count as payment though.

On the other side of the equation, directors are generally only taxed on payments from their company when they receive them (again, a credit to the director's loan account counts as receipt).

This applies to salary, bonuses, and interest paid to the director (as well as dividends, although these do not attract CT relief). The only potential exception is rent, where the position depends on whether the director is taxed on their property income under the cash basis, or under traditional accruals basis accounting.

So, where does all this leave us with the effective rate of Corporation Tax relief for payments made to, or on behalf of, directors in 2026/27?

Generally, if something is paid monthly, it will be a periodic cost. Some things are always a periodic cost, even if paid annually.

Rent and interest are always periodic costs and thus will generally attract CT relief at the rates for the relevant accounting period or periods, as in our example above.

Salaries and pension contributions paid monthly will usually also be periodic costs, attracting CT relief at the rates for the relevant accounting period or periods.

Salaries, bonuses, and pension contributions paid annually or as a one-off may not be periodic costs, but this depends on the circumstances.

The position for salaries is discussed further below; pension contributions are discussed in Chapter 41.

Where payments are NOT periodic costs, they will generally attract CT relief at the company's marginal rate for the accounting period in which they are paid: although, as we shall see later, there are some important exceptions to this.

Salaries in the Current 2026/27 Tax Year

The current tax year for *individuals* runs from 6th April 2026 to 5th April 2027. For most companies, whose marginal tax rate does not change, it will be simple to calculate the CT relief on salaries and other regular payments made to directors: generally, 19%, 26.5%, or 25%. Where the company's marginal CT rate changes during the 2026/27 Income Tax year, the calculation is more complex.

Example: *Average Company Ltd has an accounting period that runs from January to December. It makes monthly salary payments to the directors.*

For the accounting period ending 31st December 2026, the company makes a profit of £50,000 and hence will enjoy CT relief at just 19% on the salary payments it makes.

For the accounting period ending 31st December 2027, the company makes a profit of £100,000, and hence will enjoy 26.5% CT relief on any additional salary payments.

The 2026/27 tax year falls into both of these accounting periods, so the company will enjoy the following tax relief on its salary payments:

April to December 2026	*9/12 x 19%*	*14.250%*
January to March 2027	*3/12 x 26.5%*	*6.625%*
Total Corporation Tax relief		*20.875%*

The company will enjoy a total of 20.875% CT relief on salary payments made during the current 2026/27 tax year.

Note this assumes the payment of the salary does not itself alter the company's marginal CT rate for either accounting period.

The outcome may be different where the director's salary is paid in a single annual lump sum, rather than monthly.

Example: *Annpay Ltd has an accounting period that runs from January to December. In the year ending 31st December 2026, it makes a profit of just £50,000, but in the year ending 31st December 2027 profits increase to £100,000. The director, Anne, takes her salary in a single lump sum in March each year. The salary she takes in March 2027 is accounted for as an expense in the accounts for the year ending 31st December 2027 and will thus provide CT relief at 26.5%.*

If we compare the results in the last two examples, we can see that a single lump sum payment (as for Annpay Ltd) may produce a different overall rate of tax relief to regular monthly payments:

Average Company Ltd (monthly pay):	Relief at 20.875% on average
Annpay Ltd (lump sum):	Relief at 26.5%

In both cases, we are talking about salary falling into the same *Income Tax* year: 2026/27. However, such single annual lump sum payments are not always accounted for as an expense of the company accounting period in which they are paid.

It would have been equally acceptable for Annpay Ltd to have accrued part of the cost of the salary paid to Anne in March 2027 as an expense of its accounting period ending 31st December 2026, with the remainder treated as an expense of the accounting period ending 31st December 2027. The split would be done on a time apportionment basis, with the end result being that the CT relief for Anne's salary would be the same as for the monthly payments made by Average Company Ltd.

The proper accounting treatment of a lump sum payment like this is really a question of whether Anne's lump sum salary paid in March 2027 is seen as a reward for her efforts as company director over the period from April 2026 to March 2027, or as a bonus paid in recognition of her continuing service to the company.

In many cases, the decision how to treat the director's annual lump sum salary in the accounts will have been made some years ago. If so, it could be difficult to argue for a different treatment this year just because the company's marginal CT rate is changing. There is, however, a way to control the timing of relief for a director's salary (when paid as a lump sum), which may be beneficial where the company's marginal CT rate fluctuates from one accounting period to the next. We'll look at this useful technique in Chapter 2.

Chapter 2

Getting the Best Tax Relief for a Director's Salary or Bonus

For tax purposes, a director's bonus is effectively the same as a lump sum salary payment. For the purposes of the technique we are going to cover in this chapter, it is better to refer to it as a bonus, however.

It is possible to secure CT relief for a director's bonus in an accounting period that has already ended before the director is paid (or deemed to be paid: see Chapter 5).

The first step is to hold a directors' board meeting before the end of the old accounting period and minute the fact the directors have agreed to pay themselves a bonus in respect of their performance during that accounting period. The amount is not specified at this time (as we will see in Chapter 5, this could trigger an immediate Income Tax liability, which the company would have to put through the payroll and pay via the PAYE system).

While no Income Tax liability or payroll reporting obligation under PAYE has been created yet, the company now has a commitment to pay the bonus for that accounting period. As long as the director is paid (or deemed to be paid: see Chapter 5) within nine months after the accounting date, the company can accrue the cost in its accounts and secure CT relief in the earlier period.

Let's say, for example, a director's optimal salary (or bonus) for 2026/27 is £12,570 and they plan to take this as a single lump sum in March 2027. The company has a 31st December accounting date and usually makes profits somewhere between £45,000 and £75,000 before taking account of the director's salary.

Once the company's profits for the year ending 31st December 2026 are known, it can decide how much bonus to pay. In the scenarios that follow, 'profit' means the company's taxable profit before taking account of the director's bonus or salary (for 2026/27). We'll also ignore employer's National Insurance for the sake of illustration.

Scenario 1: The company's profit for the year ending 31st December 2026 turns out to be £50,000 or less. The company pays a bonus of £1 to honour its commitment in respect of that accounting period.

A further £12,569 can then be paid, as a separate, routine lump sum salary payment, later (but by 5th April 2027) and this will obtain CT relief in the year ending 31st December 2027, possibly at 26.5%.

Scenario 2: The company's profit for the year ending 31st December 2026 is between £50,001 and £62,569. The company pays a bonus equal to the amount of profit in excess of £50,000, obtaining CT relief at 26.5% on this amount. A further sum to bring the director's total salary and bonus (combined) for 2026/27 to £12,570 can then be paid as a separate routine lump sum salary payment later (but by 5th April 2027), which will obtain CT relief in the year ending 31st December 2027, possibly also at 26.5%.

Scenario 3: The company's profit for the year ending 31st December 2026 is £62,570 or more. The company pays a bonus of £12,570 and obtains CT relief at 26.5%.

Again, all these actions should be minuted as part of a directors' board meeting: this technique requires formality to succeed!

Under scenarios 1 and 2 the company could instead choose to go ahead and pay the full bonus of £12,570. This would mean some or all of the bonus only attracts CT relief at 19% but, if the company is not confident of making profits in excess of £50,000 in the year ending 31st December 2027, it may be better to get CT relief in the earlier period as this provides a cashflow benefit.

Under scenario 3, there may be instances where a salary of more than £12,570 becomes optimal for the director (we'll see these later in the guide). This technique can again be used to pay the optimal salary by way of a bonus. The technique can also be used to fix the director's salary at the optimal level in other, more complex scenarios, such as when following the large salary method covered in Chapter 26.

Salary versus Bonus

Many directors prefer the simplicity and certainty of a regular monthly salary. However, when it comes to maximising CT relief, it will often be better to take an annual lump sum as a bonus. But it's up to you!

Chapter 3

Multiple Companies

Company owners often think about setting up a second company, to keep a new venture separate from an existing business. Often there are sound commercial reasons for using more than one company, including to:

- Reduce risk (limit liability)
- Involve different shareholders
- Enable a stand-alone sale of each business
- Make it easier to borrow money

Using more than one company allows you to reduce your risk: if one business goes bankrupt, the other venture housed in a separate company should be protected because each company has limited liability status.

Using more than one company is also ideal when you want each business to have different shareholders. It's not uncommon for business owners to engage in different projects with different people.

Using separate companies may also make it easier to exit each business. For example, someone who owns an ecommerce business and a restaurant chain may wish to keep them in separate companies to make it easier to sell each business to a different buyer in the future.

When it comes to borrowing money, it's not uncommon for property investors to put their properties in a separate, stand-alone company and lenders often insist on this. Mortgage lenders tend not to like companies that have 'trading' activities, which are perceived as being more risky than property investment.

Saving Tax

Using separate companies may also be attractive when it comes to saving CGT and Inheritance Tax: in particular when one business is a trading business and the other is not. Companies that own too many non-trading assets, like rental property, can lose important tax reliefs, including business asset disposal relief, holdover relief, and business property relief.

For example, someone who owns a software company and a property rental business may wish to keep them in separate companies so that the trading business (the software company) is not 'contaminated' by the non-trading business (the property rental business).

Conversely, under certain circumstances, keeping all your assets in one company can actually save Inheritance Tax (see the Taxcafe guide *How to Save Inheritance Tax* for more information).

Using separate companies has drawbacks too. For example, if you initially expect losses from a new trading activity, those losses can usually be set off against the profits from an existing activity, if both businesses are in the same company. This is generally not possible if the businesses are in separate companies (unless you form a group: see the Taxcafe guide *Putting it Through the Company* for details).

Following the 2023 increase in CT rates, some people may also be asking whether they can benefit from more than one company each enjoying up to £50,000 of profit taxed at just 19%. Sadly, the answer is generally 'no' if the companies are controlled by the same people.

Associated Company Rules

To prevent people artificially spreading their business activities across multiple companies, the £50,000 lower limit and £250,000 upper limit are divided up if there are any 'associated companies'.

A company is associated with another company if:

- One company controls the other company
- Both are under the control of the same person or persons

For example, if you own all the shares in two companies, these companies will be associated. Each company will start paying CT at 26.5% when its profits exceed £25,000 (i.e. £50,000/2). Each company will pay 25% tax on all its profits if its profits are greater than £125,000 (£250,000/2).

If there are three associated companies, each company will start paying CT at 26.5% when its profits exceed £16,667 (£50,000/3)... and so on.

Example: *Jamie owns Company 1, which has annual profits of £100,000. He then decides to start a second business and is trying to decide whether to house it in Company 1 or set up Company 2. Let's say the new business makes a profit of £30,000. If he keeps it in Company 1, the additional profit will be taxed at 26.5% producing a total tax bill of £30,700.*

If Jamie decides to house the new business in Company 2, the two companies will be associated (if we assume he controls them both). The companies will pay CT as follows:

Company 1: £25,000 x 19% + £75,000 x 26.5% = £24,625
Company 2: £25,000 x 19% +   £5,000 x 26.5% = £6,075
Combined tax bill: £30,700

The total CT bill will be the same whether Jamie uses one company or two. Jamie will still benefit from having £50,000 of profits taxed at 19% (£25,000 in each company).

However, if Company 2 has profits of less than £25,000, Jamie will effectively be penalised for running two companies. For example, if Company 2 breaks even (i.e. has a profit of exactly £0) he will pay £1,875 more tax with two companies. This is because Company 1 will have just £25,000 taxed at 19%, instead of £50,000.

For further details on the associated company rules, including situations where company shareholdings owned by your spouse, another close family member, or a business partner, may have to be counted when applying these rules, see the Taxcafe guide *Putting It Through the Company*.

Corporation Tax Quarterly Instalments

The associated company rules will also be relevant in deciding whether a company has to pay CT in quarterly instalments. Instalments are generally payable by companies whose profits exceed £1.5 million but this amount will be divided up if there are any associated companies. Whereas most companies only have to pay CT nine months after the end of their accounting period, companies subject to instalments have to start paying tax half way through their accounting period.

Chapter 4

Investment Companies

In tax jargon, a 'trading' company is one involved in, for want of a better word, 'regular' business activities, e.g. a company that sells goods online, a catering company, or a firm of garden landscapers.

Common types of *non-trading* company include those that hold substantial investments in property or financial securities, or earn substantial royalty income.

Corporation Tax

Before 1st April 2023, companies engaged mainly in non-trading activities paid CT at the same 19% rate as most other companies.

However, some of these companies now have to pay CT at the main rate of 25% on all their profits. This is because a company classed as a close investment holding company (CIC) cannot benefit from the small profits rate. It has to pay CT at the main rate on all its profits.

For example, a company that is set up to hold stock market investments will pay CT at 25%, even if it only makes a small amount of profit. (Having said that, companies do not pay CT on dividend income: but they do on capital gains or other forms of investment income.)

Fortunately, companies that mainly derive their profits from renting property to unconnected third parties (i.e. not to family members, etc) are excluded from the CIC provisions. Hence, the vast majority of property investment companies will enjoy the 19% small profits rate where appropriate.

Capital Gains Tax

If a company has too many non-trading activities (including most property investment and property letting) it may lose its trading status for CGT purposes.

This will result in the loss of two important CGT reliefs:

- Business asset disposal relief
- Holdover relief

Business asset disposal relief allows you to pay CGT at a reduced rate when you sell your company or wind it up (see Chapter 44).

Holdover relief allows you to give shares in the business to your children, common-law unmarried partner, or other individuals and postpone CGT. (You don't usually need holdover relief to transfer shares to your spouse because such transfers are generally exempt.)

Clearly, if the company's only business is property investment or property letting (or any other form of investment activity) then it will not be classed as a trading company and the relevant CGT reliefs will not be available.

Where a company has both trading and non-trading activities, it will only lose its trading status for CGT purposes if its non-trading activities are 'substantial'. HMRC generally accepts the non-trading activities are not substantial where neither non-trading income nor non-trading assets exceed 20% of the totals for the company as a whole. However, this test is only a yardstick and is not conclusive. In a recent tax case, it was held that non-trading activities would only be regarded as substantial where they were of material or real importance in the context of the company's activities as a whole.

Nonetheless, to avoid any argument over the issue, it is wise to keep both non-trading income and non-trading assets below 20% to safely preserve the company's trading status wherever possible.

Inheritance Tax

Shares in trading companies generally qualify for business property relief, which means they can enjoy special Inheritance Tax treatment. However, if the company holds investments (including rental property) this could result in the loss of business property relief. The qualification criteria are more generous than for CGT purposes and a company generally only loses its trading status for Inheritance Tax purposes if it is 'wholly or mainly' involved in investment related activities. Significant changes to business property relief were made in April 2026: for more information, see the Taxcafe guide *How to Save Inheritance Tax.*

Chapter 5

How Directors Are Taxed: Employment Income

When HMRC and tax professionals talk about 'employment income', they are referring to salaries and bonuses.

Salaries and bonuses are subject to Income Tax and National Insurance (NI). They are also generally a tax-deductible expense for the company.

Income Tax

For the 2026/27 tax year, starting on 6th April 2026, most individuals pay Income Tax as follows on their salaries:

• 0%	on the first	£12,570	Personal allowance
• 20%	on the next	£37,700	Basic rate band
• 40%	above	£50,270	Higher rate threshold

If you earn more than £50,270, you are a higher rate taxpayer; if you earn less, you are a basic rate taxpayer.

The number £50,270 is important to remember because it will be mentioned repeatedly in the chapters that follow.

Transferable Personal Allowance

It is possible to transfer 10% of your personal allowance to your spouse or civil partner (£1,260 during the current tax year). Only basic rate taxpayers can benefit from this tax break, known as the 'marriage allowance', so the maximum potential tax saving is currently £252 (£1,260 x 20%).

Unmarried couples are excluded: this was the rather feeble attempt by David Cameron to use the tax system to reward marriage. Married couples can only benefit from the maximum potential saving of £252 if:

- One person earns less than £11,310 (not including savings interest of up to £6,000 or dividends of up to £500) and is therefore wasting at least £1,260 of their personal allowance,
- The other person earns no more than £50,270 (£43,662 in Scotland), but at least £13,830, and
- Both individuals were born after 5th April 1935.

You have to register to use it at: www.gov.uk/marriageallowance

Potential winners are married couples where one person does not work (e.g. full-time parents) or only has a part-time job.

Example: *During the current tax year, Bill earns a salary of £30,000 and his wife Daphne earns £6,000 working part time. Daphne has £6,570 of unused personal allowance. She can transfer £1,260 of this to Bill, which means Bill no longer has to pay tax on £1,260 of his income. This will save him £252 in tax (£1,260 x 20%).*

The saving is, in fact, given to the transferee by way of a £252 non-refundable tax credit. And, provided the couple qualify, it's always £252 (unless the transferee is a Scottish taxpayer, when it may be up to £265).

This means married couples running a company together can sometimes benefit, even if they both have income in excess of the personal allowance (but they must both be basic rate taxpayers).

Example: *Claire and Debbie are a married couple running a company together. They have no other income from outside the company. In 2026/27, they each take a salary of £5,000 and dividends of £20,000.*

Claire transfers £1,260 of her personal allowance to Debbie. This means Claire suffers an additional £135 in Income Tax on her dividend income (£1,260 x 10.75%). Debbie, however, gets a tax credit of £252 meaning that, overall, the couple are £117 better off.

It's a nice little tax saving under the right circumstances. However, both of the couple have to be basic rate taxpayers and this, in turn, will usually mean salaries of £12,570 should be taken and not £5,000 (as we will see later).

Dropping one salary to £11,310 might enable the £117 Income Tax saving to be achieved, but this means forgoing CT relief on £1,260. If the company's CT rate is only 19% and dropping the salary leads to an employer's NI saving it might, just about, be worthwhile. But with a maximum overall net saving of just £30, it's not really worth the effort.

So, it's an interesting quirk, but I think we'll ignore it for the rest of the guide.

Income over £100,000
When your taxable income exceeds £100,000, your personal allowance is gradually withdrawn.

For every additional £1 you earn, 50p is taken away. When your income reaches £125,140, your personal allowance will have completely disappeared. This means individuals with salary income between £100,000 and £125,140 face a marginal Income Tax rate of 60%.

Example: *Caroline, a company director, has received salary income of £100,000 so far during the current tax year. If she receives an extra £100 of salary, she will pay an extra £40 of Income Tax. She will also lose £50 of her Income Tax personal allowance, so £50 of previously tax-free salary will be taxed at 40%, adding £20 to her tax bill. All in all, she pays £60 tax on her extra £100 of salary, so her marginal Income Tax rate is 60%.*

Income above £125,140
Once your taxable income exceeds £125,140, you pay 45% Income Tax on any extra employment income. This is known as the additional rate of tax. The threshold was previously £150,000, but was reduced to £125,140 for 2023/24 and subsequent years, aligning it with the point where your personal allowance is completely withdrawn.

National Insurance

In recent times, the main rate of Class 1 NI paid by directors and other employees has been reduced from 12% to 8%. NI is currently payable as follows on employment income:

- 0% on the first £12,570 Primary threshold
- 8% on the next £37,700
- 2% above £50,270 Upper earnings limit

The way NI is calculated is different if you're a company director.

For regular salaried employees paid monthly, NI is calculated using monthly thresholds. So, although the thresholds for the whole year are £12,570 and £50,270, it is the monthly thresholds of £1,048 and £4,189 that are used to calculate how much NI is payable in any specific month.

If a regular salaried employee received a salary payment of £12,570 at the start of the tax year in April, they would pay 0% on the first £1,048, 8% on the amount between £1,048 and £4,189 and 2% on the amount over £4,189: £419 in total.

By contrast, company directors' NI is calculated on a *cumulative annual basis*. Thus, a director who receives a salary payment of £12,570 at the start of the tax year in April will pay no NI at all because his or her total pay for the year will not yet exceed the £12,570 primary threshold.

If the director receives any additional salary payments in the months that follow, they will pay 8% NI on the whole amount, up to an additional £37,700: after that, they will pay 2%.

As we can see, these thresholds and bands are the same as those for Income Tax: perhaps one of the few pieces of genuine tax simplification the Government has ever managed to achieve.

However, for many directors, things are not as simple as they may seem, as the NI thresholds apply purely to their salary, whereas the Income Tax thresholds apply to ***all*** their income. For example, a director who also has rental income of £5,000, can receive a salary of £12,570 free from employee's NI, but only £7,570 free from Income Tax.

Combined Tax Rates

The combined marginal rates of Income Tax and NI applying to director's salaries in 2026/27 are as follows:

Up to £12,570	0%
£12,570 to £50,270	28%
£50,270 to £100,000	42%
£100,000 to £125,140	62%
Over £125,140	47%

The Tax Threshold Freeze

In the November 2025 Budget, it was announced that the above thresholds would be frozen until the end of the 2030/31 tax year on 5th April 2031. As explained in the Introduction, however, there now appears to be a possibility that the personal allowance may be increased from next year, 2027/28.

Nonetheless, we would not expect any increases in the higher-rate tax threshold, or the £100,000 threshold for withdrawal of the personal allowance. What will happen to the additional rate tax threshold is anybody's guess. Whether an increase in the personal allowance also means an increase to the NI primary threshold is also unclear.

In summary, regardless of any potential increase in the personal allowance, the other threshold freezes are likely to remain, and will mean that many people will see more and more of their income taxed at a higher rate, even if it only increases with inflation.

Employer's National Insurance

Most employees don't lose sleep over their employer's NI bill. However, for company owners this extra tax is an important consideration.

From 6th April 2025 for salaries that exceed the 'secondary threshold' of £5,000, the rate of employer's NI is 15%. The threshold used to be £9,100 and the rate was 13.8%.

Employer's NI is a tax-deductible expense. So, if a company pays £100 of NI, this will reduce its taxable profits by £100, saving the company between £19 and £26.50 in CT. Thus, the overall net cost is actually somewhere between £73.50 and £81.

There is no employer's NI on salaries of up to £50,270 paid to under 21s, or apprentices under 25. The exemption is not lost if the employee earns more than £50,270: employer's NI is then simply payable on the excess.

There is also an NI holiday for employers taking on military veterans. The holiday is for the employee's first year of civilian employment. The exemption again applies to salary up to the higher rate threshold of £50,270. This exemption has been extended until 5th April 2028.

The Employment Allowance

Most businesses qualify for the employment allowance, which has risen from £5,000 to £10,500 from 6th April 2025.

Previously the allowance was not available to employers whose NI bill was £100,000 or more in the previous tax year. This restriction only affected fairly big companies and, in any event, has been abolished from 6th April 2025.

The reason for covering the employment allowance in this guide is because it may affect some company owners' own salary choice. For example, two company owners who have no other employees can pay themselves a salary of £40,000 each this year without having to pay any employer's NI.

But is it a good idea to take this much salary to avoid wasting the employment allowance? We'll answer this question in Chapter 12. In this section, we'll take a brief look at some of the employment allowance rules.

One Man Band Companies

Unfortunately, the employment allowance is not available to 'one man band' companies where there is just one director who is the only employee.

According to HMRC guidance, the employment allowance also cannot be claimed if there are other employees BUT the director's salary is the only one that exceeds the £5,000 secondary threshold. This is to prevent directors of one-man band companies employing friends or family and paying them a token amount in order to claim the employment allowance for their own salaries.

At least one of the additional employees must be paid more than the secondary threshold. For example, a company that employs a seasonal worker who earns above the secondary threshold in a week (£96 for 2026/27) will be eligible for the employment allowance for the whole tax year.

The second employee can be another director (e.g. your spouse/partner) provided both directors' salaries exceed the *annual* secondary threshold (£5,000 for 2026/27, but reduced pro rata if the directorship begins after the tax year has started).

If circumstances change during the tax year and the director becomes the only employee paid above the secondary threshold, the employment allowance can still be claimed for that tax year.

If a company with just one director who earns less than the NI threshold employs just one other person (not a director), the company can claim the employment allowance if the employee earns more than the NI secondary threshold.

In short, as a company owner/director, it is always necessary to pay at least one other person a salary in excess of the secondary threshold (for at least one pay period in the case of non-directors) in order to secure entitlement to the employment allowance.

This can, however, be done without actually using any of the employment allowance on that other person's salary by employing someone aged under 21, or an apprentice aged under 25, and paying them a salary more than the secondary threshold of £5,000, but no more than £50,270 (or the weekly or monthly equivalents in the case of regular, non-director employees).

Other Employment Allowance Rules

The employment allowance can only be used against Class 1 NI and not against Class 1A NI. Class 1A is due on most taxable benefits in kind provided to employees, e.g. company cars.

If your company belongs to a group of companies, only one can claim the allowance. If your business runs multiple PAYE schemes, the allowance can only be claimed against one scheme.

The allowance is claimed as part of the payroll process. The full £10,500 can be claimed in month one of the tax year if your employer's Class 1 NI exceeds £10,500 per month.

You can start claiming the allowance after the tax year has started and make a catch-up claim which can also be offset against your other PAYE costs.

If you claim the allowance at the end of the tax year and your remaining PAYE costs are not sufficient to use the entire allowance, the unclaimed balance can be carried forward to the next tax year.

Naturally, the amount claimed can never exceed the amount of employer's NI which would otherwise arise in the tax year.

Connected Companies

A company cannot claim the employment allowance if a connected company already claims it.

Companies are connected if one company has control of the other company, or both companies are controlled by the same person or persons.

A person is generally considered to have control of a company if they hold more than 50% of the company's share capital or voting power, or if they are entitled to more than 50% of the company's distributable income or assets if the company is wound up.

For example, if you own all the shares in two companies, you will only be entitled to one employment allowance, even if the two companies are completely separate businesses with, for example, separate premises and staff.

If the company that claims the employment allowance has employer's Class 1 NI of less than £10,500, the balance cannot be claimed by the other company.

Under certain circumstances, the shareholdings of close relatives and other 'associates' may have to be added together to determine whether two or more companies are controlled by the same person or group of persons.

For example, if you own all the shares in company X and your spouse owns all the shares in company Y, your spouse's holding in company Y could be attributed to you, so that you are treated as controlling both companies, as is your spouse.

However, this treatment is only applied where there is 'substantial commercial interdependence' between two or more companies (see the Taxcafe guide *Putting It Through the Company* for details of what this means and how this rule is applied in practice).

If the two companies are completely unrelated, then two employment allowances can be claimed. If there is substantial commercial interdependence between the companies then only one allowance can be claimed.

How Far Does the Employment Allowance Go?

The £10,500 employment allowance will fully cover the employer's NI payable on the following salaries paid to directors and employees:

	Salary
One director/employee*	£75,000
Two directors/employees	£40,000
Three directors/employees	£28,333
Four directors/employees	£22,500

* The employment allowance is not available to 'one man band' companies where one director is the only employee paid over the secondary threshold.

For example, if a company has four directors and no other employees, they can each be paid a salary of up to £22,500 this year with no employer's NI cost.

As we will see in Chapter 14, this does not necessarily mean it is a good idea to pay this salary. However, there are some exceptions, which we will come across later in the guide.

Case Study: Total Tax Payable on Salary

Jane, a director, earns a salary of £60,000. Her Income Tax for the current 2026/27 tax year can be calculated as follows:

- 0% on the first £12,570 = £0
- 20% on the next £37,700 = £7,540
- 40% on the final £9,730 = £3,892

Total Income Tax bill: £11,432

Her NI for 2026/27 can be calculated as follows:

- 0% on the first £12,570 = £0
- 8% on the next £37,700 = £3,016
- 2% on the final £9,730 = £195

Jane's National Insurance bill: £3,211.

Her company claims the £10,500 employment allowance, but this is used up on other employees. Her company's NI bill on her salary is therefore:

- 0% on the first £5,000 = £0
- 15% on the next £55,000 = £8,250

The company's NI bill is £8,250. The company will enjoy CT relief at up to 26.5%, so its NI bill, net of CT relief, will be £6,064 at best, and possibly a bit higher (see Chapter 1).

The total tax paid by Jane and her company is as follows:

Income Tax	£11,432
Employee's National Insurance	£3,211
Employer's National Insurance	£6,064
Total taxes	£20,707

When you include employer's NI, it's startling how much tax is paid on Jane's income. Her £60,000 salary is not low but you wouldn't describe her as a high earner either. Nevertheless, an amount equivalent to at least 34.5% of her salary is paid in direct taxes on her *whole* income.

Table 2 shows the total tax on a range of salaries. We assume the employer's NI attracts 25% CT relief and does not benefit from the employment allowance. Once again, it's startling how much tax is paid on salaries, especially when you look at the overall tax rate (the last column).

TABLE 2
Total Tax Payable on Salary 2026/27

Salary	Income Tax	Employee NI	Employer NI	Total	%
£10,000	£0	£0	£563	£563	6
£20,000	£1,486	£594	£1,688	£3,768	19
£30,000	£3,486	£1,394	£2,813	£7,693	26
£40,000	£5,486	£2,194	£3,938	£11,618	29
£50,000	£7,486	£2,994	£5,063	£15,543	31
£60,000	£11,432	£3,211	£6,188	£20,830	35
£70,000	£15,432	£3,411	£7,313	£26,155	37
£80,000	£19,432	£3,611	£8,438	£31,480	39
£90,000	£23,432	£3,811	£9,563	£36,805	41
£100,000	£27,432	£4,011	£10,688	£42,130	42
£110,000	£33,432	£4,211	£11,813	£49,455	45
£120,000	£39,432	£4,411	£12,938	£56,780	47
£130,000	£44,703	£4,611	£14,063	£63,376	49
£140,000	£49,203	£4,811	£15,188	£69,201	49
£150,000	£53,703	£5,011	£16,313	£75,026	50
£160,000	£58,203	£5,211	£17,438	£80,851	51
£170,000	£62,703	£5,411	£18,563	£86,676	51
£180,000	£67,203	£5,611	£19,688	£92,501	51
£190,000	£71,703	£5,811	£20,813	£98,326	52
£200,000	£76,203	£6,011	£21,938	£104,151	52
£225,000	£87,453	£6,511	£24,750	£118,714	53
£250,000	£98,703	£7,011	£27,563	£133,276	53
£275,000	£109,953	£7,511	£30,375	£147,839	54
£300,000	£121,203	£8,011	£33,188	£162,401	54

Scottish Income Tax

The Scottish Parliament can set Income Tax rates and thresholds for most types of income including salaries, self-employment income, rental income, and pensions.

It does NOT have the power to tax interest and dividend income (including small company dividends). These types of income continue to be taxed using UK rates and thresholds. The Scottish Parliament also does not have the power to set the personal allowance. NI and most other taxes, including CT, CGT and Inheritance Tax, also remain the preserve of the UK Government.

Scottish Income Tax 2026/27
The following Income Tax rates apply:

£0 - £12,570	0%	Personal allowance (PA)
£12,570 - £16,537	19%	Starter rate
£16,537 - £29,526	20%	Basic rate
£29,526 - £43,662	21%	Intermediate rate
£43,662 - £75,000	42%	Higher rate
£75,000 - £100,000	45%	Advanced rate
£100,000 - £125,140	67.5%	PA withdrawal
Over £125,140	48%	Top rate

Coupled with NI (set by the UK Government), the combined tax rates on salary income for directors are as follows:

£0 - £12,570	0%
£12,570 - £16,537	27%
£16,537 - £29,526	28%
£29,526 - £43,662	29%
£43,662 - £50,270	50%
£50,270 - £75,000	44%
£75,000 - £100,000	47%
£100,000 - £125,140	69.5%
Over £125,140	50%

Table 3 compares Scottish Income Tax with the rest of the UK. 'Income' does not include dividends or interest.

Many Scottish taxpayers pay more tax than those in the rest of the UK. For example, someone earning £50,000 in Scotland will pay £1,496 more tax than someone living elsewhere in the UK, someone earning £100,000 will pay £3,300 more tax.

Those with income below £33,493 pay slightly less than their counterparts elsewhere in the UK, with a maximum saving of £39.67, or a little over 76p per week!

TABLE 3
Income Tax: Scotland vs Rest of UK 2026/27

Income	Scottish Taxpayer	Rest of UK	Difference
£20,000	£1,446	£1,486	-£40
£30,000	£3,451	£3,486	-£35
£40,000	£5,551	£5,486	£65
£50,000	£8,982	£7,486	£1,496
£60,000	£13,182	£11,432	£1,750
£70,000	£17,382	£15,432	£1,950
£80,000	£21,732	£19,432	£2,300
£100,000	£30,732	£27,432	£3,300
£125,000	£47,607	£42,432	£5,175
£150,000	£59,634	£53,703	£5,931
£175,000	£71,634	£64,953	£6,681
£200,000	£83,634	£76,203	£7,431

Who is a Scottish Taxpayer?

Someone is a Scottish taxpayer if their sole or main place of residence is in Scotland. For example, someone who rents a flat in London where they work during the week will probably be treated as a Scottish taxpayer if their spouse/partner and children live in the family home in Edinburgh and most of their friends and other social links are also in Edinburgh.

In some cases, it may be difficult to establish where the main residence is located. Where no close connection to Scotland can be identified, Scottish taxpayer status will be determined through day counting. You will then be a Scottish taxpayer if you spend more days during the tax year in Scotland than you spend in England, Wales, or Northern Ireland (taking each country separately).

Throughout this guide, where we refer to a Scottish taxpayer, or a Scottish company owner, we are using this definition. As far as tax is concerned, it doesn't matter where you were born or who you support in the Six Nations (apart from Inheritance Tax perhaps).

Scottish Company Owners

Scottish company owners who pay themselves a small tax-efficient salary (see Chapter 12) and take the rest of their income as dividends are generally completely immune from Scottish Income Tax. They usually pay the same amount of tax as company owners living in the rest of the UK. This is because the Scottish Parliament cannot change the Income Tax personal allowance, NI thresholds, or tax dividends.

This assumes the company owner does not have any other income subject to Scottish Income Tax (e.g. rental income).

Being subject to Scottish Income Tax is not necessarily a bad thing. It's only when Scottish company owners have salary and other income subject to Scottish tax rates of more than £33,493 that they will pay more tax than those living elsewhere in the UK.

Welsh Income Tax

Since April 2019, the Welsh Parliament (Senedd Cymru) has been able to vary the Income Tax rates payable by Welsh taxpayers. However, this year (2026/27) Welsh taxpayers will pay exactly the same Income Tax as those in England and Northern Ireland.

As in Scotland, the Welsh powers are limited, with the UK Government retaining responsibility for the Income Tax personal allowance, tax on savings and dividend income, and most other taxes.

Timing Directors' Salary Payments

Directors' salaries, like other employee's pay, are subject to all the rules of the PAYE system. This can cause cashflow issues as payments made earlier in the tax year could trigger Income Tax that can only be recovered when another payment is made later in the tax year, or even later via self-assessment.

Assuming the director has a 'normal' PAYE code, these irritations can generally be avoided by either paying the salary in equal monthly instalments or in a single lump sum paid between 6th March and 5th April (assuming the company is using monthly pay periods for payroll purposes).

Generally, any salary or bonus payment is treated as paid for tax purposes when it is either paid in cash or posted as a credit to the director's loan account. However, it is important to be aware that, as soon as the ***amount*** of a payment is established and recorded anywhere in the company's records (e.g. in the minutes of a director's board meeting) this is deemed to represent payment for tax purposes and, if done too soon, can trigger unwanted tax liabilities.

Chapter 6

How Directors Are Taxed: Dividend Income

Dividends are subject to Income Tax but not NI. Also, the Income Tax rates on dividends are lower than the Income Tax rates on salaries because dividends are paid out of a company's *after-tax* profits: the money has already been taxed in the company's hands, whereas salaries are a tax-deductible expense.

The first £500 of dividend income you receive is tax free thanks to the 'dividend nil rate band', also known as the 'dividend allowance'. The dividend allowance was £5,000 when it was first introduced but was reduced steadily over a number of years.

From 6th April 2026, the Income Tax rates on most dividend income have been increased by 2%.

For those receiving dividends in excess of the dividend allowance, the following tax rates apply:

	2025/26	**2026/27 Onwards**
Basic rate taxpayers	8.75%	10.75%
Higher rate taxpayers	33.75%	35.75%
Additional rate taxpayers	39.35%	39.35%

For some unknown reason, the additional rate has NOT been increased by the current *Labour* Government: not yet, anyway!

Overall Tax Rates on Dividend Income

Because income paid out as dividends is taxed twice (first in the company's hands and second in the shareholder's hands) it's easy to lose sight of how much tax is being paid overall.

As a company owner, you are likely to be equally concerned about your company's tax bill as your own, so it's worth showing the overall combined tax rates on dividend income.

As we saw in Chapter 1, each company's overall CT rate is somewhere between 19% and 25%. The resultant total tax rates on dividend income are in the following ranges:

Total Tax Rate

Basic rate taxpayers	27.7% to 33.1%
Higher rate taxpayers	48.0% to 51.8%
Additional rate taxpayers	50.9% to 54.5%

Company owners whose companies have profits of £50,000 or less will face the lowest total tax rates. For example, a company with total profits below £50,000 will pay £19 CT on each £100 of profit, leaving £81 to pay out as dividends. Ignoring the dividend allowance, a basic rate taxpayer will pay £8.71 tax on this income (£81 x 10.75%), so the total tax bill on each £100 of profit is £27.71, or 27.7%.

For companies with profits over £50,000, the combined tax rates on dividend income will vary according to the amount of profit the company makes. For example, a company with profits of £100,000 will face a total CT bill of £22,750 (see Table 1), leaving £77,250 to pay out as dividends. If higher rate tax at 35.75% is payable on all of this income, the total tax bill on the £100,000 profit will be £50,367, which is 50.4%.

Owners of companies with profits of £250,000 or more will face the highest total tax rates. For example, a company with total profits of £250,000 will pay £25 CT on each £100 of profit, leaving £75 to pay out as dividends. An additional rate taxpayer will pay £29.50 tax on this income (£75 x 39.35%), so the total tax bill on each £100 of profit is £54.50, which is 54.5%.

The combined total tax rates on dividend income are higher than the regular Income Tax rates that apply to most types of income (20% for basic rate taxpayers, 40% for higher rate taxpayers, and 45% for additional rate taxpayers).

This is because the Government has been levelling the playing field between company owners (who often don't pay any NI) and self-employed business owners and regular employees, who pay NI on most of their earnings. Company owners are also much easier to target politically.

From a tax planning perspective, once a company owner has used up the £500 dividend allowance, they are usually better off paying themselves other types of income in preference to dividends, wherever possible.

Examples include rental income and interest income. Salary also fits the bill whenever there is no NI cost (or where the cost is outweighed by CT relief: see Chapters 12, 15, and 26).

TABLE 4
Total Tax Rates on Dividend Income

Profits	Tax Rate @ 10.75%	Tax Rate @ 35.75%	Tax Rate @ 39.35%
£50,000	27.71	47.96	50.87
£60,000	28.82	48.76	51.63
£70,000	29.62	49.33	52.17
£80,000	30.22	49.76	52.58
£90,000	30.68	50.10	52.90
£100,000	31.05	50.37	53.15
£110,000	31.36	50.59	53.35
£120,000	31.61	50.77	53.53
£130,000	31.83	50.92	53.67
£140,000	32.01	51.06	53.80
£150,000	32.17	51.17	53.91
£160,000	32.31	51.27	54.00
£170,000	32.43	51.36	54.08
£180,000	32.54	51.44	54.16
£190,000	32.64	51.51	54.23
£200,000	32.73	51.57	54.29
£210,000	32.81	51.63	54.34
£220,000	32.88	51.68	54.39
£230,000	32.95	51.73	54.43
£240,000	33.01	51.77	54.47
£250,000	33.06	51.81	54.51

Table 4 contains the total tax rates that apply at different profit levels and different Income Tax rates. In all of these calculations, we ignore the dividend allowance.

Some of these tax rates are unrealistically low if we assume that all of the company's profits are paid out in a single year to a single director.

For example, if a company has pre-tax profits of £200,000, it would be impossible for its after-tax profits of £150,750 to be paid out to just one director in one tax year with just 10.75% basic rate Income Tax payable (resulting in a total tax rate of just 32.73%).

However, this tax rate could be payable if dividends are paid to several directors who are all basic rate taxpayers, or if the profits are paid out over a number of years.

Similarly, some of the total tax rates are unrealistically high if the director does not have income from other sources. For example, if a company has pre-tax profits of just £50,000 this would never result in additional rate tax at 39.35% being payable if the director has no other sources of income.

If, however, the director does have a significant amount of income from other sources, it is possible the total tax rate on some or all of their dividend income will be 50.87%.

Marginal Tax Rates

The total tax rates listed in Table 4 are calculated using the *total* CT and Income Tax payable if all of the company's after-tax profits are paid out as dividends.

However, for companies with profits between £50,000 and £250,000 these are not the ones we would typically use to make tax planning decisions. For these purposes we would use the company's *marginal tax rate*.

Remember, companies with profits between £50,000 and £250,000 pay 19% on the first £50,000 and 26.5% on the rest. 26.5% is the company's marginal tax rate. Its total (average) tax rate will be lower because some of its profits will be taxed at 19%.

For companies with profits of £50,000 or less, the total tax rate and the marginal tax rate are the same: 19%. Similarly, for companies with profits of £250,000 or more, the total tax rate and the marginal tax rate are also the same: 25%. (However, if the company spends enough money to take its profits below £250,000, it will start to have a marginal tax rate of 26.5%)

Marginal Tax Rate Planning and Dividends

Take a company owner who is a higher rate taxpayer and anticipates that, as things stand, their company will make a profit of £60,000. Let's say the company already pays them rent to use an office property they own personally and they want to know whether they'll be better off paying themselves an additional £1,000 of rent, or taking the money as a dividend.

If they pay themselves rent this will be a tax-deductible expense for the company, so the whole £1,000 will be paid out and after paying 40% Income Tax this year, they will be left with £600.

Alternatively, the company will pay 26.5% CT on this final £1,000 of profit, leaving £735 to pay out as dividend income. After paying Income Tax at 35.75%, the owner will be left with £472.

The total tax payable on the additional dividend income is £528, which is 52.8%. Clearly in this case additional rental income is more attractive. (And it will remain more attractive from 6th April 2027 onwards, when the Income Tax rates applying to property income are increased by 2%: see Chapter 38.)

Note, 52.8% is higher than the 48.76% rate shown in Table 4 for a company with profits of £60,000. That total tax rate is calculated using the company's *total* CT rate. Most of its profits are taxed at just 19%, so the total tax rate in the table is lower.

The rate we've used in this example, however, is the company's 26.5% *marginal* tax rate, the rate which applies to the final £1,000 of profit we are looking at.

In summary, the total tax rates listed in Table 4 give you some idea of the total amount of CT and Income Tax that will be payable if all of a company's after-tax profits are paid out as dividends. But, when it comes to choosing between a dividend and some other type of income, the marginal tax rate is more relevant.

For company owners whose companies have profits between £50,000 and £250,000, the combined marginal tax rate (CT and Income Tax) on dividend income will be as follows:

	Combined Marginal Tax Rate
Basic rate taxpayers	34.40%
Higher rate taxpayers	52.78%
Additional rate taxpayers	55.42%

The Dividend Allowance

Company owners do not enjoy an additional standalone amount of £500 tax free. Instead, the dividend allowance typically uses up some of your basic rate band.

The dividend allowance only uses up your basic rate band if, like many company owners, you have dividend income subject to basic rate tax. It works differently if you have a lot of other income and all your dividends are subject to higher rate tax.

Dividend Taxation Examples
Let's take a look at some sample dividend tax calculations for the current 2026/27 tax year. To keep things simple, we'll assume the company owners take a small salary of £12,570 and the rest of their income as dividends. There may be £1,136 of employer's NI payable by the company, but see Chapter 12 for a discussion of why a salary of £12,570 will generally still be most tax efficient, even if this is the case.

We'll also assume the company owners have no other taxable income. These examples apply equally to Scottish company owners.

Example: Basic-Rate Taxpayer
Stuart is a company owner with a salary of £12,570 and dividend income of £20,000. His total income is thus £32,570.

His salary is tax-free because it is covered by his personal allowance. The first £500 of his dividend income is tax free thanks to the dividend allowance. The remaining £19,500 of his dividend income is taxed at 10.75%, producing a total tax bill of £2,096.

Example: Higher-Rate Taxpayer
Robert is a company owner with a salary of £12,570 and dividend of £50,000. His total income is thus £62,570.

His salary is tax-free, covered by his personal allowance. The first £500 of his dividend is also tax-free thanks to the dividend allowance. The dividend allowance uses up £500 of his £37,700 basic rate band so just £37,200 of his dividend income is taxed at 10.75%, producing a tax bill of £3,999. The final £12,300 of his dividend takes him over the higher rate threshold and is taxed at 35.75%, producing a tax bill of £4,397. Robert's total tax bill is thus £8,396

Example: Personal Allowance Withdrawal
Alpesh is a company owner with a salary of £12,570 and dividend of £97,430. His total taxable income is £110,000. His personal allowance is reduced from £12,570 to £7,570. Thus £5,000 of his salary is taxed at 20% (£12,570 – £7,570), producing a tax bill of £1,000.

The first £500 of his dividend income is tax free, being covered by the dividend allowance. The next £32,200 of his dividend income is covered by his remaining basic rate band (£37,700 – £5,000 – £500) and taxed at 10.75%, producing a tax bill of £3,462. The remaining £64,730 of his dividend income is taxed at 35.75%, producing a tax bill of £23,141. His total tax bill is therefore £27,603.

Example: Additional-Rate Taxpayer
Maeve is a company owner with a salary of £12,570 and dividend of £200,000. Her total income is thus £212,570. Because her income exceeds £125,140, she is an additional rate taxpayer.

The first £500 of her dividend income is tax free but her Income Tax personal allowance is completely withdrawn. This means she will pay 20% Income Tax on her salary, £2,514; and her remaining basic rate band will be reduced to just £24,630 (£37,700 – £12,570 salary – £500 dividend allowance). She will thus pay 10.75% tax on £24,630 of her dividend income (£2,648).

The next £87,440 of her dividend (£125,140 less £37,700) is subject to higher rate tax at 35.75%, resulting in additional tax of £31,260. The remaining £87,430 of dividend income takes her over the £125,140 additional rate tax threshold and is taxed at 39.35%, resulting in additional tax of £34,404.

Maeve's total tax bill is £70,826.

Individuals with Significant Non-Dividend Income
The dividend allowance only forms part of your basic rate band if you have dividend income that falls into the basic rate band. It works differently if your basic rate band is completely used up by other income, e.g. salary or rental income.

The way to think about it is like this: dividends are always treated as the top slice of your income and taxed at your highest marginal rate. The dividend allowance exempts the *bottom* £500 of that income from tax. So, if you have dividend income taxed at both 10.75% and 35.75%, the dividend allowance will exempt some of the income taxed at 10.75%.

But if ALL your dividend income is taxed at 35.75% (because you have a lot of other income, e.g. rental income) the dividend allowance will be part of your higher rate band and you'll pay 0% tax instead of 35.75% tax on £500 of your dividend income.

Example: *In 2026/27 Julia has £60,000 of salary and rental income and £30,000 of dividend income. Her salary and rental income use up her personal allowance and basic rate band, taking her over the higher rate tax threshold. The first £500 of her dividend is tax free; £29,500 is taxed at the 35.75% higher rate.*

The dividend allowance does not form part of her basic rate band as none of her dividend income falls into the basic rate band.

Example: *In 2026/27 Leon has £90,000 of salary and rental income and £50,000 of dividend income. With this much income his personal allowance is completely withdrawn.*

The first £500 of his dividend income is covered by the dividend allowance, leaving £34,640 taxed at the 35.75% higher rate. Along with his salary this takes Leon up to the £125,140 additional rate threshold. The final £14,860 of his dividend is taxed at 39.35%.

Leon has dividend income taxed at both the higher rate and additional rate. The dividend allowance reduces the amount of his dividend income taxed at the 35.75% higher rate.

Tax Charges on Tax-Free Dividends and Interest

Dividends covered by the dividend allowance are still taxable income, even if they are taxed at a rate of 0%. The same goes for interest income covered by the personal savings allowance and starting-rate band (see Chapter 33). This means these supposedly tax-free amounts can give rise to tax or other similar costs as they are counted for the purposes of:

- The Child Benefit Charge
- Withdrawal of the personal allowance (income over £100,000)
- Whether any of the basic rate band is still available to reduce the rate of CGT payable on capital gains
- Reductions in the personal savings allowance where income exceeds the higher rate tax threshold or the additional rate tax threshold (see Chapter 33)
- The pension annual allowance taper (see Chapter 27)
- Student loan repayments ('student persecution payments' as my children call them)
- The Winter Fuel Charge (clawback of winter fuel payments)
- Tax-free childcare and free childcare for working parents (withdrawn if income exceeds £100,000)

The last two points, where relevant, are probably the most important, as these are effectively 'cliff edges'. For example, if your so-called 'tax-free' dividend or interest income pushes your total taxable income even just £1 over the £100,000 threshold, you lose your entitlement to tax-free childcare and free childcare for working parents altogether. These benefits are extremely valuable, often worth many thousands of pounds per year.

Use It or Lose It

Subject to the points above, and although it is now just a pathetic £500, it generally makes sense to ensure you use your dividend allowance every year, as it does not carry forward.

Hence, for the rest of this guide, unless stated to the contrary, we'll be assuming you always pay yourself at least enough dividends to use your dividend allowance.

In particular, where a salary greater than £12,570 becomes optimal conditional on you remaining a basic rate taxpayer for the year (see Chapter 15 for a scenario where this applies), dividends of up to £500 that are entirely covered by the dividend allowance can generally still be paid where this is the *only* income that takes you over the higher-rate tax threshold. The only potential exception is where you also have more than £500 of interest and savings income in the same tax year.

For example, where your optimal salary is £50,270 and you have no other income from outside the company, it remains worth taking a dividend of £500 and this will not alter your optimal salary. This may seem an unlikely scenario, but it is quite possible for a young director under 21 (see Chapter 16), among others.

Taxpayers with Other Dividend Income

Each individual gets one dividend allowance to cover all their dividend income each tax year. If you also have dividends from stock market investments, you will not be able to use the full dividend allowance against dividends from your own company.

Scottish Taxpayers

The Scottish Government can tax most types of income but not dividends or interest. It also cannot change the personal allowance or NI. This means:

- Scottish company owners pay exactly the same amount of tax on their dividend income as company owners living in the rest of the UK.
- Scottish company owners who also pay themselves a small tax-efficient salary (no higher than the £12,570 personal allowance) are generally immune from Scottish Income Tax, assuming they do not have any other income subject to Scottish tax rates.
- Scottish company owners whose salary income, rental income and other income (except interest and dividends) exceeds £12,570 will pay Scottish Income Tax. However, if this income is less than £33,493, they will pay less tax on this income than people living elsewhere in the UK. If this income exceeds £33,493, they will pay more tax. They will pay the same amount of tax on their dividend income as company owners living in the rest of the UK.

(See Chapter 23 for more information for high income earners.)

Example: *Alan is a company owner living in Scotland. He has salary and rental income of £30,000 and dividend income of £25,000.*

He is subject to Scottish Income Tax on his salary and rental income. As we saw in Table 3 in Chapter 5, this means he will pay £35 less tax on this income than someone living elsewhere in the UK; but what about his dividend income?

Although the higher rate threshold is £43,662 in Scotland, it is the UK higher rate threshold (£50,270) that applies to his dividend income.

The first £500 is tax free thanks to the dividend allowance. This leaves him with £19,770 of basic rate band (£50,270 – £30,000 – £500). This income will be taxed at 10.75%.

The remaining £4,730 of his dividend income takes him over the £50,270 higher rate threshold and will be taxed at 35.75%.

Dividend Tax Terminology

The 0% tax rate applying to the dividend allowance or dividend nil rate band is known officially as the 'dividend nil rate'. The 10.75% rate is known as the 'ordinary rate', the 35.75% rate is known as the 'upper rate' and the 39.35% rate as the 'additional rate'. We do not use these terms much in this guide, preferring the terms basic rate, higher rate, and additional rate.

Will Dividend Tax Rates be Increased Yet Again?

On 6th April 2026, the dividend tax rates applying to basic rate and higher rate taxpayers were increased by 2% to 10.75% and 35.75% respectively. The additional rate was left unchanged.

This is something we at Taxcafe warned about in the 2025/26 edition of this guide.

Dividend tax rates were also increased by 1.25% on 6th April 2022, and it's worth remembering that the 2023 increase in Corporation Tax has resulted in a further increase in the total combined tax rates on dividend income.

It must also be remembered that the freezing of the £50,270 higher-rate threshold until 5th April 2031 has an even more damaging effect than an increase in tax rates: if your income simply increases with inflation, more and more of it will be taxed at 35.75% instead of 10.75%.

Will dividend tax rates be increased again in the near future?

Until recently, we thought this was unlikely, simply because the combined tax rates are already so high: many higher rate taxpayers are already paying over 50% when you include Corporation Tax.

Following Andy Burnham's bloodless coup, however, we wouldn't rule anything out: remember Rachel Reeves has already set the precedent that company owners are not 'working people' as far as this Government's election manifesto pledges are concerned!

And, as discussed in the Introduction, if there is an increase in the personal allowance, the Government will need to find ways to recoup its lost income: a further increase in dividend tax rates seems like a prime candidate.

Dark Clouds on the Horizon

Rates and thresholds are not the only concern we have at Taxcafe when looking at the future tax treatment of small company owners' dividend income.

To us, the new reporting requirements for company owners' dividend income (see Chapter 50) are sending out a clear signal that we can expect changes to the treatment of director/shareholder's dividends at some point in the foreseeable future. The fact these dividends must now be reported on the *Employment Pages* of the tax return is particularly worrying, and suggests the Government may be considering imposing a whole new tax regime for director/shareholder's dividends: perhaps subjecting them directly to PAYE and, worst of all, NI. (As explained in Chapter 8, many dividends may effectively be *indirectly* subjected to PAYE in the near future.)

Watch this space for further developments!

Chapter 7

Don't Forget Payments on Account

In this chapter, we will cover the current payment on account system. See Chapter 8 for proposed future changes applying from 2029/30, but potentially affected by action you take in the *current year* ending on 5th April 2027.

Payments on account are currently made twice a year and allow HMRC to collect some of the tax you owe early. Common victims include sole traders and landlords, i.e. those whose Income Tax is not collected at source. Payments on account are not extra tax, but they do significantly affect your cashflow.

Most salary earners do not have to make payments on account because their tax is collected almost immediately through PAYE. However, many company owners have to make payments on account as dividend income is not taxed at source and tax has to be paid through the self-assessment system.

How Payments on Account Are Calculated

If you paid yourself a dividend during the previous 2025/26 tax year, which started on 6th April 2025 and ended on 5th April 2026, the basic rule (ignoring payments on account) is that the Income Tax is payable by 31st January 2027: almost ten months after the tax year ended.

For example, let's say a company owner paid themselves a salary of £12,570 and dividend of £20,500 and had no other taxable income. To keep the example simple, let's also assume they have never had to make any payments on account in the past.

No Income Tax was payable on their salary because it was fully covered by their personal allowance and the first £500 of their dividend income was tax free thanks to the dividend allowance.

The remaining £20,000 of their dividend income for 2025/26 is taxed at 8.75%, producing a total Income Tax bill of £1,750, which is due to be paid by 31st January 2027.

2026/27 Tax Year

Now let's move forward to the current 2026/27 tax year, which started on 6th April 2026 and ends on 5th April 2027. We will assume our company owner pays themselves a tax-free salary of £12,570 and a dividend of £24,000.

Their Income Tax bill will be £2,526 (the first £500 of dividend income is tax free, the rest is taxed at the new rate of 10.75%). However, this time they cannot wait until 31st January 2028 to pay the tax.

On 31st January 2027, when they pay their 2025/26 tax bill, they will also have to make a payment on account of £875 for 2026/27. They must also make another payment on account of the same amount on 31st July 2027. Thus, their total tax payments will be:

- 31st January 2027 — £1,750 + £875 = £2,625
- 31st July 2027 — £875

Each payment on account is normally half the previous year's self-assessment tax liability.

In January 2028, they will have to make a final tax payment for 2026/27, but will be able to deduct the two payments on account.

In this example, the company owner will have an additional £776 to pay in respect of 2026/27 (£2,526 – £1,750 payments on account) because their payments on account will not fully cover their tax bill.

Furthermore, they will usually also be paying their first payment on account for 2027/28 at the same time, so the total amount payable by 31st January 2028 would generally be £2,039 (£776 + £2,526/2).

Where the final self-assessment tax liability for the year turns out to be less than the payments on account, the excess payment can be refunded or set against the first payment on account for the following year. This might happen if a company owner takes a much smaller dividend in 2026/27 than they took in 2025/26.

Postponing Tax

Making payments on account is still much better than paying tax through the PAYE system. Take a look at our company owner's tax payments for 2026/27.

The first payment is due around *ten months* after the start of the tax year (January 2027), the second payment is due around *16 months* after the start of the tax year (July 2027), and the final balancing payment is due around *22 months* after the tax year has started (January 2028).

Under the current system, this means that if you pay yourself a dividend at the start of the tax year, you will have free use of the taxman's money for well over a year.

That money could be invested in a cash ISA or some other low-risk investment. (But see Chapter 8 if you are thinking of taking a dividend soon after 5th April 2027: there are other factors to consider!)

Who Has to Make Payments on Account?

The current payments on account system is based on the tax you paid for the *previous tax year*. You only have to make payments on account if your self-assessment tax (i.e. ignoring tax deducted at source) for the previous tax year was more than £1,000.

For example, if during the current 2026/27 tax year, you pay yourself a salary of £12,570 and a dividend of £9,500, your total Income Tax bill will be £968 and you will not have to make any payments on account in January and July 2028.

Of course, if you have income from other sources (e.g. rental income from property or taxable interest income) this will have to be factored into the equation too.

You do not have to make payments on account, however, if more than 80% of your total tax from the previous year was covered by tax deducted at source.

How to Reduce Payments on Account

Where your self-assessment liability for the current year can reasonably be expected to be less than that for the previous year, you can apply to reduce your payments on account to the appropriate level (i.e. half of the anticipated liability for the current year).

For example, if you take a much smaller dividend in 2026/27 than you took in 2025/26, you can apply to reduce your payments on account due on 31st January and 31st July 2027. You can do this when you submit your 2025/26 tax return.

You have to be careful when doing this, however. If you claim a reduction in your payments on account and then find you have more tax to pay than you expected, you will have to pay interest on the underpayment. There could also be a penalty if there is a significant underpayment and HMRC have reason to suspect you acted fraudulently, or negligently, and had no reasonable grounds for having reduced your payments on account by so much.

Remember, the tax rates on most dividends increased by 2% on 6th April 2026. As a result, your tax bill for the current year could be higher than anticipated.

Chapter 8

Future Tax Payments: Trouble Ahead

Unfortunately, it looks like the current payments on account system we examined in Chapter 7 is going to be replaced with something far, far worse. Note that the future regime we are examining in this chapter is based on proposals put forward in a recent Government consultation and has not yet been finalised. Nonetheless, while some of the details may change, the main features of these proposals are likely to come into force and will badly affect many small company owners.

However, unlike many other self-assessment taxpayers, company owners are in a position to plan ahead in anticipation of the new payment regime: which is why we are highlighting these proposals in this edition of *Salary versus Dividends*.

As we will see later, action taken in the current tax year ending on 5th April 2027 may mitigate the impact of these proposed changes. But first, let's look at what the Government has got in store for us.

From April 2029, the Government is planning to force self-assessment taxpayers who also receive sufficient PAYE income (salary income or private pensions) to pay the tax due on *all* their income through the PAYE system. In this context, your PAYE income will be regarded as sufficient to withstand this burden if it is at least twice your total tax liability for the year (including NI).

When this system starts in 2029/30, the payments taken via PAYE will be based on the individual's self-assessment tax liability for 2027/28: a two-year time lag. But it will be the tax due for 2029/30 that is being collected. The actual tax for 2027/28 will have been paid through the current system, as described in Chapter 7.

The actual self-assessment tax liability for 2027/28 will also form the basis for the payments on account due in respect of 2028/29, and these will continue to be payable under the current arrangements on 31st January and 31st July 2029, with a balancing payment (or repayment) on 31st January 2030.

In other words, 2029/30 is going to be a terrible year for taxpayers in the self-assessment system, as the Government is planning to catch up by a year, and effectively collect the tax due on two years' worth of self-assessment income, including dividends, in the space of just fourteen months!

Example 1: *Dominic, a company owner with no other sources of income takes a salary of £12,570 as a single lump sum on 31st March each year, plus dividends as follows:*

2027/28: £35,500 (giving rise to Income Tax of £3,763)
2028/29: £37,500 (giving rise to Income Tax of £3,978)
2029/30: £38,500 (giving rise to Income Tax of £4,285)

Dominic's tax payments in respect of the 2028/29 and 2029/30 tax years will be as follows:

31st January 2029	
First payment on account for 2028/29	*£1,881*
(A balancing payment for 2027/28 may also be due)	
31st July 2029	
Second payment on account for 2028/29	*£1,882*
31st January 2030	
Balancing payment for 2028/29	*£215*
31st March 2030	
*Tax for 2029/30 deducted under PAYE**	*£3,763*
31st January 2031	
Balancing payment for 2029/30	*£522*

Excluding the final balancing payment for 2029/30, the earlier payments total £7,741 over the fourteen-month period from January 2029 to March 2030: that's effectively two years' worth of tax.

** The company must pay this to HMRC by 22nd April 2030.*

The position will be different if you take your salary earlier in the tax year, or as a regular monthly payment. For example, if Dominic took his salary of £12,570 as a single lump sum on 30th April 2029, he would suffer £2,618 under PAYE at that time, meaning he suffers a total of £6,596 over a twelve-month period (January 2029 to January 2030). His payment on account due on 31st January 2031 would then be £1,667 (£4,285 – £2,618).

If Dominic took a regular monthly salary of £1,047.50 throughout 2029/30, he would suffer a deduction of £313.58 every month, leaving him with net pay of just £733.92. He might have to take extra dividends to compensate him for this shortfall meaning that, come 2031/32 (two years later), he will be suffering an even greater PAYE deduction, reducing his net pay yet further. Meanwhile, if his dividends are increasing each year, he will still have to fund balancing payments every January. The answer: more dividends, more tax... a vicious circle!

The Government claims these proposals do not amount to extra tax, but collecting two years' worth of tax in fourteen months will place a huge burden on self-assessment taxpayers, including small company owners. In fact, the Government's own forecasts suggest they will collect almost an extra £1 billion: that's a billion pounds they are going to suck out of the economy, principally from small companies and other small businesses.

PAYE Limitations

Current rules state that no more than half of a salary payment (or private pension) can be deducted under PAYE. If these rules remain in place when the new system is implemented, up to £6,285 could be deducted from a typical small company owner's salary of £12,570 (see Chapter 12 for why this salary is typical).

This, in turn, means the tax on a dividend of up to £44,094 could be collected through the PAYE system (it might be a bit more due to rounding).

But, if a company owner taking a salary of £12,570 in 2029/30 took a dividend of more than around £44,100 in 2027/28, the PAYE system could not be used to collect the estimated tax due for 2029/30. In that case, they would then fall into the payments on account system.

That sounds like great news: but here the Government has more plans in store for us. They haven't yet decided exactly how it will work, but they're thinking of introducing a new payments on account system from 2029/30. That won't stop the current system applying for 2028/29 and effectively running in parallel with the new system for the first year.

This part of the plan is considerably less well developed, but the Government is considering two options for the new system: monthly payments or quarterly payments. The current proposal for the quarterly payments is that these will be due in April, July, October, and January. Once again, the payments on account for 2029/30 will be based on the individual's self-assessment tax liability for 2027/28.

Let's assume for the moment that the Government opts for quarterly payments and take a look at how this might work.

Example 2 Part 1: *Sarah, a company owner with no other sources of income takes a salary of £12,570 each year, plus dividends as follows:*

2027/28: £60,000 (giving rise to Income Tax of £11,971)
2028/29: £65,000 (giving rise to Income Tax of £13,759)
2029/30: £70,000 (giving rise to Income Tax of £15,546)

Sarah's tax payments in respect of the 2028/29 and 2029/30 tax years will be as follows:

31st January 2029		
First payment on account for 2028/29		*£5,985*
(A balancing payment for 2027/28 may also be due)		
30th April 2029		
First payment on account for 2029/30		*£2,992*
31st July 2029		
Second payment on account for 2028/29	*£5,986*	
Second payment on account for 2029/30	*£2,993*	
Total		*£8,979*
31st October 2029		
Third payment on account for 2029/30		*£2,993*
31st January 2030		
Balancing payment for 2028/29	*£1,788*	
Fourth payment on account for 2029/30	*£2,993*	
Total		*£4,781*
31st January 2031		
Balancing payment for 2029/30		*£3,575*

Excluding the final balancing payment for 2029/30, the earlier payments total £25,730 over the twelve-month period from January 2029 to January 2030: that's effectively two years' worth of tax.

And let's not forget, Sarah will also have to make payments on account in respect of 2030/31 in April, July, and October 2030, and January 2031.

The example paints a truly horrendous picture of what is coming up in 2029/30. So, what can be done about it?

Planning Ahead

It is your self-assessment tax liability for next year, 2027/28, that will determine both your payments on account for 2028/29, and either your PAYE deduction, or your payments on account, for 2029/30.

To put it another way, you will, roughly speaking, have to pay an amount equivalent to twice your self-assessment tax liability for 2027/28 within a twelve- to fourteen-month period (plus any balancing payment due for 2028/29).

So, the best way to avoid this cashflow crisis is to minimise your self-assessment tax liability for 2027/28. For small company owners this can easily be done by reducing the dividends you take in 2027/28. If you need the income, you can take extra dividends in either the current year, 2026/27, or in 2028/29. Let's look at both of these approaches.

Example 2 Part 2: *Let's assume that in the current, 2026/27 tax year, Sarah is planning to take a salary of £12,570 and a dividend of £55,000. This will give rise to an Income Tax bill of £10,184. It will also mean she has to make payments on account of £5,092 each in January and July 2028 and a balancing payment of £1,787 in January 2029 in respect of her 2027/28 tax liability. After that, things would proceed as per Part 1 above.*

Instead, let's now suppose that Sarah increases her dividend in the current year to £77,300 (an extra £22,300), enabling her to reduce her 2027/28 dividend to £37,700, and reducing her self-assessment tax liability for 2027/28 to just £3,999. This does not give rise to any more tax overall, but it will dramatically alter Sarah's cashflow. Remember, in this context, that Sarah can apply to reduce her payments on account for 2027/28 based on her anticipated dividend income in that year of just £37,700.

I'll assume that Sarah makes payments on account in respect of 2026/27 totalling £9,094 (based on her having taken the same salary and dividends in 2025/26 as she takes in 2026/27).

Let's now see how accelerating £22,300 of dividends from next year into the current year affects the timing of her tax payments. The 'Original' column is based on dividends of £55,000 in 2026/27 and £60,000 in 2027/28; the 'Revised' column is based on dividends of £77,300 in 2026/27 and £37,700 in 2027/28; the 'Saving/(Cost)' column gives the cumulative saving or cost up to that point. Sarah's income in 2028/29 and 2029/30 remains the same as in Part 1 above but we'll assume she takes her salary as a single lump sum on 31st March each year. BP means balancing payment and POA means payment on account.

	Original	***Revised***	***Saving/ (Cost)***
31st January 2028			
BP for 2026/27	*£1,090*	*£9,062*	
First POA for 2027/28	*£5,092*	*£1,999*	*(£4,879)*
31st July 2028			
Second POA for 2027/28	*£5,092*	*£2,000*	*(£1,787)*
31st January 2029			
BP for 2027/28	*£1,787*	-	
First POA for 2028/29	*£5,985*	*£1,999*	*£3,986*
30th April 2029			
First POA for 2029/30	*£2,992*	-	*£6,978*
31st July 2029			
Second POA for 2028/29	*£5,986*	*£2,000*	
Second POA for 2029/30	*£2,993*	-	*£13,957*
31st October 2029			
Third POA for 2029/30	*£2,993*	-	*£16,950*
31st January 2030			
BP for 2028/29	*£1,788*	*£9,760*	
Fourth POA for 2029/30	*£2,993*	-	*£11,971*
31st March 2030			
*Tax deducted under PAYE**	-	*£3,999*	*£7,972*

** Under the 'Revised' scenario, the estimated tax for 2029/30, based on Sarah's self-assessment liability for 2027/28, is low enough to be collected via PAYE.*

Ultimately, the £7,972 saving as at 31st March 2030 will be eliminated when Sarah has to make her balancing payment for 2029/30 in January 2031: this will be £11,547 under the 'Revised' scenario instead of the original £3,575.

Sarah will have to make payments on account in respect of 2030/31 in April, July, and October 2030, and January 2031; but these will be the same under both the 'Revised' and 'Original' scenarios.

The downside of this planning is that the company owner will be out of pocket from January 2028 to January 2029; although the amount involved is only significant for the first six months.

Thereafter, the company owner enjoys significant savings that persist for two years, and, in this example, peak at almost £17,000, or almost three and half times the additional cost suffered for just six months.

Another way to achieve a similarly beneficial result would be to defer dividends from 2027/28 to 2028/29.

Example 2 Part 3: *Let's now say that, instead of taking extra dividends in the current year, Sarah defers £22,300 of the dividends she would have taken in 2027/28 (as per Part 1), and takes them in 2028/29. This will give her dividends of £87,300 in 2028/29, with Income Tax of £21,731 for that year.*

Once again, this does not give rise to any more tax overall, but will dramatically alter her cashflow. We need to make an assumption about Sarah's dividends in 2030/31. We'll say these are £75,000, with Income Tax of £17,334. This is important because we expect to be able to reduce payments on account under the new system where the individual's self-assessment liability is expected to be less than for the previous year, in the same way as at present (see Chapter 7).

Let's now see how deferring £22,300 of dividends from next year into the following year affects the timing of tax payments. The 'Original' column uses dividends of £60,000 in 2027/28 and £65,000 in 2028/29; the 'Revised' column uses dividends of £37,700 in 2027/28 and £87,300 in 2028/29; the 'Saving/(Cost)' column gives the cumulative saving or cost up to that point compared with Part 1 above.

	Original	***Revised***	***Saving/(Cost)***
31st January 2028			
BP for 2026/27	*£1,090*	*£1,090*	
First POA for 2027/28	*£5,092*	*£1,999*	*£3,093*
31st July 2028			
Second POA for 2027/28	*£5,092*	*£2,000*	*£6,185*
31st January 2029			
BP for 2027/28	*£1,787*	-	
First POA for 2028/29	*£5,985*	*£1,999*	*£11,958*
30th April 2029			
First POA for 2029/30	*£2,992*	-	*£14,950*
31st July 2029			
Second POA for 2028/29	*£5,986*	*£2,000*	
Second POA for 2029/30	*£2,993*	-	*£21,929*
31st October 2029			
Third POA for 2029/30	*£2,993*	-	*£24,922*
31st January 2030			
BP for 2028/29	*£1,788*	*£17,732*	
Fourth POA for 2029/30	*£2,993*	-	*£11,971*
31st March 2030			
*Tax deducted under PAYE**	-	*£3,999*	*£7,972*
POAs for 2030/31:			
30th April 2030	*£3,439*	*£4,333*	*£7,078*
31st July 2030	*£3,440*	*£4,334*	*£6,184*
31st October 2030	*£3,440*	*£4,333*	*£5,291*
31st January 2031	*£3,440*	*£4,334*	
Plus BP for 2029/30	*£3,575*	*£11,547*	*(£3,575)*

The £3,575 cost as at 31st March 2031 will be recouped in January 2032, when there will be no balancing payment for 2030/31, as opposed to the £3,575 that would have been due under the original scenario.

Arguably, this is a much better strategy than the one Sarah adopted in Part 2. There is no upfront cost, the savings last for three years, and they peak at almost £25,000. There is a twelve-month period when the company owner is out of pocket, but the amount involved is not huge and, since it only starts in January 2031, there is plenty of time to plan for it.

But the strategy does rely on two key assumptions:

i) You can afford to defer a significant part of the dividend you would otherwise have taken in 2027/28 (although you can take it as early as 6th April 2028)

ii) Dividend tax rates will not be increased again (see the Introduction and Chapter 6 for our views on this)

If you can't afford to defer quite so much income from 2027/28 to 2028/29, you could accelerate some of it into the current, 2026/27 tax year instead (i.e. adopt a blend of the strategies in Parts 2 and 3 of Example 2). The key thing is to reduce your self-assessment tax liability for 2027/28 without creating any overall additional tax costs (i.e. remaining in the same Income Tax marginal rate band). In particular, if you're usually a higher-rate taxpayer, you should keep each year's total income between £50,270 and £100,000.

No doubt other planning opportunities will emerge once we have full details of how the new system will operate. For example, it looks like there may be a cashflow advantage if you initially have an estimated tax liability that can be paid through PAYE (i.e. no more than 50% of your salary) but change your plans early in the tax year so that the final tax bill will be too much for this route to apply. It is far from certain at present whether this will work as we hope but, if you think you are likely to take a salary of £12,570 each year, limiting your dividend income in 2027/28 to no more than £44,094 will at least mean you are in with a chance.

Note that the analysis in this chapter has been based on company owners with no other sources of income. However, the proposed changes will affect everyone with self-assessment tax liabilities and massive cashflow savings can be achieved by planning ahead.

Chapter 9

Salary versus Dividends: The Basics

Unlike self-employed business owners (sole traders and partnerships), company owners are in the fortunate position of wearing two caps.

On the one hand, you can reward your work as a director; on the other hand, you can reward your entrepreneurship as a shareholder.

As a company director and shareholder, you can split your income into salary and dividends and this can generate Income Tax and NI savings.

For example, while NI is payable on salaries, it is not payable on shareholder dividends.

By structuring distributions from your company carefully and taking the 'optimum' amount of salary and dividends, you could end up with a significantly higher after-tax income than a regular salaried employee who earns a higher income before tax.

However, while saving Income Tax will be an important consideration, other factors are important too. The major differences between a salary and dividend are:

Salaries Are Tax Deductible
Salaries usually qualify for Corporation Tax (CT) relief, dividends do not. If the company pays you a salary, its taxable profits will be reduced and it will pay less CT.

Dividends are paid out of a company's after-tax profits, so paying a dividend does not reduce the *company's* tax bill.

This is an important point to remember because most company owners are concerned about both their own and their company's tax bill.

For example, if a company has a taxable profit of £10,000, it will pay £1,900 CT (19%), leaving only £8,100 to distribute as dividends. This CT must be added to any Income Tax paid by the shareholder on their dividend income when calculating the total tax suffered.

Dividends Require Profits

Only companies that have made profits can pay dividends. For this purpose, we are talking about accounting profits rather than taxable profits and, as discussed at the beginning of the guide, these are often different.

Accounting profits are usually calculated when the company's annual accounts are drawn up (often many months after the end of the company's accounting period).

So dividends will usually be paid out of profits made in a previous accounting period. It is, however, possible to pay dividends out of profits made during the current year, for example if accurate management accounts are drawn up to determine the level of the company's distributable profits (see Chapter 49).

Salaries can be paid even if the company is making losses, although a director has a duty to ensure any funds they take out of the company, in any form, do not put the company at risk of becoming insolvent.

Income Tax and National Insurance

Salaries and dividends are subject to different rates of Income Tax.

Salaries are generally subject to NI, dividends are not. Both the director and the company may be subject to NI.

Tax Payment Dates

The Income Tax and NI payable on salaries is collected almost immediately via PAYE. The Income Tax on dividends is collected via self-assessment: generally at a later date (but see Chapter 8 regarding future changes).

Earnings

Salaries are classed as 'earnings', which is important if you want to make significant pension contributions personally. Dividends are not classed as earnings.

Chapter 10

How Much Do You Keep?

At its heart this guide is all about how to keep as much of your company's profits as possible when you withdraw them. So, it really makes sense to compare how much of the company's pre-tax profit you actually get to keep when you pay yourself salary or dividends.

Subject to all the various allowances, exemptions, and reliefs, in essence the position is that:

- Profits used to pay dividends suffer Corporation Tax (CT) and Income Tax
- Profits used to pay a salary suffer Income Tax, employer's NI, and employee's NI

So, taking all these taxes into account, how much out of each £1,000 of profit do you typically get to keep?

There are a lot of variables here, so we're going to make a few assumptions to keep things simple:

- You have no other income from outside the company
- You are over 21 but under state pension age
- There is no spare employment allowance available
- You are not a Scottish taxpayer
- You are not subject to the Child Benefit Charge

We'll also ignore the dividend allowance.

We'll look at all the variations where our assumptions do not apply later but, for now, let's look at how much of that £1,000 you keep as net, after-tax income. For a salary, it's always the same amount (within each income band); for dividends, it depends on the company's CT rate. The higher the company's marginal CT rate, the less of the company's pre-tax profits you will be able to keep if you pay yourself a dividend.

TABLE 5
Amount Kept per £1,000 of Profit

Income Band	Salary	Dividend
First £5,000	£1,000	£735 to £810
£5,000 to £12,570	£870	£735 to £810
£12,570 to £50,270	£626	£656 to £723
£50,270 to £100,000	£504	£472 to £520
£100,000 to £125,140	£330	£307 to £338
Over £125,140	£461	£446 to £491

This is a massive simplification, mostly because more of each £1,000 of pre-tax profit can be paid as salary than as dividends, so the further we go up the income bands the more chance we might not be comparing like with like. Furthermore, the withdrawal of the personal allowance in the £100,000 to £125,140 income bracket has a complex effect that isn't fully reflected here.

Nonetheless, Table 5 provides a useful comparison that will assist in understanding many of the conclusions we are able to draw later in the guide.

As we can see, a salary is usual best for the first £12,570 of income, which is why this is generally considered optimal. Thereafter, dividends are best until total income reaches £50,270.

For higher and additional rate taxpayers, the position is more nuanced as either salary or dividend may be best, depending on the company's CT rate.

But you can't have dividends falling into the basic rate band and then salary taxed at the higher or additional rate, it doesn't work that way. For this reason, it generally makes sense to stick with dividends once income exceeds £12,570: but there are exceptions, as we shall see.

Chapter 11

Company Owners Can Control Their Income Tax Bills

In Chapter 9 we mentioned that a company owner can often decide whether any distribution of the company's money is classified as salary or dividend.

Another advantage of being a company owner is that you have control over *how much* income you withdraw in total. This gives you significant control over your Income Tax bill.

Unlike sole traders, who pay tax each year on ALL the profits of the business, company owners only pay tax on the income they decide to pay themselves. This allows company owners to reduce their Income Tax bills by adopting the following strategies:

- 'Smooth income'
- 'Roller-coaster income'

Smooth Income

With smooth income, the company owner withdraws roughly the same amount of money each year, even though the company's profits may fluctuate considerably.

Smooth income allows the company owner to stay below the key Income Tax thresholds that could result in a higher tax bill:

- £50,270 Higher rate tax
- £60,000 Child Benefit Charge
- £100,000 Personal allowance withdrawal

We will return to how you can plan your salary and dividend withdrawals around these key Income Tax thresholds in the chapters that follow.

The higher rate tax threshold generally increases each year in line with inflation, but has been frozen for ten years until 5th April 2031. If it had been increased with inflation as usual, it would be around £68,000 today.

The Child Benefit Charge used to kick in when the highest earner in the household had income over £50,000. However, the charge is now only payable when the highest earner's income exceeds **£60,000**. Furthermore, the charge is now levied more gradually. The full charge is only payable when the highest earner's income reaches **£80,000**.

The £100,000 threshold was introduced in April 2010 and has *never* been increased. If it had gone up with inflation you would only start losing your personal allowance with an income of around £180,000 today.

By freezing various thresholds, the Government has decided to deploy 'fiscal drag' to raise taxes. Fiscal drag occurs when an increase in your income, which is purely down to inflation, pushes up your tax rate. At Taxcafe we call fiscal drag the Silent Killer.

Less silent, but more deadly, was the decision to reduce the additional rate threshold to £125,140. The original £150,000 threshold was introduced in 2010. If it had gone up with inflation, you would only start paying 45% tax with an income of around £275,000 today. Yet, instead, it is now less than half what it should have been by this time.

With the reduction in the additional rate threshold to align it with the point where the personal allowance is completely withdrawn, this threshold is no longer relevant for the smooth income strategy; but it plays an important role in our next strategy.

Roller-Coaster Income

With 'roller-coaster income', the company owners take a bigger or smaller salary or dividend than would normally be required to fund their lifestyles. Roller-coaster income could save you tax in the following circumstances:

Avoiding Additional Tax Costs

There are two parts of the Income Tax system that create an additional tax cost for a limited band of taxable income:

- The Child Benefit Charge where income is between £60,000 and £80,000
- Withdrawal of the personal allowance where income is between £100,000 and £125,140

Where a company owner needs income above the key threshold of £60,000 or £100,000 each year *on average*, they can still avoid these additional charges in some years by using a roller-coaster income strategy. We will look at this planning technique and the potential savings available in more detail in Chapters 22 to 24.

Income Tax Rates Are Going Up or Down

If the Government announces that Income Tax rates will *rise* during a future tax year, you may wish to pay yourself more income now and less income later on. And if your tax rate will *fall* during a future tax year, you may wish to pay yourself less income now and more income later on.

Save Capital Gains Tax

It may also make sense for company owners to pay themselves less income during tax years in which they sell assets subject to CGT such as rental properties. Why? This may allow some of your basic rate band (currently £37,700) to be freed up, which means some of your capital gains will be taxed at 18% instead of 24% (see Chapter 52).

Living Abroad

If you intend to move abroad and become non-UK resident in the future, you could consider withdrawing less income from your company while you are UK resident and more income after you become non-resident. Providing you move to a country with favourable Income Tax rates this strategy could potentially save you significant amounts of UK Income Tax (but see Chapter 53 for potential dangers).

Pension Income

When you reach age 55 (57 from 2028) you may decide to start withdrawing money from any private pension plan you have, for example a self-invested personal pension (SIPP). Any amount you withdraw over and above your 25% tax-free lump sum will be subject to Income Tax.

Fortunately, with a drawdown arrangement you can vary the amount of income you withdraw from your pension scheme every year and there are no limits placed on the amount of income you can withdraw. Coupled with the fact you can vary the amount of income you withdraw from your company, this could allow you to minimise your Income Tax bill by staying below one of the key Income Tax thresholds listed earlier.

Cashflow Savings

The current payment on account system (Chapter 7) means there are currently opportunities to make cashflow savings by taking higher dividends every other year (and lower ones in the years between). However, this must now be considered in the light of forthcoming changes to the payments on account system that mean it may make sense to take more dividends in the current 2026/27 tax year than you might otherwise have intended, so that you can take less in 2027/28. Alternatively, it may make sense to defer dividends you would have taken in 2027/28 until after 5th April 2028. See Chapter 8 for a detailed examination of the potential savings.

Part 2

Tax Efficient Salaries & Dividends

Chapter 12

Tax-Free Salaries

You should now have a good understanding of how salaries and dividends are taxed. The next question is: what is the most tax-efficient mix of salary and dividends for directors who want to extract money from their companies?

In this chapter we will start looking at the 'optimal' amount of salary you should withdraw from your company this year. The good news is that, in many cases, the answer is simple. However, there are also many exceptions to this simple answer, as we will see later.

All amounts are for the current 2026/27 tax year, which ends on 5th April 2027. The answer changes almost every year, so it's important to stay up to date.

Assumption: No Other Taxable Income

We will assume for now that the company owner has no taxable income from other sources (just their company salary and dividends). This keeps the number crunching as simple as possible.

It's not a totally unrealistic assumption either. Although most company owners will have at least some other taxable income, for example bank account interest or stock market dividends, many will have no more than a few hundred pounds. In fact, if the company owner's only income from outside the company is interest income up to £5,500 and/or dividend income up to £500, this will not alter the conclusions drawn in this chapter.

For those company owners who do have significant amounts of other taxable income, for example rental profits from a portfolio of properties, more information is provided in Part 4.

Why a Small Salary is Tax Efficient

The first point to make is that most company owners should pay themselves a small salary. They should not take all their income as dividends.

The first few thousand pounds of either salary or dividend income you receive are tax free thanks to your personal allowance. However, a dividend is not as tax efficient for the *company*.

This is because dividends are paid out of the company's *after-tax* profits, once Corporation Tax (CT) has been paid. So, every dividend has a CT bill attached.

And as a company owner you should be equally concerned about your company's tax position as your own personal tax position.

A salary, by contrast, is a tax-deductible expense for the company.

In summary, a small salary is usually more tax efficient than a dividend. It's potentially tax free in the hands of the company owner and provides a CT saving for the company.

What if You Don't Need the Money?
Because a small salary is so tax efficient most company owners should take one, even if they don't need the income. The money can always be left inside the company until a decision is made to withdraw it.

The general rule is that remuneration cannot be deducted from a company's current taxable profits unless it is 'paid' within nine months of the company's accounting date. However, HMRC will generally accept that remuneration is paid when it is credited to the director's loan account. So, if you don't need the cash, there's nothing to stop you running your salary through the monthly payroll as normal and crediting the amounts to your director's loan account.

The fact that small salaries are so tax efficient is also why company owners should consider paying a salary to their spouse/partner and children (including minor children) wherever possible (see Part 5).

How Much Salary this Year?

There are three relevant thresholds for the 2026/27 tax year:

- Employer's National Insurance £5,000
- Employee's National Insurance £12,570
- Income Tax £12,570

The sharp-eyed among you will have immediately spotted that two of these thresholds are the same amount. For the moment, while we are operating under our key assumption that the director has no other taxable income from outside the company, this means we can effectively treat them as being the same thing.

Later in the guide we will need to remember the primary threshold for employee's NI and the Income Tax personal allowance, while they are the same amount, operate in different ways. In a nutshell, the primary threshold for NI relates only to the director's salary, whereas the Income Tax personal allowance can be used up by any of the director's income.

Nonetheless, while we are keeping things simple, we can quickly answer the 'optimal' salary question:

The 'optimal' salary for many directors is £12,570

The word 'optimal' is in inverted commas because every company and company owner is different. A salary of £12,570 will not be optimal for every single company owner in the land. There are many factors that may influence a salary decision.

Where the company has enough of its £10,500 employment allowance (see Chapter 5) remaining to cover the directors' own salaries, a salary of £12,570 will be completely tax free: no Income Tax and no employee's or employer's NI.

Where the company's employment allowance is already used up paying salaries to other employees, a salary of £12,570 will result in an employer's NI bill of £1,136 this year:

£12,570 – £5,000 = £7,570 x 15% = £1,136

However, the extra salary and employer's NI will attract CT relief at a rate of at least 19%:

CT relief on extra salary:	£7,570 x 19% = £1,438
CT relief on employer's NI:	£1,136 x 19% = £216

The extra CT relief (£1,654) outweighs the NI cost (£1,136) by £518. If the company has a marginal CT rate of 26.5%, this overall net saving increases to £1,171.

That's not the end of the story. To get their hands on this additional sum of between £518 and £1,171 in the company's bank account, the director will have to pay additional Income Tax.

If the director is a basic rate taxpayer, additional Income Tax of between £56 and £126 will be payable (assuming the money is taken as a dividend taxed at 10.75%). If the director is a higher rate taxpayer, additional Income Tax of between £185 and £419 will be payable (at 35.75%).

The net effect is that basic rate taxpayers will typically be between £462 and £1,045 better off by taking a salary of £12,570 instead of £5,000 and higher rate taxpayers will typically be between £333 and £752 better off.

This juggling act gets to the heart of the salary/dividend question: as a company owner you have to compare the tax cost to you *personally* with the tax cost and tax relief enjoyed by your *company*. It can get complicated, but our aim is to guide you through all the factors involved and, hopefully, provide simple conclusions that are easy to follow.

And the key conclusion at this stage is, even when there is an NI cost, it is generally still tax efficient to pay yourself a salary of £12,570.

Chapter Conclusion

The optimal salary for most small company owners to take in 2026/27 is £12,570. This generally remains the case whether there is spare NI employment allowance available or not.

Remember, however, we have assumed so far that the company owner has no taxable income from other sources. We will take a closer look at company owners with other income in Part 4.

As well as those with other income, there are some other scenarios where a higher or lower salary may be more tax efficient, including:

- Companies with a single director, but which also have all or most of their £10,500 employment allowance available (Chapter 14)
- Directors seeking to grow the company and prepared to restrict their own net, after tax income in the short-term to achieve this (Chapter 15)
- Older and younger directors (Chapter 16)
- High income earners (Chapters 23 to 25)

There are also some scenarios where a completely different approach is required to find the director's optimal salary. This generally only applies to big earners with highly profitable companies, but can also apply in a few other circumstances. We call this alternative approach the 'large salary method', and we will look at how it is done, who can benefit, and whether it is worthwhile, in Chapter 26.

Nonetheless, despite these exceptions, it is fair to say we can effectively regard £12,570 as the default, or 'baseline' optimal salary for many directors. **Hence, in many of the examples throughout this guide, we will assume directors take a salary of £12,570 during the 2026/27 tax year**.

Chapter 13

Worthwhile Savings

The 'baseline' salary of £12,570 we looked at in Chapter 12 is the most optimal salary for a director to take in many cases. It is also simple to understand and is currently better than a higher salary from a cashflow point of view (Income Tax and NI on salaries must be paid almost immediately, Income Tax on dividends falls under the payments on account system: see Chapter 7).

There are, however, many situations where a different salary is optimal and can produce savings. Sometimes though, these potential savings are not very significant. That's alright if the alternative strategy is easy to explain and implement in practice. But, if it's more complex, and may carry cashflow disadvantages, it may not be worth it unless the savings it produces are significant.

So, for these more complex strategies, we have set ourselves a minimum threshold of £500 of savings before we regard the strategy as worth mentioning. We therefore call savings of around £500 or more 'worthwhile savings'. We may mention smaller savings sometimes when they are easy to explain, but our coverage of potential savings of less than £500 will not be comprehensive.

Some readers may feel that even a £500 saving is too small to mention, but it's worth pointing out that for a higher rate taxpayer to get an extra £500 of after-tax income out of their own company will typically require more than £1,000 of additional pre-tax profit. So, saving £500 in tax is worth more than £1,000 in most other savings you might be able to make.

And if a saving of £500 still seems too small to bother with, you can choose not to follow the more complex strategy: but at least you'll know about it.

Chapter 14

Using the Employment Allowance

The increase in the employment allowance from £5,000 to £10,500 means it stretches a lot further and quite significant levels of director's salary can sometimes be paid free of employer's National Insurance (NI).

In some cases, where all the employment allowance is available, a salary of up to £75,000 can be paid, producing savings of up to £4,211 compared with our 'baseline' salary of £12,570.

However, worthwhile savings usually only arise when the salary is quite large, generally more than £50,270. Salaries any smaller than this will usually result in an overall loss:

Example: *Brian's company makes a profit of £100,000 after paying salaries totalling £60,000 to three employees, but before taking his own salary. The payments to employees use up £6,750 of the employment allowance, leaving £3,750 to cover Brian's own salary. This means Brian could take a salary of up to £30,000 free from employer's NI.*

Let's assume Brian wishes to extract all the profits as a combination of salary and dividends. We'll compare our usual baseline salary of £12,570 with Brian's maximum employer's NI free salary of £30,000.

	Baseline Salary	***employer's NI-Free***
Company's tax	***£***	***£***
Company profit	*100,000*	*100,000*
Less: Salary	*12,570*	*30,000*
Net Profit	*87,430*	*70,000*
*Less: Corporation Tax**	*19,419*	*14,800*
After-tax profit/Dividend	*68,011*	*55,200*
Director's tax		
Total income	*80,581*	*85,200*
Income Tax	*14,835*	*18,099***
National Insurance	*0*	*1,394*
After-tax income	*65,746*	*65,707*

* 19% on the first £50,000; 26.5% on the remainder (see Chapter 1)

** A little lower for Scottish taxpayers

As we can see, increasing Brian's salary to the amount covered by the employment allowance has left him £39 worse off in this case (£65,746 – £65,707).

It's a tiny difference, and Brian might be reasonably happy with this outcome. But, sticking with the baseline salary of £12,570 may be better from a cashflow point of view.

Another reason why it may be better sticking with the baseline £12,570 is because a bigger salary may cost you significantly more than £39 in some circumstances. It depends on how much profit your company is making (and you may not know how much profit your company is making when you decide how much salary to pay yourself).

The reason profits matter is because they may affect how much Corporation Tax (CT) relief your company enjoys on your salary: if your salary reduces the company's profits below £50,000, some of your salary will only enjoy 19% CT relief instead of 26.5%.

For example, if Brian's company was making profits of just £60,000, he would end up £879 worse off with a salary of £30,000 instead of £12,570.

If you are extracting all of the company's profits, a higher salary may also push more of your income into a higher tax bracket. This is because salaries always increase your taxable income more than dividends (dividends are smaller because they are paid out of profits that are first taxed in the hands of the company).

For example, if Brian's company was making profits between around £123,000 and £158,500, he would end up worse off by *at least* £500 and possibly £1,078. At these profit levels a higher salary will push more of his income over the £100,000 threshold, resulting in the withdrawal of his Income Tax personal allowance.

Salaries between £50,270 and £75,000

The example above shows that a salary higher than £12,570 may be *less* tax efficient, even if no employer's National Insurance is payable thanks to the employment allowance.

However, the outcome starts to change when the salary rises above the £50,270 higher-rate threshold.

At this point the extra salary starts to be taxed at 42% which is better than dividends, which have an overall marginal tax rate somewhere between 47.96% and 52.78% (if you include Corporation Tax).

However, it takes a fair amount of extra salary before any *worthwhile* savings are achievable, which means the company must have a lot more of its employment allowance available for the director's own salary.

The potential saving/cost is illustrated in the table below:

			Salary			
Profits	**£50,270**	**£55,000**	**£60,000**	**£65,000**	**£70,000**	**£75,000**
£60,000	-£1,776	-£1,494	-£1,196	n/a	n/a	n/a
£70,000	-£1,418	-£1,136	-£838	-£540	-£243	n/a
£80,000	-£936	-£654	-£356	-£59	£239	£537
£90,000	-£454	-£172	£125	£423	£721	£1,019
£100,000	£28	£309	£607	£905	£1,203	£1,501
£110,000	£41	£550	£989	£1,097	£1,205	£1,313
£120,000	-£1,014	-£755	-£481	-£207	£67	£175
£130,000	-£1,892	-£1,633	-£1,359	-£1,085	-£811	-£537
£140,000	-£1,708	-£1,449	-£1,175	-£901	-£618	-£127
£150,000	-£1,166	-£702	-£211	£280	£772	£1,263
£160,000	£223	£687	£1,178	£1,670	£2,161	£2,652
£170,000-£250,000	£309	£774	£1,265	£1,756	£2,247	£2,739

The table shows how much better off or worse off you could end up by taking a salary of between £50,270 and £75,000 instead of our baseline £12,570, with the remaining profits extracted as dividends. In the case of a company like Brian's, with profits of £100,000, a saving of £607 is achieved with a salary of £60,000. This requires at least £8,250 of spare employment allowance. His maximum potential saving of £1,501 is achieved with a salary of £75,000, which requires all of the £10,500 employment allowance to be available for his own salary.

Some points to note from the table:

- At relatively low profit levels a higher salary will produce an overall loss because it will mostly only enjoy 19% CT relief instead of 26.5%.
- At some higher profit levels there is also an overall loss – the higher salary is pushing more of the director's income over the £100,000 threshold, resulting in a more significant loss of personal allowance.
- Once the personal allowance is fully withdrawn at the highest profit levels, a higher salary produces savings once again. In some cases, it may even be beneficial to pay an even greater salary and suffer some employer's NI. We'll look at that situation in Chapter 26.
- The outcome always improves as the salary increases from £50,270 to £75,000.

Salary of £75,000
If the company has all of its £10,500 employment allowance available for the director's own salary, a salary of up to £75,000 can be paid free from employer's National Insurance.

Although not in our table, the saving peaks at £1,783, which is achieved when profits reach £105,864 (it takes profits of more than £153,750 before greater savings can be achieved).

A taxable profit of £105,864 is the point where a director who is taking a salary of £75,000 plus all the remaining after-tax profits of £25,000 as dividends reaches a gross taxable income of £100,000. At this point, the director's net, after tax income is £70,299.

If the director is content with a net income of £70,299, they can stick to a salary of £75,000 plus dividends of £25,000, even when the company has profits of more than £105,864.

If so, the savings compared with taking a salary of £12,570 will continue to grow, and can reach £4,211 where the company's profit is between £125,000 and £250,000.

We'll look at an example later in this chapter. At profit levels over £250,000, the saving gradually reduces until bottoming out at £3,274 for profits of £325,000 or more.

Alternatively, if the director wishes to extract all the company's profits, the savings disappear when profits rise above around £120,000, making our baseline salary of £12,570 more attractive once again.

The position then changes yet again at the highest profit levels in our table, making a salary of £75,000, or sometimes even more, attractive once again: see Chapter 26.

Limitations
Of course, not every company has sufficient employment allowance available to cover the director's salary: some or all of the £10,500 allowance will often be used up on other employees' salaries.

The maximum saving of £4,211 is generally only achieved where there is just one single director and all of the employment allowance is available.

However, as explained in Chapter 5, when there is just one director the company only qualifies for the employment allowance if there is at least one other employee paid more than the secondary threshold.

Nonetheless, the full £10,500 allowance can be claimed on a single director's salary where there are other employees, but they are all young workers aged under 21, or apprentices aged under 25, paid more than the secondary threshold, but less than £50,270. And that's how our maximum saving of £4,211 can be achieved.

Example: *Stewie's company is very much like Brian's except it only employs workers aged under 21 and makes a profit of £130,000. Stewie is content to limit his after-tax income to £70,299. Let's now compare the position if he takes a normal baseline salary of £12,570 or his maximum employer's NI free salary of £75,000.*

	Baseline Salary	***employer's NI-Free***
Company's tax	***£***	***£***
Company profit	*130,000*	*130,000*
Less: Salary	*12,570*	*75,000*
Net Profit	*117,430*	*55,000*
*Less: Corporation Tax**	*27,369*	*10,825*
After-tax profit	*90,061*	*44,175*
Less: Dividend	*75,097*	*25,000*
Cash retained in company	*14,964*	*19,175*
Director's tax		
Total income	*87,667*	*100,000*
Income Tax	*17,368*	*26,191***
National Insurance	*0*	*3,510*
After-tax income	*70,299*	*70,299*

* 19% on the first £50,000; 26.5% on the remainder (see Chapter 1)
** Higher for Scottish taxpayers

In this scenario, the director's after-tax income is the same but the company has £4,211 more cash left (£19,175 – £14,964).

Another way to secure most of the £10,500 employment allowance is to employ someone paid just above the secondary threshold for a short period. As we saw in Chapter 5, it is possible to pay a temporary, part-time worker anything over £96 for a week and secure the employment allowance for the whole year. Let's say you take on a part-time helper for two weeks and pay them £250 for this period. This will use just under £9 of the employment allowance, leaving £10,491 to cover the director's salary.

The director can then take an employer's NI free salary of up to £74,940 and can achieve savings of up to £4,200 if the company's profits are high enough. With potential savings worth almost 17 times the cost of taking on the temporary helper, it's got to be worth thinking about!

Calculating the Optimal Salary

In both this chapter and Chapter 5, we've looked at a few different scenarios and calculated the maximum salary a director can take that is covered by the employment allowance. That salary will sometimes be the director's optimal salary, as shown in this chapter, but also in other scenarios we will look at later.

In many cases, that optimal salary can be calculated in a few steps.

i) Calculate the company's total wages and salaries cost for the tax year (not the accounting period), not including owner/directors
ii) Deduct amounts paid to workers under 21, and apprentices under 25
iii) Work out the number of employees the company has, excluding owner/directors, workers under 21, and apprentices under 25
iv) Divide the net total at step (ii) by the number derived at step (iii)
v) Deduct £5,000 from the amount derived at step (iv)
vi) Multiply the amount derived at step (v) by the number derived at step (iii) and then also by 15%: this is how much employment allowance has been used up, if it's £10,500 or more there is none left, if it's £9,365 or more there isn't enough left to cover a salary of more than £12,570, so you can stop here. Otherwise...
vii) Deduct the amount derived at step (vi) from £10,500
viii) Multiply the amount derived at step (vii) by 100/15
ix) Add £5,000

And that's your maximum employer's NI free salary. Like to see a demonstration?

Example:
Step (i) Griffin Ltd pays wages and salaries totalling £82,000 in 2026/27, not including Peter, the owner/director.
Step (ii) This includes £16,000 paid to Meg, a worker aged under 21, Deducting this leaves £66,000.
Step (iii) The company employs three other people, not counting Peter and Meg.
Step (iv) £66,000 divided by three equals £22,000
Step (v) £22,000 – £5,000 = £17,000
Step (vi) £17,000 x 3 x 15% = £7,650 (the amount of employment allowance used)
Step (vii) £10,500 – £7,650 = £2,850 (the amount of spare employment allowance available)
Step (viii) £2,850 x 100/15 = £19,000
Step (ix) £19,000 + £5,000 = £24,000

In this case, Peter could pay himself a salary of up to £24,000 covered by the employment allowance and free of employer's NI.

In most cases, this will not be optimal (as illustrated in the table earlier, there generally needs to be a salary significantly higher than £50,270 before any worthwhile savings arise) and Peter may be better off sticking with a salary of £12,570.

However, the £24,000 salary could be optimal for Peter if he is over state pension age (Chapter 16) or looking to grow the company (Chapter 15).

Note, the method for deriving the amount of spare employment allowance available shown above will not work if there are any workers under 21 or apprentices under 25 paid more than £50,270, workers paid less than the secondary threshold, or a different number of employees at different points in the tax year: although it will often still give a reasonable approximation.

Chapter 15

Growing the Company

A salary of more than £12,570 may be tax efficient where **all three** of the following factors are present:

- There is no employer's NI payable on the director's salary because the company's employment allowance is not used up paying salaries to other employees
- The company has a marginal CT rate of 26.5% or 25%: this will be the case where it has taxable profits of at least £50,000 *after* paying the directors' salaries
- The director remains a basic-rate taxpayer after taking additional salary income (a basic-rate taxpayer is someone whose total taxable income does not exceed £50,270)

To ensure the director remains a basic rate taxpayer, it is important to take account of their increased salary, the dividends they take from the company, and any other taxable income received from outside the company in the same tax year (e.g. pensions, interest, rental income, stock market dividends, etc).

We call this the 'growing the company' scenario because it requires the director to ensure their total taxable income for the year does not exceed £50,270, while the company will generally need to be making profits of more than £62,570 before paying the director's salary.

Note, this is a different scenario to the position we looked at in Chapter 14, where the director is a higher rate taxpayer and there is sufficient employment allowance available to pay an employer's NI free salary of more than £50,270.

Example: *Sushila and her son Robbie own and run a camper van company that makes profits of around £200,000 per year and therefore faces a marginal CT rate of 26.5% (satisfying factor two above).*

The pair wish to extract income of no more than £50,270 each to avoid paying higher-rate tax and leave enough cash in the company to help it grow. To keep the example simple, we'll also assume they do not have any other taxable income from outside the company. Both these points mean factor three above is satisfied.

We'll also assume the company does not have any other employees, so all of the company's £10,500 NI employment allowance is available for the directors' own salaries.

How much salary income should Sushila and Robbie pay themselves this year?

As explained in Chapter 5, the full £10,500 employment allowance will cover two directors' salaries of £40,000 each. So, Sushila and Robbie should pay themselves a salary of no more than £40,000 each (satisfying factor one above) and make up the balance with a dividend of £10,270 each:

£50,270 less £40,000 salary = £10,270 dividend

Sushila and Robbie will pay 20% Income Tax and 8% employee's NI on a significant portion of their salary income but this is better than the 34.4% combined tax rate on dividend income (see Chapter 6).

But if they pay themselves salaries of more than £40,000, the additional salary will also suffer 15% employer's NI, which is why they are better off taking the additional £10,270 as dividend income.

If the company DOES have other employees, those salaries will use up some or all of the company's £10,500 employment allowance. If all of the employment allowance is used up paying salaries to other employees, the directors should pay themselves a salary of £12,570 each, as explained in Chapter 12.

If only some of the employment allowance is used up paying salaries to other employees, the directors should reduce their salaries accordingly.

For example, if the company has just one employee earning £25,000 this will use up £3,000 of the company's employment allowance:

£25,000 – £5000 = £20,000 x 15% = £3,000

This will leave £7,500 of employment allowance remaining for the directors' own salaries or £3,750 each. This will allow the directors to pay themselves a salary of £30,000 each with no employer's NI (satisfying factor one above):

£30,000 – £5,000 = £25,000 x 15% = £3,750

They should then take a dividend of £20,270 each to make up the balance of their income:

£30,000 salary + £20,270 dividend = £50,270 higher-rate threshold

But if the company has three employees earning £25,000 each this will use up £9,000 of the company's employment allowance, leaving just £1,500 of employment allowance remaining for the directors' own salaries, or £750 each.

In such a case our 'baseline' salary of £12,570 remains optimal. This amount of salary results in £1,136 of employer's NI and therefore uses up all of the remaining employment allowance. If the directors pay themselves a bigger salary, factor one above will no longer be satisfied.

For more information on how to calculate the amount of spare employment allowance available to cover director's salaries, see Chapter 14.

As we can see, there are cases where paying a salary of more than £12,570 is tax efficient. It will appeal most to profitable, growing companies run by couples with no other employees.

It could also work well where there is a single director/shareholder with only a few low-paid employees, such as Peter in our last example in Chapter 14 (remember, the employment allowance is not available if a single director/shareholder is the only employee). For another illustration of the benefits of this strategy, based on a single director, see Chapter 19.

The strategy is, however, generally only for those company owners who are committed to growing their company. While it is most tax efficient overall, taking account of both the directors' and the company's position (what we call 'optimal' in this guide), it is important to understand it could leave the director with less after-tax income than a lower salary might.

For instance, let's look at Sushila and Robbie from our example above. Taking a salary of £40,000 plus dividends of £10,270 will leave each of them with after-tax income of £41,539. A salary of £12,570 plus dividends of £37,700 would have left them with £46,271 each. That's £4,732 less net income each, a total of £9,464.

BUT the total cost to the company of paying the lower salaries plus higher dividends is £127,725. This includes the CT on the profits used to pay the dividends. This compares with a total cost of £107,945 to pay the higher salaries and smaller dividends.

So, while the directors are £9,464 worse off, the company is £19,780 better off. That's an overall net saving of £10,286, which means, for those looking to grow their company, this may be the better route.

Chapter 16

Older & Younger Directors

If a company director is over state pension age, there is no employee's NI payable on their salary. Employer's NI is still payable, however, unless the company has spare employment allowance to cover the directors' own salaries.

A company director can receive a fairly large salary with no NI payable at all if:

- The director is over state pension age, and
- The company has spare employment allowance

For example, where there are two directors over state pension age, and no other employees, it will be possible for the directors to receive salaries of £40,000 each with no NI liability at all.

A larger NI free salary is usually more tax efficient than taking a smaller salary and dividends. Even larger salaries could be tax efficient for some of these directors: see Chapter 26.

Older Directors: No Spare Employment Allowance

Where employer's NI is payable because the company does not have any spare employment allowance, the position for these older directors depends on the company's marginal CT rate.

If the company's marginal CT rate remains either 25% or 26.5% after paying the director's increased salary, the larger salary is generally more tax efficient than taking a small salary plus dividends.

There are a few exceptions where the larger salary would result in the director losing more of their personal allowance than taking a small salary plus dividends. These depend on several factors, but can obviously be avoided by limiting the director's total taxable income to no more than £100,000. Alternatively, at high profit levels, the large salary method covered in Chapter 26 becomes optimal.

The position is different for older directors subject to Scottish Income Tax rates. For these directors, if there is no spare employment allowance available, a large salary will generally only produce savings, even if the company's marginal CT rate is 25% or 26.5%, *if* the director remains a basic or intermediate rate taxpayer once all their income for the tax year is taken into account (including dividends from the company). In most other cases, the best salary for these directors to take will usually be £5,000.

Where the company is only paying CT at 19%, the most tax efficient salary for an older director living anywhere in the UK, where no spare employment allowance is available, will generally be £5,000. This is assuming the director has income from outside the company of at least £7,570, which will generally be the case when they are in receipt of a state pension. If they have no income from outside the company, a salary of £12,570 will generally be optimal.

Reaching State Pension Age

The exemption from employee's NI begins immediately when you reach state pension age. Hence, if you will reach state pension age during the current tax year, and plan to take a salary in excess of £12,570 (either as a result of the guidance given above, or for some other reason) it will generally make sense to defer some or all of your salary until after the date you reach state pension age.

Beware, however, that employee's NI continues to be payable where a salary payment *should* have been paid before you reached state pension age. HMRC might therefore seek to apply employee's NI where you defer payments that are normally made on a regular monthly basis, or as a lump sum earlier in the tax year. Changing this pattern a few years before reaching state pension age might avoid such a problem.

Remember also that a director's salary is deemed to be paid as soon as the amount is recorded anywhere in the company's records.

Conversely, for those reaching state pension age this year, your ability to add another qualifying year to your record for state pension entitlement purposes (without having to pay for it) ends on the date you reach state pension age. Hence, if you have not yet secured your maximum state pension entitlement, it will probably make sense to pay yourself at least £6,708 of salary before you reach state pension age (see Chapter 17).

It also generally makes sense to ensure your NI is calculated on the default, cumulative basis (see Chapter 5) in the tax year you reach state pension age and not on the alternative basis where you can choose to be treated like a regular employee until the final pay period.

Younger Directors

Surprisingly, someone can be a company director from as young as 16. Less surprisingly, they also become subject to *employee's* NI from the same age.

However, for a director (or any employee) under 21, there is no *employer's* NI payable on a salary up to the higher rate threshold (currently £50,270). For a larger salary, employer's NI is only payable on the excess. Hence, a salary of up to £50,270 becomes optimal for a young director aged under 21 in *either* of the following scenarios:

- The company has a marginal CT rate of 26.5% or 25% after paying the director's salary (there are some exceptions where the director's total income for the year exceeds £100,000), *or*
- The director has a salary of at least £50,270 from another job (way to go, kid).

For young directors subject to Scottish Income Tax rates: under the first scenario, the director generally needs to remain a basic or intermediate rate taxpayer once all their income for the tax year is taken into account (including dividends from the company).

Even greater salaries may sometimes be optimal for young directors under 21 with more profitable companies: see Chapter 26 for details.

Chapter 17

Salaries: Pension Benefits

Apart from being tax efficient, a salary confers two extra benefits on the director/shareholder:

- State pension entitlement
- Ability to make private pension contributions

State Pension Entitlement

To obtain the necessary credit for state pension entitlement purposes, you need to pay yourself a salary at least equal to the NI lower earnings limit, which is £6,708 for 2026/27. Many company owners wishing to extract company profits tax efficiently will already take an optimal salary of £6,708 or more in any case.

However, subject to the points considered below, if you would not otherwise be taking a salary of at least £6,708, it is generally worth taking this minimum level of salary in order to secure state pension entitlement.

Even when the employment allowance is not available, the employer's NI cost of paying yourself a salary of £6,708 is only £256, or between £188 and £208 net of CT relief. As the basic state pension is currently £241.30 *per week*, most commentators would regard this as an excellent investment!

But this cost is either irrelevant or unnecessary if you are either already over state pension age, or obtaining a credit for state pension entitlement purposes by:

- Receiving a salary of at least £6,708 from another job
- Making trading profits of at least £7,105 from self employment
- Claiming child benefit for a child under 12

Under the current system, those who have already clocked up at least 35 qualifying years for state pension entitlement purposes will not generally see any additional benefit from obtaining further credits. This means the cost described above may again be unnecessary for some company owners aged 51 or more.

However, there are transitional rules applying to many people that could mean you need more than 35 qualifying years to get your maximum state pension: so it would be wise to check your state pension forecast first. There's also the possibility they might change the rules again!

Those with trading profits under £7,105 and some individual landlords with a sufficiently active business can pay voluntary Class 2 NI of £190 per year. Where available, this will be cheaper than a salary that suffers both Income Tax and employer's NI.

Where an individual is not entitled to pay voluntary Class 2 NI and is not getting a credit by any other means, they can only secure state pension entitlement by paying voluntary Class 3 NI at £957 a year. Paying yourself a salary of £6,708 will be cheaper!

To keep things simple, for the rest of this guide, we will generally assume company owners need to pay themselves a salary of at least £6,708 to secure state pension entitlement, and will usually set this as the minimum salary level to be paid, rather than anything lower (e.g. £5,000).

This will not, however, apply where we know the director is over state pension age or in receipt of another salary of £6,708 or more.

Private Pension Contributions

Everyone under 75 can make a pension contribution of £3,600 per year. The actual cash contribution would be £2,880, with the taxman adding £720. If you want to make bigger pension contributions, the contributions you make *personally* (as opposed to contributions made by your company) must not exceed your 'relevant UK earnings'. Salaries count as earnings but dividends, rental income, and interest income do not.

For a company director taking an 'optimal' tax-free salary of £12,570, the maximum pension contribution he or she can make is £12,570. This is the maximum *gross* contribution. The director would personally invest £10,056 (£12,570 x 80%) and the taxman will top this up with £2,514 of basic rate tax relief.

Company owners can also get their companies to make pension contributions, instead of making them personally. As we shall see in Chapter 42, company pension contributions are more tax efficient than personal contributions in many circumstances.

Chapter 18

Tax-Free Dividends

If a company owner needs more income than their 'optimal' salary, as most probably do, the most tax-efficient solution is generally to take a dividend rather than a bigger salary.

In this chapter, we'll take a look at how much tax-free dividend income you can take and then, in the next chapter, we'll look at how much dividend income you can take taxed at just 10.75%.

We know from Chapter 6 that dividends attract no NI and are free from Income Tax if they're covered by the director's personal allowance or their dividend allowance.

As we saw in Chapter 12, the 'optimal' salary for most small company owners in 2026/27 is £12,570. This uses up their personal allowance, meaning the only tax-free dividend they can take is the measly £500 covered by their dividend allowance. Combined with their salary, this gives the director/shareholder a maximum total 'tax-free' income of £13,070.

However, when we look at the *company's* tax position, we see that this income is not truly tax free. Firstly, where the company has no spare employment allowance then, as we saw in Chapter 12, there is £1,136 of employer's NI payable on this level of salary. Secondly, although a dividend of £500 can generally be paid with no tax consequences for the director/shareholder, dividends are paid out of a company's profits after paying CT.

Nonetheless, despite the tax costs, this is still generally the best way for most director/shareholders to get the first £13,070 they need out of the company.

The fact that dividends always have a CT bill attached is an important point to remember, especially if you want to grow your business rather than extract income from it. If, for example, a company with a marginal CT rate of 26.5% incurs £10,000 of tax-deductible expenditure before the end of its accounting period, its CT bill will be reduced by £2,650. This will leave less after-tax profit to distribute as dividends but such a strategy may appeal to some business owners who would prefer to re-invest profits and minimise all taxes, including CT.

The fact that dividends come with a CT bill is also why company owners should consider other profit extraction strategies, for example paying interest or making company pension contributions (Chapters 39 and 41). Some payments like these can be both tax free in the hands of the director and provide CT relief. This is the best-case profit extraction scenario.

Doubling the Tax-Free Income

Many companies are started and run by married or unmarried couples. The salaries and tax-free dividends outlined above can then be doubled up. So, where salaries of £12,570 are taken:

Tax-free salaries	£25,140
Tax-free dividends	£1,000
Total tax-free income	£26,140

Spouses/Partners Brought into the Business

Not all companies are started or managed by couples. In these cases, the questions from a tax planning perspective are:

- Can a spouse/partner be employed in the business?
- Can company shares be transferred to a spouse/partner?
- How much tax will these strategies save?

We'll return to these important tax planning issues in Chapter 35.

Company Directors' Tax Returns

Even if you don't have any Income Tax to pay on your salary and dividends, you may still have to complete a tax return. All company directors have this duty where they either have taxable income or have been issued with a notice to file a tax return. In fact, HMRC seem to be under the impression that all company directors must file a tax return, even if they have no taxable income. In practice, it's probably easier to file a tax return than to get into an argument with them over this point. See Chapter 50 for more information about small company director's tax returns.

The Next Step: Taxable Dividends

The tax-free salaries and dividends listed above will not provide enough income for the vast majority of company owners. Those that require more income will have to pay Income Tax on any additional dividends withdrawn, as we shall now see.

Part 3

How to Extract More Income Tax Efficiently

Chapter 19

The Next Step: Dividends Taxed at Just 10.75%

So far, we've shown that a company owner who has no other income and takes a tax-free salary of £12,570 this year can also take a tax-free dividend of £500 for a total tax-free income of £13,070. These amounts can be doubled up where the company is owned by a couple.

Of course, most company owners will require more income and the most tax-efficient route is normally to take a bigger dividend.

Any additional dividend income you take will be taxed. However, as long as your total income does not exceed the £50,270 higher rate threshold, you will pay just 10.75% Income Tax. If you take any more dividend income, the tax rate jumps to 35.75%!

If you've taken a salary of £12,570 and tax-free dividend of £500, the maximum amount of additional dividend income you can take taxed at just 10.75% is £37,200. The Income Tax payable on this additional dividend income will be £3,999.

In summary, you can take a salary of £12,570 and a total dividend of £37,700 for a total pre-tax income of £50,270. After paying £3,999 tax you'll be left with after-tax income of £46,271.

These amounts can be doubled up if the company is owned by a couple, leaving them with total after-tax income of £92,542 and a total Income Tax bill of £7,998.

Salary vs Dividends
No Employment Allowance Available

Even though the additional dividend income is taxed, it is generally still more tax efficient than taking a bigger salary. To end up with the same after-tax income of £46,271 in 2026/27, a director/shareholder would require an additional salary payment of £48,144, on top of the £12,570 already paid and the maximum tax-free dividend of £500.

The director would end up with the same amount of after-tax income but the company would end up with around £3,500 less cash. This is because the company has to make such a large salary payment to cover all the extra tax, especially NI.

The table below illustrates this effect in two companies: one paying a small salary and dividends, the other paying a big salary plus a £500 tax-free dividend. For the sake of illustration, we will look at companies with sufficient profits to ensure the big salary attracts CT relief at the highest possible rate of 26.5%.

In each case, the director ends up with £46,271. The company paying the big salary ends up with £3,493 less cash.

	Small Salary	**Big Salary**
Company's tax	**£**	**£**
Company profit	125,000	125,000
Less: Salary	12,570	60,714
Less: Employer's NI	1,136	8,357
Net Profit	111,294	55,929
Less: Corporation Tax*	25,743	11,071
After-tax profit	85,551	44,858
Less: Dividend	37,700	500
Company cash	47,851	44,358
Director's tax		
Total income	50,270	61,214
Income Tax	3,999	11,718**
National Insurance	0	3,225
After-tax income	46,271	46,271

* 19% on the first £50,000; 26.5% on the remainder (see Chapter 1)
** Higher for Scottish taxpayers

Salary vs Dividends
Spare Employment Allowance Available

The position is less clear-cut where there is spare employment allowance available, as this reduces the cost of a salary in excess of £12,570 considerably.

There are two scenarios where increasing the director's salary to the amount covered by the employment allowance can produce savings. The first, for higher rate taxpayers with most of the employment allowance available to cover their salary, was covered in Chapter 14. That chapter also provides guidance on how to calculate the amount of spare employment allowance available.

The other scenario applies where the company is enjoying CT relief at 25% or 26.5% and the director does not also take enough dividends to make them a higher rate taxpayer. In this case, a salary that uses up the employment allowance might be beneficial.

For example, with a salary of £45,000, a director/shareholder could take a dividend of £5,270 before becoming a higher rate taxpayer. After Income Tax and NI of £9,080 on the salary and Income Tax of £513 on the dividend, the director would be left with £40,677 of after-tax income.

If the director is willing to limit their income in this way, a higher salary that is free of employer's NI can save the company money.

By way of illustration, let's look at another two companies. One company pays a salary of £45,000 plus dividends of £5,270, the other pays a small salary of £12,570 plus sufficient dividends to give the director the same after-tax income of £40,677.

We will again assume the companies have sufficient profits to ensure the big salary attracts CT relief at the highest possible marginal rate of 26.5%. This time, however, we will also assume the companies have sufficient spare employment allowance to allow the larger salary to be paid without incurring any employer's NI liability.

	Small Salary	Big Salary
Company's tax	**£**	**£**
Company profit	125,000	125,000
Less: Salary	12,570	45,000
Net Profit	112,430	80,000
Less: Corporation Tax*	26,044	17,450
After-tax profit	86,386	62,550
Less: Dividend	31,432	5,270
Company cash	54,954	57,280
Director's tax		
Total income	44,002	50,270
Income Tax	3,325	6,999**
National Insurance	0	2,594
After-tax income	40,677	40,677

* 19% on the first £50,000; 26.5% on the remainder (see Chapter 1)
** Higher for Scottish taxpayers

The saving produced by following this strategy is £2,326 (£57,280 – £54,954).

However, this strategy is really only for directors who want to grow their companies and are willing to keep their personal income to a lower level to achieve it. For a further analysis of the benefits of this strategy, see Chapter 15.

Bigger Salaries for Other Reasons

Of course, not all company owners take the most tax efficient or 'optimal' salary. Some take a bigger salary because it suits them to do so for other reasons.

For example, a company owner who takes a salary of £30,000 can still take a tax-free dividend of £500 plus additional dividend income of up to £19,770 taxed at 10.75% (£50,270 – £30,000 – £500).

A company owner who takes a salary of £50,000 can still take a tax-free dividend of £500. However, because their total taxable income exceeds the higher rate threshold, any additional dividend income will be subject to tax at the higher rate of 35.75%.

Chapter 20

Making the Most of the 10.75% Tax Rate

So far, we have shown a company owner who takes a salary of £12,570 can receive dividend income of £500 tax free and a further £37,200 taxed at 10.75%.

Company owners who extract more money from their companies will go over the £50,270 higher rate threshold and start paying Income Tax at 35.75% on their dividends, which is a big leap!

(Remember, at this point, to keep things simple, we are assuming the company owner does not have income from other sources.)

An important tax planning question is whether you should pay yourself as much dividend income as you can taxed at 10.75%, even if you don't need the money immediately? It's impossible to provide a definitive answer because every company owner is different. However, we will attempt to outline the main benefits and drawbacks in this chapter.

One of the main reasons why you may NOT want to pay yourself the maximum amount taxed at 10.75% this year is if you expect to be able to withdraw the same money tax free next year or in another tax year.

We've shown that a couple who take salaries of £12,570 each can also pay themselves tax-free dividends of £500 each: a total tax-free income of £26,140 in 2026/27. Although some company owners may be able to survive on the tax-free amounts, most will not and will have to withdraw at least some dividend income each year taxed at 10.75%. Arguably you then have fairly little to lose by withdrawing the maximum amount you can have taxed at 10.75% this year (£37,200 each).

The main drawback is you will end up paying Income Tax earlier than may be necessary. In other words, the extra money you pay in Income Tax will earn interest in the taxman's bank account instead of your company's bank account.

So, what are the benefits of paying tax early? By paying the maximum dividend taxed at 10.75%, you stand to protect yourself against:

- Further dividend tax increases
- Business risk
- Becoming a higher rate taxpayer

In previous editions of this guide, we warned that dividend tax rates could be increased. This has happened twice in recent years. The rates were all increased by 1.25% from April 2022, and the basic and higher rates were increased by a further 2% this year. The dividend allowance has also been slashed to a pathetic £500.

In our opinion, further increases cannot be ruled out under the current Government, as discussed in the Introduction and Chapter 6. If you are concerned that dividend tax rates could be increased again, it may be better to withdraw as much income as you can taxed at 10.75% in case the rate is increased to, say, 12%.

Of course, it's also possible that dividend tax rates could be reduced at some point, but this seems highly improbable for the foreseeable future in light of recent Government announcements.

Some company owners may wish to remove cash from their companies to protect against business risk (arguably your money is at greater risk in the company's bank account than your own).

But perhaps the best reason to pay yourself the maximum dividend taxed at 10.75% is if you think you may become a higher rate taxpayer in the future. In other words, it may be better to *definitely* pay 10.75% tax this year rather than *possibly* 35.75% in a future tax year.

Why would you expect to become a higher rate taxpayer in the future? Perhaps you expect the profits of your business to grow or you expect to receive more income from other sources, for example an inheritance.

It's likely many basic rate taxpayers will become higher rate taxpayers, even if their income simply increases because of inflation. This is because the higher rate threshold has been fixed at £50,270 for ten years (until 5th April 2031).

Although you might never become a higher rate taxpayer, you arguably have very little to lose by paying yourself the maximum dividend taxed at 10.75%. If you do become a higher rate taxpayer you will save 25% (by paying 10.75% tax this year rather than 35.75% in the future).

If you don't become a higher rate taxpayer you will probably lose nothing because you will pay 10.75% tax this year instead of 10.75% in the future.

Another reason to make the most of the 10.75% rate this year may be to use this as a method to reduce your self-assessment tax liability for next year, 2027/28. As we saw in Chapter 8, this could have significant cashflow benefits in the near future.

Reasons to Pay Smaller Dividends

A company owner may decide to not withdraw the maximum dividend taxed at 10.75% for several reasons:

- The company hasn't made enough profit
- The company needs the cash to grow
- The company owner doesn't need the money
- The company is forced to restrict its dividends
- The company owner has taxable capital gains
- To avoid the Winter Fuel Charge

The Company Hasn't Made Enough Profit

The company doesn't need to have made any profit to pay *salaries* and tax-efficient salaries should be paid wherever possible because they are also a tax-deductible expense and reduce the company's CT bill (even if this is only at a later date if the company is currently not making profits). For example, a salary of £12,570 will reduce a company's tax bill by *at least* £2,388.

Dividends, on the other hand, can only be declared if the company has sufficient distributable profits. It is not necessary for the company to actually make a profit in the year the dividend is paid, as long as there are sufficient accumulated profits (after tax) from previous years. (See Chapter 49 for more information on this issue.)

The Company Needs the Cash to Grow

Even if the company has made sufficient profits, the directors may wish to keep the cash in the company to grow the business. In these circumstances it may be possible for a dividend to be declared but not paid out. The dividend can simply be credited to the director's loan account and withdrawn at a later date when it is more convenient. This may be more tax efficient than reducing dividends during one year and then declaring bigger dividends taxed at 35.75% in another year.

Note that the director will be subject to Income Tax on any dividend that has been declared, whether it is paid out or not. In practice, this means it may be necessary to pay out a small portion of the dividend to help the director pay their tax bill.

The Company Owner Doesn't Need the Money

A company owner may decide to take a smaller dividend if they have other resources such as inherited money or proceeds from selling another business or from selling other assets like property or shares. The company owner may also have a spouse/partner who earns enough income to support the family.

In these circumstances the company owner may believe it is sensible to limit the amount taken as dividends to avoid paying tax at 10.75%. In reality, however, the company owner may simply be storing up an Income Tax problem for the future. If accumulated profits are eventually paid out as a large dividend, an Income Tax charge of 35.75% or 39.35% could be payable on a significant portion of any dividend declared.

If income is withdrawn on a more regular annual basis, even if not required immediately, Income Tax can be restricted to 10.75%.

There is one important exception. If the company owner has taxable income from other sources, it may be prudent to take a smaller dividend. So far, we have assumed the company owner has no other taxable income. If there is other taxable income that uses up some or all of the director's basic rate band, it may be necessary to restrict dividends to avoid paying Income Tax at 35.75%. (More about directors with other income in Part 4.)

The Company is Forced to Restrict its Dividends

Lenders may place restrictions on dividend payments to protect their interests (i.e. to stop cash leaking out of the company that should be going to them). In these circumstances it may be difficult for the company owners to structure their dividend payments to mitigate tax.

The Company Owner Has Taxable Capital Gains

If you have taxable capital gains you may want to reduce the amount of income you withdraw from your company to free up some of your basic rate band. This may allow you to pay less CGT: see Chapter 52.

Avoiding the Winter Fuel Charge

Winter fuel payments are not exactly worth a fortune (between £100 and £317 this year), but you have to pay them back if your income strays even just £1 above the £35,000 Winter Fuel Charge threshold.

So, for some older directors, it may be worth restricting your dividends to avoid the charge.

It's probably not worth worrying about if you were planning to take £40,000 or more out of the company, but it would be crazy to end up with taxable income only just over £35,000!

Alternatives to Dividends

Although paying tax at 10.75% is a lot better than paying tax at 35.75%, it's important to remember that dividends are paid out of income that has already been subjected to CT. Thus, if you are a basic rate taxpayer, the true effective tax rate on your dividends is at least 27.71%, not 10.75% (see Chapter 6). Thus dividends are less tax efficient than some other types of income you may be able to extract from your company.

Take rental income for example. If your company pays you rent of £10,000, the amount will be a fully deductible expense (providing the rent is a reasonable market rate for the company's occupation of a property you own personally). If you are a basic rate taxpayer, you will pay 20% tax on the amount received, leaving you with £8,000.

On the other hand, if your company does not pay you rent it will have extra profits of £10,000 on which it will pay at least 19% CT, leaving £8,100 at most to distribute as dividends. After paying 10.75% tax you will be left with £7,229 at most.

Clearly, rental income is a fair bit more tax efficient than dividend income in this situation (see Chapter 38 for more information).

Another example is pension contributions. If your company contributes £10,000 to your pension it can claim CT relief. Ignoring investment growth, when you retire you will be able to withdraw 25% tax free and the rest could be taxed at just 20% if you are a basic rate taxpayer.

After tax you'll be left with £8,500, compared with £7,229, at most, from a dividend (see Chapter 41 for more on pension contributions).

It's worth bearing all this in mind before you pay yourself any dividends, as these may effectively limit your ability to make other tax efficient payments. We'll take a closer look at this potential conflict in Chapter 49.

Furthermore, paying dividends may also limit the financial resources available to the company to make other tax efficient payments, e.g. rent or pension contributions.

Chapter 21

Making the Most of the 35.75% Tax Rate

So far, we have shown that a company owner who takes a tax-free salary of £12,570 can extract a tax-free dividend of £500 and a dividend of £37,200 taxed at 10.75%, leaving them with an after-tax income of £46,271.

The company owner's gross, taxable income is then £50,270, meaning they are on the cusp of being a higher rate taxpayer.

These amounts can be doubled in the case of companies owned and run by couples.

If you generally do not require more income, you may be able to adopt an 'income smoothing' strategy: taking the maximum tax-free salary and dividend plus the maximum dividend taxed at 10.75% every year where possible, regardless of whether the company has made bigger than normal profits or lower than normal profits.

Taking Bigger Dividends

If you want more income, the optimal strategy is usually to take additional dividends rather than salary, in order to avoid the NI payable on employment income. However, now that you have reached the £50,270 higher rate threshold, you will pay a whopping 35.75% Income Tax on any additional dividend income you take.

You also have to watch out for two further tax stings:

- Child Benefit Charge: income over £60,000
- Personal allowance withdrawal: income over £100,000

In this chapter, we will assume neither the company owner, nor any other member of their household, is claiming any child benefit. We will return to child benefit in the next chapter.

If no child benefit is being claimed, the next threshold to watch out for is £100,000, where your personal allowance starts to be withdrawn. The personal allowance currently saves many higher rate taxpayers up to

£5,028 in Income Tax; it often saves company owners up to £5,657, so many company owners will want to keep their income below £100,000 to avoid losing it.

Maximum Income

With total income of £50,270 the director can take additional dividend income of up to £49,730 taxed at 35.75% before the £100,000 threshold is breached.

A director who takes a salary of £12,570 and the rest of their income as dividends will be left with total after-tax income of £78,223:

£12,570 salary + £87,430 dividend – £21,777 tax = £78,223

If the company is owned and managed by a couple this can potentially be doubled up.

Don't Forget the Corporation Tax Bill!

It's tempting to think that company owners who pay themselves any of the above amounts are paying relatively little tax. After all, a total of £100,000 is being extracted from the company with a total Income Tax bill of just £21,777. The effective Income Tax rate is only 21.78%!

However, it's important to remember that dividends are always paid out of a company's *after-tax* profits.

To pay a dividend of £87,430, the company will have had to make taxable profits of at least £113,850. This would result in a CT bill of at least £26,420 (the first £50,000 at 19%, the remainder at 26.5%: see Chapter 1). Coupled with an Income Tax bill of £21,777, the total tax bill attached to the dividend is £48,197.

Alternatives to Dividends

In Chapter 6 we pointed out that, as a higher rate taxpayer, the total tax rate on your dividend income is at least 47.96%, and sometimes up to 52.78%. With the tax rate at this level, some small company owners may decide to not pay themselves any dividend income which takes them over the higher rate threshold.

They may simply roll up cash inside their companies, possibly until the business is sold or wound up.

At this point it may be possible to pay CGT at a reduced rate (18% from 6th April 2026) on the funds extracted if the company owner qualifies for business asset disposal relief. We'll explore this issue more in Chapter 44.

Other company owners may decide to pay themselves less dividend income and focus on other techniques to extract money from their companies, such as pension contributions.

For example, if your company contributes £10,000 to your pension, the payment will be a tax-deductible expense for the company. Ignoring investment growth, when you retire you can withdraw up to 25% tax free and the rest will possibly be taxed at just 20% if you are a basic rate taxpayer, as many retirees are. After tax you'll be left with £8,500. This compares with at most £5,204 if instead a dividend is taken equal to what is left of that pre-tax profit of £10,000 (after CT) and then taxed again in your hands at 35.75%. (See Chapter 41 for more information on company pension contributions.)

Many company owners who are higher rate taxpayers now face a combined marginal tax rate on dividend income of 52.78% (see Chapter 6). This makes it even more attractive to extract other types of income from your company (for example rental income or interest), or focus on other profit extraction techniques, such as pension contributions.

Having said this, company owners whose company currently has profits low enough to pay CT at just 19%, but who expect to have higher profits in future, and thus a marginal CT rate of 25% or 26.5%, may wish to consider postponing certain types of discretionary spending where possible so as to enjoy more CT relief in the future.

In most cases, it is not possible to postpone paying yourself things like rent (if your company uses a property you own) or interest (if your company owes you money). For CT purposes, these types of expense are generally allocated to the period they relate to. It may, however, be possible to postpone making pension contributions and various other expenses.

Bringing Dividends Forward

In some cases, where you regularly extract dividends taxed at the higher rate, you might want to consider paying yourself additional dividend income taxed at 35.75%; unless you can extract money from your company in a more tax efficient way.

Why? With the public finances in such a poor state, it seems unlikely the 35.75% higher rate will be reduced in the foreseeable future, it may even be increased.

One group who should certainly consider paying themselves as much dividend income as they can taxed at 35.75% are company owners whose taxable income is getting close to £100,000.

This is because, once your income rises above £100,000, your marginal Income Tax rate will typically rise from 35.75% to an effective rate of 58.25% (see Chapter 23).

For example, if you expect your taxable income to be, say, £85,000 this year, it may be better to pay yourself an additional £15,000 now, instead of in a future tax year when your income may have already risen to around £100,000.

The £100,000 threshold has not been increased since it was introduced in 2010 and we don't expect it to be increased any time soon. As a result, more and more taxpayers will probably have their personal allowances withdrawn in the years ahead.

See also Chapter 8 for another reason you may benefit from bringing dividends forward into the current, 2026/27 tax year.

Sample Tax Bills

For company owners who want to withdraw more than £50,270 *this year*, Table 6 contains some sample Income Tax bills. It's assumed that a tax-free salary of £12,570 is taken, with the remaining income taken as dividends. The table goes up to £100,000: beyond that your personal allowance is withdrawn.

The numbers are fairly easy to calculate. The first £12,570 is tax free thanks to your personal allowance and the next £500 of dividend income is also tax free thanks to the dividend allowance. The next £37,200 of dividend income is taxed at 10.75%, resulting in tax of £3,999. At this point the company owner has income of £50,270 and is on the higher rate threshold. Any additional dividends will be taxed at 35.75%.

Someone who extracts £75,000 will pay £3,999 on the first £50,270 and £8,841 on the final £24,730 (£24,730 x 35.75%), resulting in a total tax bill of £12,840.

The amounts listed in Table 6 can be doubled for companies owned and run by couples. For example, a couple can withdraw £150,000 (£75,000 each) with a total Income Tax bill of £25,680 (£12,840 each).

TABLE 6
Income between £50,270 and £100,000

Income	Income Tax	After-tax Income
£50,270	£3,999	£46,271
£55,000	£5,690	£49,310
£60,000	£7,477	£52,523
£65,000	£9,265	£55,735
£70,000	£11,052	£58,948
£75,000	£12,840	£62,160
£80,000	£14,627	£65,373
£85,000	£16,415	£68,585
£90,000	£18,202	£71,798
£95,000	£19,990	£75,010
£100,000	£21,777	£78,223

Income Smoothing

If your company makes bigger than normal profits during one accounting period you may be tempted to pay yourself a bigger dividend, even if this results in Income Tax being payable at a higher rate.

Paying a bigger than normal dividend is perfectly acceptable from a tax planning perspective IF you expect the company's profits to remain at a higher level, or continue to grow, AND expect to extract those profits as dividends each year.

If, however, you expect the company's profits to fall back, it may be wiser to 'smooth' your income and withdraw any bumper profits gradually, paying tax at no more than 10.75%.

Chapter 22

How to Protect Your Child Benefit

If you wish to withdraw more than £60,000 income from your company *and* you are the highest earner in a household that receives child benefit, you will be subject to two tax stings:

- 35.75% tax on your dividend income, and
- The Child Benefit Charge

The Child Benefit Charge is payable when the highest earner's income exceeds **£60,000**. However, the full charge is only payable when the highest earner's income reaches **£80,000**. This means families where the main breadwinner earns between £60,000 and £80,000 can hold onto at least some of their child benefit payments.

The Child Benefit Charge has important implications for company owners who want to determine how much income to withdraw from their companies during the current and future tax years.

How Much is Child Benefit Worth?

Child benefit is a valuable *tax-free* handout from the Government. Those who qualify receive the following payment in 2026/27:

- £1,407 for the first child
- £931 for each subsequent child

Depending on the number of children, a family can expect to receive the following total child benefit payment this year:

Children	Total Child Benefit
1	£1,407
2	£2,337
3	£3,268
4	£4,199

plus £931 for each additional child

Child benefit generally continues to be paid until your children are 16 years old. The payments will continue until age 20, if the child is enrolled in full-time 'non-advanced' education, including:

- GCSEs
- A levels
- Scottish Highers
- NVQ/SVQ level 1, 2 or 3
- BTEC National Diploma, National Certificate, 1st Diploma

So, if your child is aged between 16 and 19, and enrolled in one of the above courses, child benefit will continue to be paid. Once the child is 20 years old, all child benefit payments will cease.

The following courses do NOT qualify:

- Degrees
- Diploma of Higher Education
- NVQ level 4 or above
- HNCs or HNDs
- Teacher training

In other words, if your children are aged 16 or more, and enrolled in any of these courses, you will ***not*** receive any child benefit.

Total Value of Child Benefit

Child benefit payments continue for between 16 and 20 years. Based on the current child benefit rates the total amount you can expect to receive over the total period your child qualifies is:

- £22,506 to £28,132 tax free for the first child
- At least £14,893 tax free for each additional child

These are very much 'back of an envelope' figures because they are based on the rates applying for a single year, 2026/27, and ignore fluctuations due to inflation and changes of Government policy.

Furthermore, the amount received for second and subsequent children will vary from family to family. When your first child ceases to qualify, your second child will step into their shoes and qualify for the higher payment. In other words, when you stop receiving £1,407 for your first child, the payment for your second child will increase from £931 to £1,407 (at current rates).

Thus, families will receive different overall amounts depending on the age difference between their children and where they study.

The above overall figures nevertheless illustrate how valuable child benefit is over many years and why it's worth protecting.

How the Child Benefit Charge is Calculated
For every £200 of income over £60,000, an Income Tax charge equivalent to 1% of the child benefit is levied on the highest earner in the household.

For example, if the highest earner in the household has income of £65,000, the tax charge will be equivalent to 25% of the child benefit claimed. If the highest earner has income of £75,000, the tax charge will be equivalent to 75% of the child benefit. And if the highest earner has income of £80,000 or more, the tax charge will be equivalent to 100% of the child benefit.

Marginal Tax Rates
Once your income goes above £60,000, you may face the Child Benefit Charge *and* 35.75% tax on your dividend income.

For the highest earner in the household, the Child Benefit Charge creates the following marginal tax rates on dividend income in the £60,000 to £80,000 tax bracket:

Children	Marginal Tax Rate on Dividends
1	42.78%
2	47.44%
3	52.09%
4	56.75%
5	61.40%

Example: *David, a company owner, has taken a salary and dividends totalling £60,000 so far in 2026/27. He is the highest earner in a household claiming child benefit for two children.*

David decides to withdraw additional dividend income of £20,000. His total income will be £80,000, so he will face the maximum Child Benefit Charge. The tax payable on the additional dividend is £9,487, calculated as follows:

£20,000 dividend x 35.75%	*£7,150*
£2,337 child benefit x 100%	*£2,337*
Total additional tax	*£9,487*

The overall tax rate on the additional £20,000 dividend is 47.44%.

The dividend tax rates listed above actually understate the total tax payable. When you include CT, the total tax rates rise significantly (remember dividends are paid out of a company's profits after CT has been paid).

For example, for a company with a marginal CT rate of 26.5%, the total tax rates are as follows:

Children	Total Tax Rate
1	57.95%
2	61.37%
3	64.79%
4	68.21%
5	71.63%

Income between £80,000 and £100,000

If you have more than £80,000 of income, you will already be paying the maximum Child Benefit Charge. Hence, dividends falling into the income bracket between £80,000 and £100,000 are simply taxed at 35.75%.

Once your income rises above £100,000, you face a fresh tax sting: withdrawal of your Income Tax personal allowance.

Why You Should Always Claim Child Benefit

Where you regularly have income in excess of £80,000, it may be tempting not to claim child benefit in the first place, since you will only have to pay it back in Income Tax. Think again!

If you claim child benefit in respect of a child aged under 12, you will get a credit for state pension purposes. You can also apply to transfer this credit to your spouse/partner.

If you are getting a state pension credit (or had it transferred from your spouse/partner), this will mean it isn't necessary to take *any* salary from your company for this purpose. We won't always mention this possibility when discussing minimum salaries in the rest of this guide, but it's worth bearing in mind.

If you don't want to get hit with the Child Benefit Charge, you can claim child benefit but apply to stop the payments. This still provides the state pension credit, where relevant. It also allows you to claim the stopped payments later, any time within two years of the end of the relevant tax year. If you hadn't claimed in the first place, you could only backdate a future claim by a maximum of three months.

But frankly, why not just take the cash, even if you have to pay it back later. Stick it in an ISA in the meantime and earn some tax-free interest!

How to Avoid the Child Benefit Charge

Company owners arguably have the most flexibility when it comes to reducing or avoiding the Child Benefit Charge because they can often adopt the following strategies:

- **Smooth income** – Pay just enough dividend income to stay below the £60,000 threshold every year.

- **Roller-coaster income** – Pay big dividends in some tax years and smaller dividends in other tax years, thereby avoiding the Child Benefit Charge every second year.

- **Income Splitting** – Split your income with your spouse or partner by gifting them shares in the company.

Let's take a company owner who pays themselves a tax-free salary of £12,570 (see Chapter 12) and the rest of their income as dividends.

We'll also assume they have no income from other sources and they are the highest earner in a household receiving child benefit.

The Income Tax payable on their income is as follows:

- First £13,070 Tax free (£12,570 + £500 divi allow)
- £13,070-£50,270 10.75%
- £50,270-£60,000 35.75%
- £60,000-£80,000 42.78% to 61.40% (1 to 5 children)
- £80,000-£100,000 35.75%
- £100,000-£125,140 58.25% (PA withdrawal)
- £125,140+ 39.35%

Income Smoothing

Where possible, company owners should try to keep their total income below £50,270 to avoid the big jump in Income Tax from 10.75% to 35.75% that occurs when you become a higher-rate taxpayer.

As discussed in Chapter 20, if the income you withdraw is currently somewhere below £50,270 and you expect your company's profits and your own income to continue growing, you should consider extracting approximately £50,270 for several tax years, where possible, even if this is more than you need.

This is because it's better to pay 10.75% tax now rather than 35.75% in the future.

Similarly, those who already pay themselves £50,270 but expect their company's profits and their own income to continue growing may wish to consider paying themselves an income of up to £60,000 per year, where possible.

They will have to pay 35.75% tax on an additional £9,730 of dividend income but, by doing so, may be able to avoid the Child Benefit Charge in future years.

Roller Coaster Income

With the roller-coaster income strategy, you pay yourself a bigger than normal income one year and a smaller than normal income the next year.

If you plan to withdraw £80,000 per year from your company, you could consider taking £100,000 in year one and £60,000 in year two. Instead of paying the maximum Child Benefit Charge every year you will only have to pay it every second year.

What about someone who plans to withdraw £70,000 per year from their company? Such a person will effectively lose 50% of the family's child benefit every year: over a three-year period, they'll lose 3 x 50% = 150%. They could instead consider paying themselves £90,000 in year one and £60,000 in years two and three. They'll lose 100% of their child benefit in year one but nothing in years two and three. The net saving is 50% which currently equates to £1,169 for a household with two children.

Those thinking about using the roller-coaster strategy to avoid the Child Benefit Charge have to watch out for the £100,000 threshold where the marginal tax rate on dividend income rises to 58.25% as a result of the personal allowance being withdrawn.

For example, if you normally pay yourself income of £90,000, you might instead consider paying yourself £120,000 in year one and £60,000 in year two. You will completely avoid the Child Benefit Charge in year two, but in year one you will also lose most of your Income Tax personal allowance, which would usually outweigh any child benefit saving.

Income Splitting

Keeping your income below £50,270 or £60,000 is possibly easier said than done. The higher-rate threshold has been the same since 2021 and many company owners will need to extract much more than £50,270 to pay their bills. Some will also have to extract more than £60,000, which means they may struggle to escape the horrendous tax rates that kick in when the Child Benefit Charge becomes payable.

However, those who own their companies with a spouse or partner are in a more fortunate position because they can effectively double up the amount of income taxed at the lower rates.

For example, where the company is owned equally by a couple a total of £100,540 can be taken out as income (£50,270 each) and tax of just 10.75% will be payable on the dividend income.

If that's not enough income the couple can pays themselves a total of £120,000 (£60,000 each). They'll pay 35.75% on £19,460 of their combined dividend income but will avoid the higher tax rates that kick in when the Child Benefit Charge becomes payable.

Other Issues

When paying yourself dividends that are smaller than normal or bigger than normal there may be lots of other issues to consider.

For example, you can only declare bigger dividends if the company has sufficient distributable profits.

If you postpone taking some of your dividends until a future tax year, you may leave yourself exposed to any future increase in tax on company owners. Remember tax rules are constantly changing.

If you take a smaller than normal dividend this may have other financial repercussions, for example it may affect the size of mortgage you are able to get.

Chapter 23

Income over £100,000

So far, we have shown that a director/shareholder can extract a tax-free salary of £12,570 and a dividend of £87,430 (with £500 tax free, £37,200 taxed at 10.75%, and £49,730 taxed at 35.75%). Total pre-tax income: £100,000. Total after-tax income: £78,223.

The salary may give rise to employer's NI of £1,136 but this cost can be avoided if the company has sufficient employment allowance available. Both the salary and employer's NI will attract CT relief at up to 26.5%.

The above amounts can be doubled up if the company is also owned and run by your spouse/partner.

The Child Benefit Charge is payable if the highest earner in the household has income of more than £60,000 (see Chapter 22).

Income between £100,000 and £125,140

Many company owners will be satisfied with a net after tax income of around £78,000.

For those who wish to extract more cash, a dividend is often the best option. However, now you face an additional tax sting: withdrawal of your Income Tax personal allowance.

Once your taxable income rises above £100,000, your personal allowance is gradually withdrawn at the rate of £1 for every £2 of additional income.

In other words, if you have income of £101,000 your personal allowance will be reduced by £500. Once your gross taxable income reaches £125,140, you will have no personal allowance left at all.

Company owners with income in the £100,000 to £125,10 bracket could end up paying Income Tax at an effective rate of 58.25% on any additional dividends they withdraw.

Example: *Annabel, a company owner, has already taken a salary of £12,570 and dividend of £87,430. Total income: £100,000. She decides to pay herself additional dividend income of £25,140. She will pay 35.75% Income Tax on the additional dividend: £8,988. She will also lose all her personal allowance, which means her salary of £12,570 will now be taxed at 20%. Additional tax: £2,514.*

In addition, her salary now uses up £12,570 of her basic rate band, which means £12,570 of dividends will be taxed at 35.75% instead of 10.75%. Additional tax: £3,142.

The total additional Income Tax is £14,644, which is equivalent to 58.25% of the £25,140 dividend.

Don't Forget the Corporation Tax Bill!

As always, it's important to remember that dividends are paid out of a company's *after-tax* profits.

To pay an additional dividend of £25,140, a company with a marginal CT rate of 26.5% will have had to make additional profits of £34,204, resulting in CT of £9,064. Coupled with an Income Tax bill of £14,644, the total tax bill on the £34,204 of profit is £23,708, or a staggering 69.3%!

These extortionate tax rates do not apply to all dividend income over £100,000: only income between £100,000 and £125,140. Once your income exceeds £125,140, your personal allowance will have disappeared altogether and any further dividends will simply be taxed at the additional rate of 39.35%.

Losing Tax-Free Childcare

It is also important to note that having total taxable income in excess of £100,000 will mean you lose your right to claim tax-free childcare.

Although we do not factor this into our analysis in this guide, this may be a significant additional cost for some company owners, and should be taken into account when deciding how much income to extract from your company. Even income of £100,001 will mean the tax-free childcare is lost, so be careful!

How to Avoid 58.25% Tax

Unlike regular salaried employees or owners of unincorporated businesses (sole traders and partnerships), company owners can avoid this extortionate tax rate by simply not paying themselves salary and dividends in excess of £100,000 per year.

Thus, a company owner taking a salary of £12,570 could extract dividends not exceeding £87,430.

A company owner whose income may fluctuate from year to year, in line with the company's profits, may want to consider smoothing income to avoid the £100,000 threshold. In other words, if possible, try not to pay yourself a salary and dividend of £80,000 in year one and £120,000 in year two. It may be better to pay yourself £100,000 during both tax years, to preserve all your Income Tax personal allowance in year two.

Bigger Companies

Owners of companies earning substantial profits face a dilemma. While they may choose to extract no more than £100,000 per year, ultimately they may end up with a lot of surplus cash inside their companies.

For example, if you are the only shareholder in a company that is making an after-tax profit of £200,000 per year, you may not wish to extract just £100,000 per year indefinitely, especially if the surplus cash is not needed to help grow the business.

Company owners who wish to pay themselves more than £100,000 per year may be able to keep their personal allowances in some years by using the 'roller-coaster' strategy: paying bigger dividends in some tax years and smaller dividends in other years.

Remember, once your income exceeds £125,140, your personal allowance will have disappeared altogether and the only penalty for taking further dividends is that these will be subject to additional rate tax at 39.35%: far better than the punitive effective rates of up to 58.25% applying to income between £100,000 and £125,140.

For example, let's say you had been planning to withdraw a salary of £12,570 and dividend of £112,430 both this year and next year (total income £125,000 in each year). With this level of income almost all your personal allowance will be withdrawn in both years.

If instead you pay yourself a total of £150,000 this year, but only £100,000 next year, this will allow you to keep all your personal allowance in 2027/28. Potential net tax saving across the two years: £4,699.

For more potential savings based on the roller-coaster strategy, see Chapter 24.

Couples Can Keep One Personal Allowance

Where a couple own a company together, it is usually most beneficial for them to split income equally, in order to make the best use of allowances, basic rate bands, etc. However, where the couple's total combined income exceeds £200,000, savings may sometimes be possible by having a non-equal split.

Example: *Jack and Gwen own a highly profitable company based in Cardiff. So far in 2026/27, they have not taken any income out of the company, but are planning to each take a salary of £6,708 and dividends of £139,500, making them additional rate taxpayers and lose their personal allowances.*

Alternatively, if Jack were to transfer some of his shares to Gwen before taking dividends, so that she owned two thirds of the company and he owned one third, his total income for 2026/27 would fall to £99,708 (salary of £6,708 plus dividends of £93,000), meaning he retained most of his personal allowance.

Jack's Income Tax bill would fall by £22,497 (from £44,170 to £21,673). This saving is made up as follows:

Dividends no longer taxed at 39.35% (Note 1)	
£21,068 x 39.35%	*£8,290*
Dividends no longer taxed at 35.75% (Note 2)	
£25,432 x 35.75%	*£9,092*
Personal allowance restored (Note 3)	
Tax saved on salary	
£6,708 x 20%	*£1,342*
Tax saved on dividends	
£5,862 x 35.75%	*£2,096*
£6,708 x 25% (35.75% - 10.75%)	*£1,677*
Total	*£22,497*

Gwen, on the other hand, now has £46,500 more dividends taxed at 39.35%, leading to an £18,298 increase in her Income Tax bill.

Nonetheless, by restoring one personal allowance (Jack's in this case, but it could equally have been Gwen's if their roles were reversed), the couple have saved £4,199 overall (£22,497 – £18,298), with similar savings possible in future years if their total income remains broadly the same.

Notes

1. Doesn't save anything, Gwen is taxed at the same rate on these dividends
2. Gives rise to an overall cost at 3.6% on these dividends (Gwen is taxed at 39.35% instead of Jack's 35.75%) BUT it's a price worth paying because...
3. Restoring Jack's personal allowance saves £5,115, far outweighing the additional cost of £916 under (2) in this case

The saving achieved by restoring a full personal allowance for one person in 2026/27 will always be £5,115 as per Note 3 when the salary taken is £6,708. For a salary of £12,570, the saving would be £5,657, for a salary of £5,000 it would be £4,956.

The cost arising under Note 2 will vary between different couples and different years, and may need to be monitored year on year.

While some savings are possible whenever the couple's total income exceeds £200,000, the best savings can only be achieved when their total income is £250,280 or more. Savings are maximised by keeping the total income of the person with the lower income as close to £100,000 as possible (slightly under is better than slightly over). For 2026/27, the best possible *overall net saving*, where the lower income is exactly £100,000 in total, including a salary of £12,570, is £4,751. For more on saving tax by transferring shares, and on how and when the transfer itself can be carried out tax free, see Chapter 35.

Salary vs Dividends

Apart from a few people with five or more qualifying children suffering the Child Benefit Charge, the marginal tax rate on income between £100,000 and £125,140 is the highest in the personal tax system. In general, company owners would therefore be wise to avoid having their total income for the year falling into this bracket, and we have seen several methods for achieving this already.

However, if your income does fall into this punitive tax bracket, what does this mean for the salary versus dividends question? Remember, our analysis here is based on the assumption the director has no income from outside the company.

Where at least £1,136 of spare employment allowance is available, the position is fairly simple: a salary of £12,570 usually remains optimal (except in some cases where more than £7,500 of spare employment allowance is available: see Chapter 14).

No Employment Allowance Available

The rest of our analysis below is based on the assumption there is no spare employment allowance available.

In these cases, company owners with income over £100,000 may face three potential salary choices: what is optimal (most tax efficient) in the short term; what may be sensible in the long run; and what is simplest.

Keeping it Simple
Some company owners may prefer to stick with the simple, 'baseline' salary of £12,570 we saw in Chapter 12 (the optimal salary for most small company owners). This may not be most tax efficient, or 'optimal' when your total income falls into the £100,000 to £125,140 bracket, but it will not cost you a great deal of extra tax overall.

Optimal Salary
The theoretical optimal salary in 2026/27 for those with total income in excess of £100,000, and no spare employment allowance available is sometimes £5,000: the employer's NI threshold. The maximum saving is, however, a mere £506, or a measly £211 in the case of full profit extraction.

While this modest saving is not exactly spectacular, it may suit some company owners, for example owners of 'one man band' companies that aren't entitled to the employment allowance, and who don't need a credit for state pension entitlement purposes.

Protecting Your State Pension
There are various tax and non-tax reasons why you may not want to reduce your salary to just £5,000. In other words, what may be mathematically 'optimal' or save the most tax in the short-term, does not always make for sound overall financial planning.

As discussed in Chapter 17, in order to keep building your state pension record, you may need to take a salary of at least £6,708 in 2026/27.

Taking a salary of £6,708 will cut your maximum potential saving (compared with a salary of £12,570) to just £392, or a pathetic £164 in the case of full profit extraction.

Looked at another way, taking enough salary to protect your state pension entitlement will cost between £47 and £114 (compared with taking a salary of £5,000 when this is theoretically optimal), which has to be regarded as a pretty good investment!

Scottish Company Owners
In previous chapters, we have stated that company owners in Scotland who take a small salary and the rest of their income as dividends are completely immune from Scottish Income Tax.

However, those with income over £100,000 will have their personal allowances gradually taken away, which means their salaries will become subject to Scottish Income Tax. Their dividends will continue to be taxed using UK rates and thresholds.

As it happens, this is not necessarily a bad thing. As long as your salary and other income subject to Scottish tax rates (e.g. rental income) is less than £20,923 this year, you will pay a bit less tax than company owners living elsewhere in the UK, even if you lose your personal allowance.

In this way, the SNP Government has unwittingly handed a tax cut to company owners who have big dividends but only small salaries!

Chapter 24

Income over £125,140

Once your income rises above £125,140, your personal allowance will have been completely withdrawn, and you will also become an additional rate taxpayer.

Most people are familiar with the 45% tax rate that applies to most types of income above this threshold. If you are a company owner though, it's likely it will be your dividends that take you over the £125,140 threshold (dividends are always treated as the top slice of income: see Chapter 29). Technically, once your dividend income rises above £125,140, the Income Tax rate rises from 35.75% to 39.35%.

However, as we saw in Chapter 23, the *effective* tax rate on dividend income between £100,000 and £125,140 is often 58.25%. So, once your dividend income rises above £125,140, the effective Income Tax rate generally *falls* from 58.25% to 39.35%.

Don't Forget the Corporation Tax Bill

Although 39.35% is lower than the 45% rate most people associate with high income levels, we mustn't forget that dividends are paid out of profits that have already been taxed.

For example, a company paying CT at 25% will pay £250 tax on every £1,000 of profit. That leaves £750 to distribute as a dividend. If the director/shareholder then pays 39.35% Income Tax on the £750 distribution, the additional tax comes to £295. The total tax paid by the director and the company is £545, which is 54.5%!

Avoiding the 39.35% Tax Rate

The simplest way to avoid paying 39.35% tax on your dividends is to keep your taxable income below £125,140 (e.g. by extracting higher than normal profits over more than one tax year).

But frankly, this is not really what you should be aiming to do. Since the effective tax rate on dividends actually *falls* once your income exceeds £125,140, it is the punitive rates applying to income between £100,000 and £125,140 you should really be trying to avoid.

In other words, if you're going to keep your income below £125,140, it makes sense to keep it below £100,000: at least in most years, anyway.

Some company owners will be able to do this, and we looked at tax planning for these director/shareholders in Chapter 23.

In Chapter 23, we also looked at tax planning for company owners who can't, or don't wish to, keep their income to a maximum of £100,000 every year, including the savings available by employing the roller-coaster strategy. In effect, that strategy involves using the 39.35% rate in some years in order to avoid punitive effective rates of up to 58.25% in other years.

Owners of more profitable companies (who don't want to roll up profits inside the company indefinitely) should remember that going over the additional rate threshold is very different to going over other key thresholds.

When your income rises above £50,270 the dividend tax rate goes up from 10.75% to 35.75% and you start paying an extra £250 tax on every additional £1,000 of dividend income you receive. When your income rises above £100,000, you start to lose your personal allowance and you may end up paying up to £225 extra on every additional £1,000 of dividend income.

But when your income rises above £125,140, the effective tax rate on dividend income generally *reduces* from 58.25% to 39.35% and you pay £189 *LESS* on every additional £1,000 of dividend income.

In short, unlike the other key Income Tax thresholds, the additional rate tax threshold is really nothing to fear. In fact, sometimes it is to be embraced!

When Paying 39.35% is a Good Idea

In many cases, it is better to pay the 39.35% tax rate during one tax year in order to protect your Income Tax personal allowance during another tax year. This is because losing your Income Tax personal allowance is generally more costly than paying the additional rate.

Example: *Sam owns a successful chain of gyms. In 2026/27, she decides to take a salary of £12,570 and a dividend of £137,430. Her total taxable income is £150,000, so she pays the 39.35% additional rate of tax on the top £24,860 of her income.*

She has been withdrawing £150,000 for several years now. With this much income, she also loses her Income Tax personal allowance every year. As a result, her total Income Tax bill for 2026/27 will be £46,204.

In 2027/28, Sam takes the same salary and dividend again, giving her the same Income Tax bill. Hence, over two years, her total tax bill will be £92,408.

Sam could instead consider withdrawing £200,000 in 2026/27 and £100,000 in 2027/28: the same total income, but split differently. If she does this, her Income Tax bills will be £65,879 and £21,777 respectively: a total tax bill of £87,656.

Sam saves £4,752 by following this strategy. In 2026/27, she has to pay Income Tax at 39.35% on an extra £50,000 of dividend income: £19,675. However, in 2027/28, her taxable income falls by £50,000 to £100,000, so her Income Tax personal allowance is fully retained. She would have paid 58.25% tax on the first £25,140 of that income (see Chapter 23) and 39.35% on the final £24,860: a total of £24,426. The difference is £4,751 (£24,426 – £19,675).

Sam could repeat this strategy, withdrawing income of £100,000 every second year in order to protect her personal allowance. The bi-annual saving of £4,751 amounts to around 4.6% of Sam's annual after-tax income, so it's well worthwhile and shows how company owners can use 'roller-coaster income' (see Chapter 11) to lower their tax bills.

If both Sam and the company meet the necessary conditions, even more might be saved by varying income over a longer cycle. If Sam withdraws income of £250,000 in tax year one, and £100,000 in each of tax years two and three, she would save £9,503 over the three years compared with taking income of £150,000 in each year.

Following this pattern for six years would produce total savings of £19,006 over that period, compared with £14,253 using a bi-annual strategy: so we can see the potential benefits of a longer cycle. All of this naturally assumes current Income Tax rates continue to apply for the foreseeable future.

Using the rollercoaster strategy and paying more tax at 39.35% in the current, 2026/27 tax year to make overall savings by paying less tax in future years, has two further advantages:

- Paying less tax in 2027/28 could lead to substantial cashflow savings in the near future: see Chapter 8
- Extra dividends taken in 2026/27 will escape any future increase in dividend tax rates

Salary versus Dividends
The 'optimal' salary for most company owner/directors with income in excess of £125,140 in 2026/27 is £12,570 (Jack and Gwen in Chapter 23 obviously didn't know this).

In some cases, however, much greater salaries may be optimal, as we will see in Chapter 26.

Couples
Couples with combined income of £250,280 or more (i.e. at least £125,140 each if split equally) can make annual savings of up to £4,751 following the method we examined in Chapter 23.

Chapter 25

The Cost of Taking Larger Salaries

Some company owners may desire the convenience of a larger salary, even if this is not strictly speaking 'optimal'. Some may take a bigger salary for other reasons.

While these factors could sometimes outweigh tax considerations, it's worth understanding the additional tax cost arising. In some cases, it may be a lot more than the company owner realises.

For example, if the owner of a company making profits of £150,000 takes a salary of £30,000 this year instead of the usual 'baseline' salary of £12,570, and extracts the company's remaining profits as dividends, he or she will be £1,881 worse off.

If the owner of a company with profits of £250,000 takes a salary of £50,000 instead of the usual 'baseline' salary of £12,570, he or she will be £2,204 worse off.

These extra tax costs represent a significant additional burden. To make up for the extra tax suffered, the first director would need to make at least £6,130 of extra pre-tax profit in their company. The second director would need to make an extra £4,845.

So, what's easier, changing the level of salary you take so you can pay around £2,000 less tax, or finding a way to make over £4,800, or even over £6,000, of additional profit?

Interestingly, despite all this, large salaries are more tax efficient than dividends in some cases, particularly where the employment allowance is available (we've assumed it isn't in this chapter). We've seen some examples of this already, and we're going to see some more in Chapter 26.

Chapter 26

Big Earners and the Large Salary Method

As discussed in Chapter 12, in some scenarios, a director's optimal salary can be much higher than the usual 'baseline' salary of £12,570, and is derived using a completely different approach, which we call the 'large salary method'.

Under the large salary method, the director typically takes most of their income as salary: the reverse of our usual approach where it is generally more beneficial for the director to take most of their income as dividends. Let's be clear though: the small salary/large dividend method we have been looking at so far is the most tax efficient method in most cases, and should be seen as the 'default' method for establishing a director's optimal salary. What we are looking at in this chapter are the exceptions where a large salary may be more beneficial.

The large salary method is also different to the approach we looked at in Chapter 14, which applies at lower profit levels, or where the director is willing to restrict their gross taxable income to no more than £100,000.

In this chapter, we will compare the large salary method with taking the 'baseline' salary of £12,570 and, unless stated to the contrary, the savings illustrated here are based on this comparison. Where a third alternative is optimal, however, we will point this out.

The large salary method can only be beneficial where the company has a marginal CT rate of 26.5% or 25% before paying the director's salary. This generally means it needs profits over £50,000 (or over £62,570 before paying the usual 'baseline' salary of £12,570). In fact, profits usually need to be much higher than this, as we will see later. It also follows that the director must be a higher or additional rate taxpayer: the large salary method is not suitable for basic rate taxpayers.

Furthermore, the large salary method is generally only worthwhile where one or more of the following factors also apply:

- There is spare employment allowance available
- The director is over state pension age
- The director is under 21
- The company is highly profitable and the director wishes to withdraw all or most of the profits in the current year

For example, where all or most of the £10,500 employment allowance is available, the large salary method may produce savings if the company has taxable profits of more than around £138,500 and the owner/director wishes to extract them all by way of salary and dividends.

It's also worth pointing out at this stage that the large salary method is not generally suitable for Scottish taxpayers and is only worthwhile at very high profit levels if there is more than one owner/director aged over 21 but under state pension age.

How Does the Large Salary Method Work?
Under the right circumstances, the director's optimal salary will be the salary that reduces the company's profits to the point where it pays CT at just 19%. That point is usually £50,000, unless the company has any associated companies.

To calculate this salary, we need to take account of employer's NI, so it is not simply a case of deducting £50,000 from the company's profits.

Example: *Marcus's company makes a profit of £185,000 before tax. He wishes to withdraw all his after-tax profits as a combination of salary and dividends. Apart from Marcus himself, the company employs a few staff aged under 21, each paid less than £50,270 (but more than £5,000). Hence, the whole £10,500 employment allowance is available to cover Marcus's salary. As we saw in Chapter 5, this means he can take a salary of £75,000 free from employer's NI, reducing the company's taxable profit to £110,000. This exceeds our target profit level by £60,000 (£110,000 – £50,000). To work out Marcus's 'optimal' salary, we first divide this figure by 1.15 (one plus the current 15% rate of employer's NI).*

£60,000/1.15 = £52,174

We now add back the £75,000 that is free from employer's NI, to produce Marcus's optimal salary: £127,174.

Having derived the optimal salary, let's now compare the outcome of either taking this large salary, or a small salary of £12,570. In both cases, we will assume Marcus takes the company's remaining after tax profits as dividends.

	Small Salary	Large Salary
Company's tax	**£**	**£**
Company profit	185,000	185,000
Less: Salary	12,570	127,174
Less: Employer's NI	-	7,826
Net Profit	172,430	50,000
Less: Corporation Tax	41,944	9,500
After-tax profit/dividend	130,486	40,500
Director's tax		
Total income	143,056	167,674
Income Tax	43,471	59,171
National Insurance	-	4,554
After-tax income	99,585	103,949

Taking the large salary leaves Marcus with £4,364 more after-tax income (£103,949 – £99,585).

To get that same additional £4,364 of after-tax income following the small salary/large dividend method, Marcus's company would need to make an extra £9,790 of pre-tax profit, so the large salary method is well worthwhile in this case.

Why Does the Large Salary Method Work?

The reason we sometimes see a tax saving by paying large salaries is because of the difference in marginal tax rates at higher income levels. We can demonstrate this by revisiting Table 5 (Chapter 10) but, this time, assuming the company has a marginal CT rate of either 26.5% or 25%.

TABLE 7 (TABLE 5 REVISITED)
Amount Kept per £1,000 of Profit

Income Band	Salary	Dividend
£50,270 to £100,000	£504	£472 or £482
£100,000 to £125,140	£330	£307 or £313
Over £125,140	£461	£446 or £455

See Chapter 10 for the relevant assumptions made here. As we can see, when the director's income exceeds £50,270, the salary starts beating a dividend: provided the salary is getting CT relief at 26.5% or 25%.

But that doesn't mean the large salary method becomes beneficial immediately. Paying that first £50,270 of income as salary will have led to a higher overall tax cost, either directly, or sometimes indirectly (by pushing dividends over the higher-rate tax threshold).

So, it will usually take a much higher salary than £50,270 before the large salary method becomes beneficial and that, in turn, means we need high company profits.

Nonetheless, once profits are sufficiently large to give the director enough income to overcome the disadvantage of paying the first £50,270 of salary, the table shows us that further salary will provide the director with more after-tax income than dividends.

The more the company's profit increases above this critical threshold, the greater the savings yielded by following the large salary method. If Marcus's company was making a profit of £250,000, his saving would increase to £5,345; at a profit of £300,000 it would be £5,759.

When Does the Large Salary Method Produce Savings?

For the large salary method to produce savings, the company's profits generally need to exceed a certain critical threshold. That threshold depends on a number of factors. As we have already seen, the critical threshold when the whole employment allowance of £10,500 is available is around £138,500.

For a worthwhile saving of at least £500 to be achieved in this scenario, profits need to be more than around £141,500.

Set out below are some more profit thresholds required before the large salary method produces worthwhile savings. In each case, it is assumed the director wishes to extract all of the company's profits by way of salary and dividends and, unless stated to the contrary, has no other income. It is also assumed that there are no associated companies, only a single director, and the director is not a Scottish taxpayer.

- £144,500: where there is £9,365 of spare employment allowance available (one employee over 21 paid £12,570)
- £150,000: where £7,500 of spare employment allowance available
- £157,000: where £5,000 of spare employment allowance available
- £182,000: where £2,500 of spare employment allowance available
- £215,000: where £1,136 of spare employment allowance available
- £216,000: where there is no spare employment allowance available

It's worth us taking a closer look at the last scenario, as it is quite common: namely where a highly profitable company has no spare employment allowance available.

Example: *Elon's company makes a profit of £300,000 before tax. He wishes to withdraw all his after-tax profits as a combination of salary and dividends. The company has no spare employment allowance. Hence, following the large salary method, Elon should take a salary of: £300,000 – £250,000 – £5,000 = £245,000, divided by 1.15, which gives £213,044 plus £5,000, which equals £218,044. Let's now see how that compares with taking a small salary of just £12,570.*

	Small Salary	**Large Salary**
Company's tax	**£**	**£**
Company profit	300,000	300,000
Less: Salary	12,570	218,044
Less: Employer's NI	1,136	31,956
Net Profit	286,294	50,000
Less: Corporation Tax	71,574	9,500
After-tax profit/dividend	214,720	40,500
Director's tax		
Total income	227,290	258,544
Income Tax	76,618	100,063
National Insurance	-	6,371
After-tax income	150,672	152,110

Taking the large salary leaves Elon with £1,438 more after-tax income (£152,110 – £150,672).

It's not a huge saving for such a profitable company, but it's worth pointing out that to get that same additional £1,438 of after-tax income following the small salary/large dividend method, Elon's company would need to make an extra £3,161 of pre-tax profit, so it is actually quite worthwhile.

As before, the greater the profit, the great the saving the large salary method will produce. For example, with a profit of £400,000, the large salary method would produce a saving of £2,036 in this scenario, with a profit of £500,000, the saving would be £2,635.

However, while the savings continue to increase with profits, the rate at which those savings increase slows down considerably once profits exceed £250,000. In fact, the additional saving per £1,000 of profit in excess of £250,000 is only £6.

Here are some other profit thresholds where the large salary method begins to produce worthwhile savings, based on the same assumptions as before. Unless stated to the contrary, it is also assumed there is no employment allowance available.

- £152,000: where the director is under 21
- £136,500: where the director is under 21 and the whole £10,500 employment allowance is available. However, in this scenario, the maximum salary covered by the employment allowance (£120,270) is optimal where this is greater
- £147,000: where the director is over state pension age
- £97,000: where the director is over state pension age, in receipt of the standard state pension of £12,548, and has no other income from outside the company

Where the director is over state pension age and there is any spare employment allowance available, the optimal salary will generally be the *greater* of the amount under the large salary method and the amount covered by the available employment allowance (see Chapters 14 and 16).

Using the Large Salary Method in Practice

To enable the director to get the right optimal salary under the large salary method in practice, it will generally be necessary to adopt the technique covered in Chapter 2, whereby the intention to pay a bonus is declared before the company's accounting date, but the amount of that bonus is only decided when the accounts for that period are being finalised. This is because you need to know the level of your company's taxable profits before deciding whether it is worthwhile paying yourself a higher salary, and to calculate what that salary should be.

Alternatively, a hybrid approach will often be possible, especially where the director has a reasonable idea of roughly what sort of profit their company is going to make. For example, Marcus (the first example in this chapter) could take a regular salary of £5,000 per month (£60,000 for the year) and then pay himself a bonus of £67,174 (using the method in Chapter 2).

The hybrid approach will appeal to many directors but it carries two significant disadvantages.

Firstly, if it transpires that the company's profits turn out to be significantly less than expected, the large salary method may prove disadvantageous. For example, if Marcus's company only made a profit of £125,000, his salary of £60,000 would leave him £1,216 worse off than if he had taken a salary of £12,570. Oddly, he could cut his losses to £394 by still taking a bonus of £15,000. In fact, his best approach might be to take the £15,000 bonus and restrict his dividends to just £25,000 (see Chapter 14).

Secondly, the hybrid approach carries cashflow disadvantages, as Income Tax and NI will have to be paid on the regular salary much earlier than on a bonus. By using the bonus method from Chapter 2 to pay all or most of the director's salary, the cashflow position is greatly improved.

Cashflow Optimisation

At present, using the large salary method will often accelerate tax liabilities. This could all change in the near future (see Chapter 8) but, in this chapter, we will concentrate on the current position.

Income Tax and NI due on a salary is payable under PAYE by the 22nd of the month following payment. The CT relief for these costs doesn't follow until nine months after the end of the company's accounting period (in most cases: see Chapter 3 regarding large companies making profits in excess of £1.5m).

By contrast, the tax due on a dividend under the self-assessment system is currently generally payable in two instalments on 31st January during the tax year and the following 31st July (see Chapter 7).

If the salary is paid monthly, the cashflow impact is both complex and significant: it would generally mean the overall saving needs to be quite large to make the large salary method worthwhile at present.

However, the cashflow impact is both simpler and vastly improved if the salary (or most of it) is paid as a single lump sum bonus after the end of the accounting period (but within nine months) using the method we examined in Chapter 2.

Let's say, for example, Marcus's company has a June accounting date and his salary, or bonus, of £127,174 (or £12,570) in respect of the year ending 30th June 2026 is paid in a single lump sum in March 2027 (after the 5th).

To be fair, let's also say his dividends are paid during 2026/27 and the Income Tax arising is payable in two equal instalments on 31st January and 31st July 2027 (it won't usually be this simple, but it's a reasonable approximation in most cases: see Chapter 7).

Let's now compare the tax cash inflows/(outflows) under the two methods:

	Small Salary	Large Salary	Cumulative Saving/(Cost)
31/1/2027 (1)	(£20,478)	(£7,870)	£12,608
1/4/2027 (2)	£3,331	£35,775	£45,052
22/4/2027 (3)	(£2,514)	(£55,811)	(£8,245)
31/7/2027 (4)	(£20,479)	(£7,870)	£4,364

1. First payment on account under self-assessment in respect of dividend income
2. Reduction in the amount of CT paid due to tax relief for Marcus's salary and related employer's NI
3. Income Tax and NI paid under PAYE
4. Second payment on account under self-assessment in respect of dividend income

As we can see, Marcus and his company are £8,245 out of pocket for a little over three months; but they are at least £12,608 ahead for a similar (albeit slightly shorter) period. Hence, all in all, the cashflow impact is broadly neutral.

Similar results can be achieved for companies with other accounting dates although, in some cases, this will mean the large salary/bonus is paid, and taxable, in the next tax year. That may be alright in principle, but it will be important to assess the overall impact of the strategy across both tax years. In some cases, it may be preferable to pay the large salary/bonus in the current tax year. This won't be as good from a cashflow perspective, but the overall saving achieved by the large salary method will still be obtained.

Is the Salary Justified?

An important point to bear in mind is that the large salaries discussed in this chapter are only worthwhile if the company obtains CT relief for them (and at a marginal rate of at least 25%).

This means the remuneration paid to the director (their salary) must be justified by the work they do in the company's business.

While this issue is seldom challenged by HMRC, we have to consider whether, for example, the work done by someone like Marcus warrants a salary of over £127,000. And remember, it is the director's total remuneration package we need to consider, including any company pension contributions made on their behalf and other benefits provided.

I would, however, make two key points in this context:

- If the director is actively running the company, there is a strong argument that its high profits are entirely down to his efforts, and any salary covered by those profits must therefore be justified.
- In a case like Marcus's, HMRC are collecting over £70,000 in Income Tax and NI: there is very little incentive for them to challenge the way a director in this situation has chosen to structure their pay.

Partial Extraction

So far in this chapter, we have only looked at director/shareholders who wish to extract all their company's after-tax profits by way of salary or dividend.

At higher profit levels many company owners may not be extracting all the profits and will reinvest part of them to fund future growth.

Large salaries can still be beneficial under these circumstances: provided the director/shareholder wishes to extract a substantial sum. Let's say a company has a profit of £300,000 and £8,000 of spare employment allowance available. The director could extract all the profits using the large salary method and be left with net income of £155,796 (£4,607 more than taking a salary of £12,570 and the rest as dividends).

But let's say the director is content to restrict their net, after tax income to £100,000. Let's see how they might do this:

	Small Salary	**Large Salary**
Company's tax	**£**	**£**
Company profit	300,000	300,000
Less: Salary	12,570	165,497
Less: Employer's NI	-	16,075
Net Profit	287,430	118,428
Less: Corporation Tax*	71,858	27,633
After-tax profit	215,572	90,795
Less: Dividend	131,171	500
Company cash	84,401	90,295
Director's tax		
Total income	143,741	165,997
Income Tax	43,741	60,677**
National Insurance	-	5,320
After-tax income	100,000	100,000

* 25% with the small salary; 19% on the first £50,000 and 26.5% on the remainder with the large salary
** Higher for Scottish taxpayers

Rather than the director enjoying £4,607 extra after-tax income, the company retains £5,894 (£90,295 – £84,401) extra cash. The saving is increased, and is effectively transferred from the director to the company.

Savings can sometimes still be achieved where there is no spare employment allowance available, but will be greatly reduced. For example, in the case of a company with profits of £300,000, where the director wishes to take net, after-tax income of £100,000 out of the company, the saving would be just £865.

For companies with profits not exceeding £250,000, worthwhile savings will only arise where the director wishes to take net, after-tax income of at least around £88,500.

The minimum net income requirement for worthwhile savings at higher company profit levels (where there is no spare employment allowance available) is as follows:

Profit	**Minimum Net Income**
£300,000	£93,500
£350,000	£107,000
£400,000	£121,000
£450,000	£135,000
£500,000	£149,000

As with full profit extraction, there are various other scenarios we might consider. For example, where the company's profits do not exceed £250,000 and the whole £10,500 employment allowance is available, a director aged over 21 but under state pension age will generally see a worthwhile benefit from taking a large salary where they wish to take more than around £79,750 in net, after-tax income out of the company.

Younger or older directors might benefit from a large salary when looking to take less after-tax income than this.

Partial Extraction: What Salary?

We know how to work out your optimal salary under the large salary method if you plan to take all the company's profits by way of salary and dividends, but what is your optimal salary if you are not extracting all the company's profits?

To recap, this is only worthwhile if you have a company making profits over the relevant critical threshold (as outlined above) and plan to take enough income out of it, as discussed above. This generally means you will be taking enough income to make you an additional rate taxpayer.

Let's say you would like net income of £120,000 from your company. To use your dividend allowance (always worthwhile for an additional rate taxpayer), at least £500 of that needs to be a dividend, so up to £119,500 can come from salary.

For any director under state pension age, the first £125,140 of salary will leave them with net, after tax income of £78,111. So, to get the required £119,500, they need another £41,389 of net income. As an additional rate taxpayer, they suffer 47% in combined Income Tax and NI leaving them with just £53 for every £100 of salary paid. Hence, the additional salary they need is: £41,389 x 100/53 = £78,092.

So, the required salary in this case appears to be £125,140 + £78,092 = £203,232.

BUT we're not quite finished yet. If the director's optimal salary under the large salary method (with full profit extraction) would be less than £203,232, they should only take that lower optimal salary and get the rest of the net income they require by way of dividends.

For example, if the optimal salary under the large salary method would be £190,000, the director should take that salary and a further £19,898 in dividends (i.e. total dividends of £20,398). After Income Tax at 39.35%, the £19,898 of extra dividends provides the additional £13,232 of net income that is needed.

Multiple Directors

Where there is more than one director, much higher company profit levels will be required before the large salary method is beneficial.

For example, where a company is co-owned by a couple and profits are shared equally, the large salary method can only produce worthwhile savings where company profits exceed around £307,000: and that's where the whole £10,500 employment allowance is available.

The large salary method may be worthwhile at lower profit levels where the directors are over state pension age or under 21, especially if there is some spare employment allowance available.

Associated Companies

Where there are associated companies, the optimal salary under the large salary method becomes the amount that reduces the company's profit to the point where its CT rate drops to 19%: that's £25,000 where there is one associated company, £16,667 where there are two... and so on.

On the other hand, the amount of CT saved by paying a large salary will generally reduce. Furthermore, the company may not be entitled to the employment allowance (see Chapter 5), which will often mean the large salary method is not worthwhile (a company profit of at least £271,000 would generally be required).

However, if the company is entitled to the employment allowance, the impact of associated companies may not be too great and the large salary method could still be worthwhile. For instance, if Marcus's company in our example near the start of the chapter had one associated company, but was still entitled to the employment allowance, his optimal salary would increase to £148,913, which would save him £4,310 (compared with £4,364 previously).

Where there is one associated company, the large salary method can produce worthwhile savings when the whole employment allowance is available and the company has profits between around £79,500 and £122,250, or over £139,500.

Where there are two associated companies, the large salary method can produce worthwhile savings when the whole employment allowance is available and the company has profits between around £71,500 and £121,500, or over £140,500.

Other Income

Apart from the standard state pension (where applicable), our analysis so far in this chapter has been based on the assumption the director has no other income.

Where a director has other income, this could mean the large salary method becomes beneficial at much lower profit levels. For example, if a director also has rental income of £30,000, the large salary method starts to produce worthwhile savings once the company's profits exceed around £169,000: even when there is no spare employment allowance available.

If someone like Marcus had rental income of £30,000, the large salary method would save them £5,076, i.e. £712 more than we saw in the original example above.

Pension or self-employment income will have a similar effect. Employment income from another source may bring another beneficial factor into play, which we will look at in Chapter 33.

In some cases, where a director has interest income, the large salary method could lead to them losing out on the starting rate band (see Chapter 33). This could cost up to £1,000 in extra Income Tax (£1,100 from 2027/28 onwards), but there may still be savings overall.

Dividend income from another source will not generally make any difference to the savings available under the large salary method.

Once other income from outside the company (excluding dividends) exceeds around £81,000, there is an opposite effect and higher profit levels will be required before the large salary method is beneficial.

See Chapter 32 for more examples of the impact of other income on whether the large salary method is beneficial.

In Summary

There are far too many potential combinations of different factors for us to examine every possibility here. However, with potential savings running to several thousand pounds, the large salary method is certainly worth looking into for high earners, especially where:

- Some spare employment allowance is available,
- The director is over state pension age,
- The director is aged under 21, or
- The director has other income up to £80,000

Savings can arise at lower profit levels where these factors are present. But the savings will be reduced, or often eliminated, if there is more than one director, and are not generally available to Scottish taxpayers at all.

Finally, although we have seen how, at high income levels, a salary could be better than dividends, it is still a very costly way for an additional rate taxpayer to take money out of a company, with an overall tax burden of 53.9% in most cases. It is therefore generally only worth looking at these larger salaries after other options have been considered.

Chapter 27

Alternative Profit Extraction Strategies

Company owners faced with losing their personal allowance or paying additional rate tax on their salary or dividends may wish to consider alternative profit extraction strategies, including:

- Gifting shares in the company to family members, including family members who are higher rate taxpayers (see Part 5).
- Making personal or company pension contributions (see Chapters 41 and 42).
- Keeping cash inside the company until the business is sold or wound up (see Chapter 44). At this point, it may be possible to pay CGT at a reduced rate of 18% on the extracted funds.

Pension Contributions

Company owners who pay themselves small salaries can only make small pension contributions *personally*: your pension contributions cannot generally exceed your earnings (dividends don't count as earnings).

For example, if you pay yourself a salary of £12,570, you can only make a pension contribution of £12,570 personally (£10,056 contributed by you, with a further £2,514 added to your pension by the taxman).

Company owners who wish to make bigger pension contributions can either pay themselves higher salaries or get their companies to make the contributions. A higher salary usually comes with a punitive NI bill, so company contributions are often preferable. Company pension contributions also enjoy CT relief, providing they are not excessive (see Chapter 42).

The Pension Taper

High income earners face another restriction: the annual allowance. This is the maximum amount that can be invested in a pension each year and, for high earners, it can be reduced from £60,000 to just £10,000.

The first thing you have to calculate is your 'threshold income'. If your threshold income is no more than £200,000, you are completely exempt from tapering and can make pension contributions just like anyone else.

Your threshold income is, broadly speaking, your total taxable income. This includes your salary, dividends, rental profits, interest income and any other taxable income you receive.

From this, you deduct any pension contributions you have made *personally* (you deduct the gross contributions). You can also deduct qualifying loan interest (see Chapter 39), relief for trading losses, most other forms of loss relief, and a few other, more obscure reliefs, as listed in Section 24 of the Income Tax Act 2007.

Employer pension contributions are ignored when calculating threshold income. But you must add back any salary sacrificed in exchange for employer pension contributions.

Example 1: *Dirk takes a salary and dividend income totalling £200,000 out of his company. He has no other income. His company makes a pension contribution on his behalf but we ignore that when calculating his threshold income. He doesn't make any pension contributions personally, so his threshold income is exactly £200,000. Dirk is unaffected by the tapered annual allowance. This means his annual allowance for the current tax year is £60,000.*

Example 2: *Beric is a company owner who pays himself salary and dividend income totalling £200,000. He also has taxable rental profits of £50,000, so his total taxable income is £250,000.*

His company makes a pension contribution of £50,000 on his behalf, but we ignore this when calculating his threshold income. He doesn't make any pension contributions personally.

Beric's threshold income is therefore £250,000. Because this exceeds £200,000, he is potentially affected by the tapered annual allowance.

If your threshold income exceeds £200,000, the next thing you have to calculate is your 'adjusted income'. Broadly speaking, your adjusted income is your total taxable income *plus* any pension contributions made by your company (your employer).

You also add back any contributions to an occupational pension scheme under a net pay arrangement (where your contributions are deducted from your salary before calculating PAYE).

As with threshold income, you can again deduct qualifying loan interest, relief for trading losses, most other forms of loss relief, and other reliefs listed in Section 24 of the Income Tax Act 2007.

Your £60,000 pension annual allowance will only be reduced if your adjusted income exceeds £260,000. Your annual allowance is then reduced by £1 for every £2 your adjusted income exceeds £260,000. For example, an individual with adjusted income of £290,000 will have their annual allowance reduced by £15,000 (£30,000/2), giving them an annual allowance of £45,000.

The annual allowance cannot fall below £10,000: this is the minimum level of the allowance for those affected by the taper.

Pension contributions that exceed the tapered annual allowance face the annual allowance charge. The excess contributions will be added to your income and taxed. If the charge exceeds £2,000, it may be possible to have it paid out of your pension savings. This may only be possible if total contributions to the scheme in question exceed the £60,000 annual allowance.

Example 2 continued: *As we saw earlier, Beric has total taxable income of £250,000 and his company makes a contribution of £50,000 on his behalf. His adjusted income is therefore £300,000 (£250,000 + £50,000). His annual allowance is cut by £20,000 (£300,000 – £260,000 = £40,000/2), and is therefore £40,000 (£60,000 – £20,000). He faces an annual allowance charge on £10,000 (£50,000 – £40,000).*

Beric can avoid the charge by getting his company to make a smaller pension contribution (no more than £43,333). Alternatively, he may be able to extract less income from his company (no more than £180,000) to ensure his total taxable income reduces to £230,000 and he is able to benefit from a tapered annual allowance of £50,000. Company owners may find it easier than others to control their taxable income to reduce their threshold income and adjusted income. However, if they do this, they may have to be wary of triggering a special anti-avoidance rule (see below).

Company owners will find it fairly easy to calculate their adjusted and threshold income when it comes to salaries and dividends.

Problems may arise when the company owner has other income that is less predictable, for example rental income from properties. Company owners who are also landlords may not know precisely how much taxable income they have earned (and thus their tapered annual allowance) until *after* the tax year has ended. By then it will be too late to make pension contributions.

Those who wish to benefit from pension contributions and think they may be affected by the tapered annual allowance may need to estimate their taxable income *before* the end of the tax year.

The Tapered Annual Allowance and Carry Forward

All is not lost if your pension contributions exceed your tapered annual allowance for the year. Those affected by the tapered annual allowance can still carry forward any unused annual allowance from the three previous tax years. For example, if your annual allowance this year is reduced from £60,000 to £40,000 and you make a £25,000 pension contribution, you will have £15,000 left to carry forward to next year (£40,000 – £25,000).

Carry forward could act as a lifeline for those whose pension contributions accidentally exceed the tapered annual allowance in any given year. Beric in the above example will avoid the annual allowance charge if he has at least £10,000 of unused annual allowance from the three previous tax years.

Example: *Mario is a company owner with taxable income of £200,000. He gets his company to make an £80,000 pension contribution (utilising £20,000 of unused annual allowance carried forward from previous years). His adjusted income is £280,000 but his threshold income is £200,000, so his annual allowance for the current year is not reduced.*

If your threshold income does not exceed £200,000, you cannot be subject to the tapered annual allowance, even if your adjusted income is greater than £260,000.

Anti-Avoidance Rule

There is an anti-avoidance rule to prevent anyone entering into an arrangement that involves reducing their adjusted or threshold income and increasing their income in a different tax year.

The anti-avoidance provisions apply when it is reasonable to assume the main purpose, or one of the main purposes of the arrangement, is to reduce the impact of the tapered annual allowance. If the anti-avoidance provisions apply, then the relevant arrangement will be ignored for the purposes of calculating the tapered annual allowance.

It is unclear how this anti-avoidance rule could be applied to company owners who vary their income from year to year.

Enjoying over 55% Tax Relief

Many additional rate taxpayers are unaffected by the tapered annual allowance and can make fairly big pension contributions with full tax relief.

Any company owner with taxable income of no more than £200,000 can get their company to make a pension contribution of up to £60,000 every year. Other high earning company owners can make the following maximum pension contributions:

Taxable Income	**Maximum Contribution***
£230,000	£50,000
£260,000	£40,000
£290,000	£30,000
£320,000	£20,000
£350,000+	£10,000

* Ignores potential carry forward from previous tax years.

Additional rate taxpayers currently face a combined marginal tax rate of up to 55.4% on their dividend income (CT and Income Tax). After tax, a company owner could be left with just £446 from each £1,000 of pre-tax profit.

By contrast, with a pension contribution, the whole £1,000 can be paid into the director's pension fund. Income Tax will be payable when they eventually take the money out, but the effective tax rate could be between 15% and 30%, leaving them with between £700 and £850 after tax. (See Chapter 41 for an explanation of how these tax rates are calculated.)

Thus, the director can choose between £446 today and £700 to £850 in the future. It's easy to see why pensions are such powerful tax shelters!

Chapter 28

Using a Company versus Self-Employment

Most company owners probably realise that if they take all of their income as salary, they could end up paying significantly more tax than a self-employed person (sole trader or partner) with the same income. This is because of the additional employer's NI payable on most salary income.

It's interesting to note that, even if a company owner structures their pay in the most tax efficient manner, taking most of their income as dividends (generally), they could still end up paying significantly more tax than a self-employed person. This situation arises in most cases where the company owner withdraws all or most of the company's profits each year.

Table 8 compares the total after-tax income of a company owner with that of a self-employed business owner at different profit levels. It is assumed the business owner has no other taxable income in both cases.

The table is based on 2026/27 tax rates, and takes account of the recent increase to dividend tax rates.

For the company owner, it is assumed the 'optimal' salary for 2026/27 is taken and all the remaining after-tax profits are extracted as dividends. At most profit levels up to £175,000, that 'optimal' salary is £12,570. However, there is an exception for profits of £150,000, where a salary of £5,000 is theoretically optimal (but note the points in Chapter 17 regarding state pension entitlement).

At higher profit levels of £200,000 or more, the large salary method (Chapter 26) becomes 'optimal' and that has been used in this table.

The 'Extra Income' column is the additional income enjoyed by the *self-employed* person. For example, when profits are £100,000, a self-employed person will enjoy £4,102 more after-tax income than a company owner.

TABLE 8
After-Tax Income Compared
Company Owner vs Self Employed

Profits	Company Owner	Self-Employed	Extra Income
£30,000	£24,403	£25,468	£1,065
£40,000	£31,633	£32,868	£1,235
£50,000	£38,862	£40,268	£1,406
£60,000	£46,091	£46,111	£20
£70,000	£51,042	£51,911	£869
£80,000	£55,765	£57,711	£1,947
£90,000	£60,487	£63,511	£3,024
£100,000	£65,210	£69,311	£4,102
£110,000	£69,932	£73,111	£3,179
£120,000	£74,654	£76,911	£2,257
£130,000	£78,973	£81,440	£2,468
£140,000	£82,041	£86,740	£4,699
£150,000	£85,321	£92,040	£6,719
£175,000	£94,621	£105,290	£10,670
£200,000	£106,022	£118,540	£12,518
£225,000	£117,544	£131,790	£14,246
£250,000	£129,066	£145,040	£15,974
£300,000	£152,109	£171,540	£19,431
£350,000	£175,153	£198,040	£22,887
£400,000	£198,196	£224,540	£26,344
£500,000	£244,283	£277,540	£33,257

Notes:
1. Company owner withdraws all the profits of the business
2. Company owner takes optimal salary (see above) and remaining income as dividends
3. No spare employment allowance available
4. No associated companies
5. Business owner is under state pension age but over 21 in both cases
6. Self-employed tax includes Income Tax and NI
7. Self-employed tax bills are higher in Scotland (see Table 10 below)

As we can see, this year's dividend tax increase is the 'last nail in the coffin' for the whole idea of forming a company simply to save tax where you wish to extract all the profits every year.

The picture changes over the years: twenty years ago, using a company could lead to significant tax savings at many profit levels. That may happen again but, for the time being, we wouldn't suggest self-employed business owners form a company just to save tax if they need all their profits to live on every year.

But there are many other reasons to form a company, and the non-tax benefits, such as limited liability protection, could often outweigh the tax considerations. There are also many opportunities to reduce your tax burden when using a company, as we have seen, and will continue to see, throughout this guide. The position is also different for Scottish taxpayers (see below).

Furthermore, none of this necessarily means all company owners would be better off self-employed. If profits are kept inside the company to help it grow, the only tax payable will be CT. Clearly, paying CT at 25% or 26.5% is a lot better than the 47% tax paid by self-employed additional rate taxpayers (50% in Scotland).

It is in these circumstances, when profits are reinvested, that companies are most powerful as tax shelters. For example, where a company has profits of £500,000 and only half the profits are paid out using the method explained in Chapter 26 (i.e. mostly as salary), the total tax bill will be around £37,500 less than the tax paid by a self-employed person.

Would the Employment Allowance Help?

Where there is at least £1,136 of spare employment allowance available, the usual 'baseline' salary of £12,570 can be paid free from employer's NI. This improves the position a little for small company owners, but there are still only savings compared with the self-employed person in a narrow band of profit, from £54,400 to £66,900, and these peak at a maximum of just £674 (at profits of around £59,120).

At higher profit levels, the 'optimal' salary may be greater when there is spare employment allowance available, leading to overall savings compared with the baseline salary of £12,570. We looked at these savings in Chapters 14 and 26, but the savings we saw in those chapters are not enough to leave the company owner better off than the self-employed person.

Partnership versus Company

Table 8 above is based on a comparison between a sole trader and a single company director. If we compare a partnership to a company with more than one director, the company becomes even less favourable. For example, a couple in partnership together who each have a profit share of £150,000 would each enjoy after tax income of £92,040, as shown in Table 8.

If they formed a company, however, and both extracted half the after-tax profits by way of salaries of £5,000, with the remainder taken as dividends, their after-tax income would be £84,599 each.

Hence, staying in partnership would mean they had £7,441 (£92,040 – £84,599) of extra income each, rather than the £6,719 shown in Table 8 for a sole trader with profits of £150,000.

Nonetheless, a company could again yield tax savings when the couple limit the amounts they withdraw each year. For example, if they each took a salary of £12,570 plus a quarter of the company's after-tax profits as dividends (£51,110 in this case), there would be an overall tax saving of just over £28,000 compared with operating as a partnership. At the same time, the couple would have a healthy £109,774 of after-tax income between them.

The employment allowance would again improve the position for the company owner couple, and it is more likely to be available where there are two directors. However, if we go back to our initial assumption that all profits are extracted, the difference the employment allowance makes is too small to make a company worthwhile at any profit level.

Scottish Business Owners

The higher Scottish Income Tax rates on self-employed business owners mean there is a very different picture in Scotland, as shown by Table 9. In fact, it's so different that, this time, the 'Extra Income' column means the extra after-tax income enjoyed by the *company owner*.

As we can see, at many profit levels, there are worthwhile savings to be had by using a company for Scottish business owners. In fact, there is some saving at any profit level between around £50,000 and £86,000, or between around £105,000 and £145,000. As with other taxpayers in the rest of the UK, the savings will be slightly greater if some spare employment allowance is available.

The picture for Scottish couples in business together (and other Scottish partnerships) is again considerably less favourable than for sole traders, although savings remain available for a two-director company with profits between around £114,000 and £137,000, or between around £224,000 and £282,000.

TABLE 9
After-Tax Income Compared
Company Owner vs Self Employed: Scottish Taxpayers

Profits	Company Owner	Self-Employed	Extra Income
£30,000	£24,403	£25,503	(£1,100)
£40,000	£31,633	£32,803	(£1,170)
£50,000	£38,862	£38,772	£90
£60,000	£46,091	£44,361	£1,730
£70,000	£51,042	£49,961	£1,081
£80,000	£55,765	£55,411	£354
£90,000	£60,487	£60,711	(£224)
£100,000	£65,210	£66,011	(£802)
£125,000	£77,016	£73,636	£3,379
£150,000	£85,322	£86,109	(£787)
£175,000	£94,650	£98,609	(£3,949)
£200,000	£105,794	£111,109	(£5,304)

Notes:
1. Company owner withdraws all the profits of the business
2. Company owner takes optimal salary of £12,570 (except in the case of profits of £150,000, when the optimal salary is £5,000); and remaining income as dividends
3. No spare employment allowance available
4. No associated companies
5. Business owner is under state pension age but over 21 in both cases

A Word of Warning

Everything in this chapter is based on current tax rates. A change in rates will tip the balance, and one change we may see is a further increase in dividend tax rates, making companies less attractive, whatever their profit level (even if you're a Scottish taxpayer).

Property Businesses

This chapter has also focussed exclusively on trading businesses. Property letting or property investment businesses are quite different. For a thorough analysis, see the Taxcafe guide *Using a Property Company to Save Tax*.

Part 4

Company Owners with Income from Other Sources

Chapter 29

The Impact of Other Income

So far, we have mostly (though not exclusively) looked at director/shareholders with no income from outside their company. The existence of other income impacts the 'salary versus dividends' question in a number of ways, some of which may not be immediately apparent.

The effect of having other income from outside the company depends on both the amount and type of that other income. To understand these effects, it is first important to appreciate that personal income received by an individual is taxed in a specific order.

The Order in which Income is Taxed
For most Income Tax purposes, income is currently taxed in the following order:

- Non-savings income:
  - Employment income
  - Self-employment trading income
  - Pension income (including state pension income)
  - Property income (rental income, etc)
- Savings income (interest, etc)
- Dividend income

Most importantly for the purposes of this guide, dividends are always treated as the top slice of income.

In the current 2026/27 tax year, all of an individual's non-savings income (as defined above) can effectively be bundled together for Income Tax purposes, as it will ultimately be taxed as if it were a single lump sum. There are, however, some quirks to each type of income, which we will examine in more detail in Chapter 33.

From 2027/28 onwards, property income will no longer be bundled in with other non-savings income and will be taxed separately (but before savings income and dividends). We'll look at the impact of that in our next edition.

This ordering of income for Income Tax purposes does not affect how income is treated for NI purposes. Both employer's and employee's NI are seldom affected by any income the director may have from outside the company.

There are two potential exceptions: firstly, where the other income is a salary from an associated company or business, and secondly, where the director has a salary of £50,270 or more from another source (we will look at this in Chapter 33).

Income from Other Sources

With the exception of self-employment and pension income, it may be possible to extract any other type of income from *your own company*: employment income, rental income, interest income, and dividend income.

We've already talked extensively about salaries (employment income) and dividends. If your company uses a property that you own personally (for example, an office or shop) it can also pay you rent; and if your company borrows money from you, it can pay you interest. In Chapters 38 and 39 we take a look at whether it is tax efficient to get your company to pay you rent or interest and how much.

In this part of the guide, however, our focus is on company owners who have income from *other sources*: i.e. income that does not come from their own company. More specifically, the focus is on company owners who have income from other sources that is subject to *Income Tax*. Some income (e.g. most interest income and stock market dividends) can be sheltered from Income Tax inside an ISA or pension scheme.

It is also possible to shelter assets from Income Tax inside another company. Many property investors do this. CT is still payable on any rental profits produced by the properties but the Income Tax position of the company owner will be unaffected, unless those profits are extracted.

For the rest of this chapter, we will also focus on non-savings income. Hence, unless stated to the contrary, when we refer to 'other income', it means employment income, self-employment trading income, rental income, or pension income received personally by the company owner, from outside the company (we'll look at interest and dividends in Chapter 33).

Other Income Less Than £12,570

The first thing other income does is to use some of the director's personal allowance. Hence, if the director were to take the usual 'baseline' salary of £12,570, some of it would suffer Income Tax. In some cases, this means the director's optimal salary will be less than £12,570, but this is not always the case, and we will look at this in detail in Chapter 31.

Other Income Between £12,570 and £50,270

Once other income reaches at least £12,570, the personal allowance has been used up and all of the salary the director takes out of the company will be subject to Income Tax, as well as any dividends in excess of the dividend allowance.

The director's theoretical optimal salary will sometimes now be just £5,000 although, as explained in Chapter 17, a salary of at least £6,708 may be advisable. Again, we will look at this scenario in Chapter 31.

But other income at this level has other effects that we need to take into account.

Firstly, the director is already closer to the key tax thresholds where their overall effective tax rates will increase significantly. This means they are able to take less income from their company before exceeding those thresholds, and we will look at this situation, and the related planning measures some directors may wish to implement, in Chapter 30.

Secondly, the director is also closer to the point where the overall tax burden, taking everything into account, may be less for a salary than it is for dividends: as demonstrated by Table 5 in Chapter 10. This means the director's optimal salary might remain £12,570, might be the amount covered by the employment allowance (where available), or might be the salary calculated under the large salary method (Chapter 26). We will explore these possibilities in Chapters 31 and 32.

Other Income of £50,270 or More

With other income at this level, the director may not need to take much, if any, income out of their company. However, it's generally worth taking dividends covered by the dividend allowance (but see Chapter 6 for a few words of caution). It may also be sensible to take a salary of at least £6,708 if you are not getting a credit for state pension entitlement purposes by any other means (see Chapter 17).

It may be worth 'topping up' your income to one of the other key thresholds (£60,000 or £100,000) in order to avoid exceeding those thresholds in later years. Any income you don't need immediately can always be lent back to the company.

Conversely, if you do not wish to lose either your child benefit or your personal allowance *this year*, it may be necessary to restrict the income you take out of the company (see Chapter 30).

With other income of at least £50,270, your basic rate band has been used up. Any dividends you take in excess of the dividend allowance will suffer Income Tax at 35.75% or more.

Any salary you take out of the company will suffer Income Tax at 40% or more, but this will not generally affect the NI on the salary (unless the other income is also salary), so combined Income Tax and NI rates of 48% or 53% become possible.

However, once this hurdle has been overcome, any further salary (i.e. salary in excess of £50,270 from the director's company) will be more tax efficient than dividends whenever the company's marginal CT rate is 26.5% or 25% (as shown by Table 7 in Chapter 26). Hence, the large salary method will often be the best way to take significant amounts of income out of the company. We'll explore this further in Chapter 32.

Chapter 30

Keeping Income Below the Key Thresholds

In Chapter 11, we explained why company owners, when deciding how much income to withdraw from their companies, need to be aware of the following Income Tax thresholds and brackets:

• Over £50,270	Higher rate tax
• £60,000-£80,000	Child Benefit Charge
• £100,000-£125,140	Personal allowance withdrawal
• Over £125,140	Additional rate tax

Basic rate taxpayers pay 10.75% Income Tax on their dividends. Once your income exceeds £50,270, you start paying 35.75% higher rate tax. However, dividend income that falls into the final three tax brackets is taxed at much higher rates:

• £60,000-£80,000	42.78% or more
• £100,000-£125,140	58.25% in many cases
• Over £125,140	39.35%

When trying to avoid these extortionate tax rates, you must remember to include any other taxable income you receive which may force your company income, in particular your dividend income, into a higher tax bracket.

To avoid a potential tax sting, you may wish to reduce the amount of income you withdraw from your company or take other steps.

Let's say you expect to earn £10,000 of rental income during the current tax year but so far have not withdrawn any income from your company. As things stand, all your rental income will be tax free, being covered by your Income Tax personal allowance. Let's say you now decide to withdraw a salary of £12,570 and a dividend of £37,700 from your company (the maximum amount you can withdraw tax free or taxed at just 10.75%, in the absence of any other income). The decision to take a salary means you now have £22,570 of non-savings income (see Chapter 29) and your Income Tax bill will increase by £2,000:

£22,570 – £12,570 personal allowance = £10,000 x 20% = £2,000

And what about your dividends that are supposedly taxed at no more than 10.75%? Thanks to your rental income, £10,000 of your dividend income will now be pushed into the higher rate tax bracket and taxed at 35.75% instead of 10.75%, resulting in additional tax of £2,500.

In summary, having £10,000 of rental income increases the company owner's tax bill by £4,500!

Restricting Company Income

Company owners who have a significant amount of taxable income from other sources, and cannot shelter it from Income Tax, may wish to reduce the amount of income they withdraw from their company, so as to avoid paying Income Tax at some of the extortionate rates listed above.

One of the benefits of being a company owner is you can control how much income you withdraw from your business. This allows you to control your Income Tax bill from year to year.

Income from other sources is often less easy to control. For example, it may not be possible to shift it from one tax year into another tax year. You may be able to control the dividends declared by your own company, but if you own a few shares in BP, you can't force their directors to increase or lower the dividend!

Company owners who want to keep their taxable income below any of the key Income Tax thresholds may therefore have to restrict their *company income*: it may not always be possible to alter the income you receive from other sources.

For example, if you have other income of £20,000, a dividend of no more than £30,270 will prevent your income going over £50,270, which means you will avoid paying 35.75% tax.

A dividend no higher than £40,000 will ensure you avoid the Child Benefit Charge, where relevant.

A dividend of up to £80,000 will ensure your income does not exceed £100,000. A significant amount will be taxed at 35.75% and you may end up paying the maximum Child Benefit Charge, but you will not lose any of your personal allowance.

All this is equally relevant to Scottish taxpayers, because it is the *UK* thresholds that apply to your dividend income. A Scottish taxpayer with £40,000 of salary and rental income can still receive a dividend of £10,270 without paying 35.75% tax because it is the UK higher rate threshold that applies to dividend income.

We haven't included the additional rate tax threshold of £125,140 in any of this because, as explained in Chapter 24, there is no benefit in avoiding it.

Predictability

At the start of a new tax year, you may not know how much taxable income you will receive from other sources during the year. This could be problematic if you wish to withdraw dividends from your company *at the beginning of the tax year.* If you withdraw dividends from your company and your other income ends up higher than anticipated, you may end up paying more Income Tax than expected on your company dividends.

Some types of income are, however, more predictable than others. For example, interest income, stock market dividends, and pension income are arguably more predictable than, say, the profits of a sole trader business (self-employment income).

Some types of income, if not completely predictable, are more likely to end up being *less than expected,* rather than higher than expected. A rental property that normally generates £1,000 per month may lie empty for three months, thereby producing an annual income of £9,000 rather than £12,000.

If your income from other sources turns out to be less than expected, you may be able to get your company to pay you additional dividend income before the end of the tax year. If your income from other sources turns out to be *higher than expected* you generally cannot reverse any dividends you have already taken out of your company, although it may be possible to do some emergency year-end tax planning (see Chapter 34).

Company owners who have unpredictable income from other sources may therefore wish to postpone paying dividends until closer to the end of the tax year, if they are concerned that their dividend income may fall into a heavily taxed bracket.

Chapter 31

Should I Pay Myself a Lower Salary?

So far, we have shown that if you have income from other sources (e.g. rental income) you may wish to reduce your company *dividends* to avoid various tax thresholds. Another important question is, "Should I pay myself a lower salary?"

The answer to this depends on a number of factors, including:

- What you are trying to achieve
- Whether the employment allowance is available
- How much other income you have
- What type or types of other income you have

Not Exceeding the Thresholds

If you have a substantial amount of other income from outside the company (generally more than £37,700, or more than £31,092 for a Scottish taxpayer), you may want to reduce your salary in order to avoid exceeding one of the key Income Tax thresholds: £50,270, £60,000, and £100,000.

(Scottish taxpayers have two additional thresholds to be aware of: £43,662 and £75,000, but can ignore interest or dividend income for the purpose of these.)

So, for example, if you have other income of £52,000 and several small children, you might choose to reduce the salary you take from your company to £8,000 in order to avoid the Child Benefit Charge. (Or perhaps £7,500 so you can still take a £500 tax-free dividend.)

Maximising After-Tax Income

You might also wish to reduce your salary in other cases where you are seeking to maximise your total after-tax income without exceeding one of the key Income Tax thresholds.

Let's say you have rental income totalling £30,000 and a company making profits of around £125,000. You want to limit your total taxable income to £100,000 so that you retain your personal allowance.

What's the best level of salary to take during the current 2026/27 tax year? Let's look at three options:

Salary	**£0**	**£6,708**	**£12,570**
Income Tax @ 20%	£0	£1,342	£2,514
Net Salary	£0	£5,366	£10,056
Dividends	**£70,000**	**£63,292**	**£57,430**
Income Tax @ 10.75%	£2,125	£1,404	£774
Income Tax @ 35.75%	£17,778	£17,778	£17,778
Total Net Income*	£50,097	£49,476	£48,934

* This doesn't include the rental income or take account of the Income Tax on it. However, as long as total taxable income does not exceed £100,000, this is the same regardless of what salary is taken from the company.

So, in this scenario, the best after-tax income is produced by taking no salary at all. But this is far from the end of the story.

Firstly, taking no salary will mean you get no credit for state pension purposes. It may also create other problems. We'll look at these issues later in this chapter.

Secondly, we have only looked at the director's position and not the company's. A salary of £12,570 would have produced a CT saving of £3,331 in this case: that's £2,168 more than the director's £1,163 Income Tax saving. Even if it gave rise to employer's NI of £1,136, it would have produced a £3,632 CT saving and an overall £2,496 net saving for the company: still £1,333 more than the director's Income Tax saving.

So, what's best for the director personally is not necessarily best overall. And that's why we need to look at the optimal position taking all these factors into account.

Optimal Salaries with Other Income

If you intend to pay yourself a salary of £12,570, as discussed in Chapter 12, and extract the rest of the company's profits as dividends, it may be possible to save a small amount of tax by reducing your company salary. The position depends on whether the company has any spare employment allowance and on how much other income from outside the company you have.

In the analysis below, unless stated to the contrary, 'other income' means taxable income from sources outside the company, excluding dividends and interest.

We will look at what salary would be mathematically optimal. Note, however, that, if this works out at less than £6,708, it will often be sensible to take a salary of £6,708 in order to protect your state pension entitlement (see Chapter 17).

With Spare Employment Allowance

Where there is at least £1,136 of spare employment allowance available, a salary of £12,570 generally remains optimal for directors with low levels of other income. Although the salary may be subject to Income Tax, there will be no NI payable by the director or the company.

With significant amounts of other income and spare employment allowance available, higher salaries may sometimes be optimal: see Chapter 32.

No Spare Employment Allowance

Mathematically speaking, a salary of £5,000 may sometimes be optimal where the company has no spare employment allowance available and you have at least £7,570 of other income. The savings for a basic rate taxpayer are typically £237.

Some higher-rate taxpayers may experience savings of up to £367 by taking the lower salary, although the position is complicated, to say the least. In many cases, a salary of £12,570 remains optimal and a lower salary would lead to an overall cost.

For those with total taxable income in the £100,000 to £125,140 bracket, a salary of £5,000 may be optimal, although the saving compared with our usual baseline salary of £12,570 is a mere £94 at best and, again, there may be an overall cost.

In some cases, while a salary of £5,000 might be optimal, it will be sensible to take a salary of £6,708 (see Chapter 17). The savings for a basic rate taxpayer (compared with a salary of £12,570), where the director has at least £5,862 of other income, are then typically £184. Higher rate taxpayers may again experience savings in some cases: up to £284 in this case; although sometimes there may be an overall cost. The saving for those with total income in the £100,000 to £125,140 bracket is typically just £73 but, again, there may sometimes be an overall cost.

With less than £7,570 of other income and no spare employment allowance available, the optimal salary for a basic rate taxpayer is generally £12,570 less that other income. For example, with £4,000 of other income, the optimal salary will generally be £8,570. The saving for a basic rate taxpayer in this case would be £125.

The position for higher-rate taxpayers varies and a similar salary may again be optimal, but the potential savings are small and there may even be a cost in some cases.

In summary, company owners with other income may sometimes achieve small savings by taking a theoretically optimal salary of less than £12,570. But the savings arising are not what we would consider worthwhile, and some higher-rate taxpayers may even see a cost if they were to take a lower salary. In practice, many company owners will feel it is better to stick with our baseline salary of £12,570.

Where an additional rate taxpayer has other income, a lower salary will not be optimal. In fact, as we will see in Chapter 32, the other income sometimes means a higher salary will be beneficial.

Reducing Your Salary: Other Factors to Consider

Aside from the issues discussed above, there are reasons why you may not wish to reduce your salary, or why it may not be practical to do so:

- To make pension contributions personally (see Chapter 42).
- Because your income from other sources may not be known at the beginning of the year, when you may wish to start making monthly salary payments.
- Because the taxman may question any reduction in your salary (see Chapter 51).

However, when we are only looking at whether to pay yourself £5,000, £6,708, or £12,570, the second point is easily dealt with by paying yourself a monthly salary of £416.67 (£5,000/12), or £559.00 (£6,708/12) for most of the tax year. Then, if you decide the higher salary is going to be better, simply pay an extra £7,570 or £5,862 as a bonus in March.

And a mere reduction from £12,570 to either £5,000 or £6,708 is highly unlikely to give rise to any problem under the third point.

So, the main thing for most company owners to be aware of is the importance of paying yourself a salary of at least £6,708 in 2026/27 to secure state pension entitlement where necessary (see Chapter 17).

Dividends and Interest

Where your income from outside your company includes, or comprises, dividends or interest, the impact of reducing your salary will be different. We'll look at these types of 'other income' in Chapter 33.

Chapter 32

Should I Pay Myself a Higher Salary?

In Chapter 31, we looked at whether having other taxable income from outside your company might mean you should pay yourself a lower salary (less than the 'baseline' salary of £12,570).

However, having other income can alternatively sometimes mean it becomes more beneficial to pay yourself a higher salary, greater than £12,570. There are two factors that can lead to a higher salary becoming beneficial:

- The company has more than £1,136 of spare employment allowance available, *OR*
- The company has substantial profits and you wish to extract all or most of them by way of salary and dividends

We'll look at each of these in turn. It's important to stress that a higher salary may be beneficial under either scenario on its own: so, for example, the second scenario does not necessarily need there to be spare employment allowance available (although it helps).

Spare Employment Allowance AND Other Income

As we have seen in previous chapters, with at least £1,136 of spare employment allowance available, a salary of £12,570 usually remains optimal.

As we saw in Chapter 14, however, if more of the employment allowance is available, it may become optimal to pay a higher salary. This is because, for a higher rate taxpayer, an employer's NI free salary can be more tax efficient than dividends.

The presence of other income effectively provides a head start to becoming a higher rate taxpayer (or could mean you are already there) and this, in turn, means that a higher, employer's NI free salary may often be optimal. Let's look at an example.

Example: *Lois has personal rental profits of £30,000. Her company makes a pre-tax profit of £120,000 and has spare employment allowance of £5,250 available (precisely half), enough to cover a director's salary of £40,000. Lois intends to extract all the company's after-tax profits by way of salary and dividends. Let's look at her options:*

	Baseline Salary	***employer's NI-Free***
Company's tax	***£***	***£***
Company profit	*120,000*	*120,000*
Less: Salary	*12,570*	*40,000*
Net Profit	*107,430*	*80,000*
*Less: Corporation Tax**	*24,719*	*17,450*
After-tax profit/Dividend	*82,711*	*62,550*
Director's tax		
*Total income***	*125,281*	*132,550*
Income Tax	*38,884*	*42,910*
National Insurance	*0*	*2,194*
After-tax income	*86,397*	*87,446*

* 19% on the first £50,000; 26.5% on the remainder (see Chapter 1)
** Including rental profits of £30,000

As we can see, increasing her salary to the amount covered by the employment allowance has left Lois £1,049 better off in this case. This is because, when all taxes are taken into account, a higher rate taxpayer generally keeps more of an employer's NI free salary than a dividend, as shown by Table 10.

TABLE 10
Amount Kept per £1,000 of Profit: Higher Rate Taxpayer

Salary Level	**Salary***	**Dividend****
First £12,570	£600	£520, £472, or £482
£12,570 to £50,270	£520	£520, £472, or £482
£50,270 to £75,000***	£580	£520, £472, or £482

* To the extent covered by the employment allowance
** At marginal CT rates of 19%, 26.5%, and 25% respectively
*** Maximum possible salary covered by the employment allowance

Table 10 covers salary or dividends falling into the income band between £50,270 and £100,000 for a typical higher rate taxpayer under state pension age and not subject to the Child Benefit Charge. It ignores the dividend allowance. It is also assumed the company owner's other income does not include another salary of more than £12,570.

The only scenario where a higher rate taxpayer is not better off taking an employer's NI free salary out of their company is for salary between £12,570 and £50,270 that only provides CT relief at 19%.

In Lois's case, her salary provided CT relief at 26.5%, so, once she was a higher rate taxpayer, she was keeping £48 more (£520 – £472) out of every £1,000 of additional salary.

This is slightly offset by an additional overall cost of just over £2 per £1,000 of salary falling into the basic rate band in this scenario, but the salary doesn't have to extend far above the higher-rate tax threshold to more than make up for this.

In other words, it's clear that many company owners with other income and spare employment allowance available could be better off taking their maximum employer's NI free salary rather than the usual baseline salary of £12,570.

But there are other factors to consider before we can be definitive. If there is more than £6,791 of spare employment allowance available, the employer's NI free salary can exceed £50,270. The additional salary in excess of £50,270 then provides the company owner with up to £108 (£580 – £472) more after-tax income per £1,000 of employer's NI free salary.

Conversely, once the salary reduces the company's profits to £50,000, any further salary may lead to a small overall tax cost, although this will be negligible when covered by the employment allowance; and this does not apply once the salary exceeds £50,270, when a saving of £60 per £1,000 arises.

There are other complications because £1,000 of pre-tax profit can fund £1,000 of employer's NI free salary, but only between £735 and £810 of dividends. Furthermore, the position changes once the director's total taxable income exceeds £100,000 and again when it exceeds £125,140: which can sometimes mean the large salary method becomes preferable instead (see further below).

Nonetheless, here are some examples of when the maximum employer's NI free salary may become optimal:

Other Income	Spare EA Needed	Salary
£5,000	£6,010	£45,067
£10,000	£5,255	£40,033
£15,000	£4,500	£35,000
£20,000	£3,740	£29,933
£25,000	£2,985	£24,900
£30,000	£2,230	£19,867
£35,000	£1,470	£14,800

Notes:
1. 'Spare EA Needed' is the minimum amount of spare employment allowance that needs to be available for this strategy to be optimal; 'Salary' is the maximum employer's NI free salary covered by this amount of spare employment allowance
2. The company owner is assumed to be under state pension age but over 21
3. The table does not apply to Scottish taxpayers
4. Other income excludes dividends, but includes interest (see Chapter 33 for further guidance)

It is important to stress the purpose of this table is to illustrate when it *might* be optimal to take the maximum employer's NI free salary instead of the baseline salary of £12,570. It is based on two key assumptions:

- The salary provides CT relief at 26.5%: in other words, the company will be left with taxable profits of at least £50,000 (generally) after paying the salary
- The director limits their total gross taxable income to £100,000 and wishes to achieve this at the minimum cost to the company

That is not to say this strategy is not worthwhile when these assumptions are not met. In our example above, Lois still achieved a saving even when extracting all the profits of her company and having total taxable income well in excess of £100,000 as a result.

But, if the assumptions are not met, the amount of spare employment allowance required to make this strategy optimal will be more than the amount shown in the table.

In a nutshell, the table tells us when this strategy is worth considering. And the reason it only covers directors with other income up to £35,000 is that once other income is £37,700 or more, the strategy is *always* worth considering.

Another reason for our assumptions is that where the director wishes to extract all or most of the company's profits, and the company is highly profitable, another strategy may be even better.

The Large Salary Method: Directors with Other Income

For those with a company making substantial profits *and* income from other sources, the existence of that other income often means it is more likely that you will benefit from following the large salary method we looked at in Chapter 26.

On the other hand, very high levels of other income (over around £81,000) mean the large salary method can become less attractive.

Here are some examples of the profit level required before the large salary method produces worthwhile savings in the current 2026/27 tax year where the director has other income:

Other Income	**Profit Level Required**
£10,000	£192,500
£20,000	£170,000
£30,000	£169,000
£40,000	£179,000
£50,000	£188,000
£60,000	£197,000
£70,000	£206,000
£80,000	£215,500
£90,000	£224,500
£100,000	£234,000
£113,000 or more	£247,000

These figures assume:

1. Company owner withdraws all the profits of the business
2. No spare employment allowance available
3. No associated companies
4. Company owner is under state pension age but over 21
5. Company owner is not a Scottish taxpayer
6. Other income excludes dividends, but includes interest (see Chapter 33 for further guidance)

'Profit Level Required' means the minimum company profit (before tax and the director's salary) required before the large salary method produces worthwhile savings of around £500 or more, compared with taking a salary of £12,570 with the remaining profits as dividends.

Where there is spare employment allowance available, the large salary method may be beneficial at much lower profit levels. The comparison we then need to make is between the large salary method and whichever is better out of a salary of £12,570 or the maximum employer's NI free salary (as discussed above).

There are too many variables to provide a definitive answer to this complex 'three horse race', but we can give you a few guidelines.

Where the whole employment allowance of £10,500 is available, the large salary method is the winner whenever the company's profits exceed £125,000. At lower profit levels, it's between the maximum employer's NI free salary of £75,000 or the baseline salary of £12,570: see above for a detailed analysis. Chapter 14 also provides guidance.

Where half the employment allowance is available (i.e. £5,250), the salary derived by following the large salary method will be optimal when profits exceed the levels given in the table below:

Half the Employment Allowance (£5,250) Available

Other Income	**Profit Level Required**
£10,000	£132,500
£20,000	£120,000
£28,000 to £67,000	£113,000
£75,000	£121,000
£85,000 or more	£131,000

This table is based on the same assumptions as before, except that there is spare employment allowance available.

'Profit Level Required' means the minimum company profit required before the large salary method becomes optimal. In many cases, the optimal salary at lower profit levels in this scenario is the maximum employer's NI free salary of £40,000. However, the £12,570 baseline salary will sometimes be optimal instead: see above for further guidance.

Increasing Your Salary: Other Factors to Consider

Our analysis in this chapter is based on the assumption that the higher salary paid to the director is eligible for CT relief. Remember, the salary will only provide CT relief if justified by the work the director does for the company and the role they play. Furthermore, it is the director's whole remuneration package, including their salary, any company pension contributions, and any benefits provided, that must be justified.

In many cases, the existence of other income from outside the company suggests the director may not be working full time on the company's business and this will need to be taken into account.

As discussed in Chapter 26, a higher salary has cashflow implications that may need to be considered. However, this issue can be overcome by paying most of the salary as a bonus using the method described in Chapter 2. Paying a higher salary one year then reducing it to £12,570 or less the next could lead to difficulties with HMRC: although this possibility is usually pretty remote. See Chapter 51 for further details.

Chapter 33

The Different Types of Income

In this chapter, we will take a closer look at the different types of income you may earn from sources outside your company and how they may affect the income you decide to withdraw from your company.

As a general point, it's worth remembering, as discussed in Chapter 32, that significant amounts of other income from outside the company could mean the large salary method described in Chapter 26 becomes optimal for director/shareholders with highly profitable companies. This is equally true for all types of other income except dividends (with a little adjustment required where the other income is interest).

Employment Income

It is possible to have more than one source of employment income, for example:

- Salary from a second job with a separate employer, or
- Salary from a second company you own

If you have recently started out in business, it's possible you will have a second job (possibly a part-time job) to help pay the bills.

If you start a second company for a separate business venture there is, of course, nothing to stop you paying yourself a second salary.

For Income Tax purposes you are only entitled to one personal allowance (£12,570 at present). This generally means you can only have one tax-free salary (unless, of course, the two salaries, added together, total no more than £12,570). Some or all of the second salary may be taxed at 20%.

National Insurance is calculated differently. Directors who have more than one salary of £12,570 this year may not have to pay any NI *personally*. This is because the earnings from each job may be treated separately.

If the two businesses are 'in association' however, the salaries will be added together and NI may be payable. Employers are considered to be in association if:

- The businesses serve a common purpose, and
- There is significant sharing of things like premises, personnel, equipment, or customers

A second salary will generally be more tax efficient than a dividend, providing there is no NI payable.

If you wish to pay yourself two salaries, it may be necessary to obtain professional advice to satisfy yourself the companies will not be treated by HMRC as being in association, with resulting NI liabilities.

Finally, there may be other tax and non-tax reasons why you wish to pay yourself a second salary or a bigger second salary.

Salary from Other Job At Least £50,270

Where a company owner earns a salary of at least £50,270 (the upper earnings limit) from a different employment, it may be possible to reduce the employee's NI rate on the salary they receive from their own company.

In other words, instead of paying 8% NI, it may be possible to pay just 2% on all of the second salary the director receives from their own company.

This is because there is a limit to the amount of salary income on which you have to pay the main rate of NI each year. Applications to pay the reduced rate can be made using form CA72A, available from HMRC's website.

Note, employer's NI will still be payable on any amount over £5,000, unless the company has spare employment allowance available.

Nonetheless, where you are eligible to pay just 2% NI on the salary you take from your company, it will often be tax efficient to increase your company salary.

Where there is NO spare employment allowance available, a higher salary may be beneficial provided that, after paying the salary, the company will still have a marginal CT rate of 25% or 26.5% (i.e. a salary that reduces the company's profit before tax to £50,000, but no more than this: in other words, the salary under the large salary method we saw in Chapter 26).

Where there IS spare employment allowance available, the optimal salary will be the *greater* of the amount covered by the employment allowance, or the amount using the large salary method.

As usual, this assumes all remaining after-tax profits are taken as dividends. The position may differ in other cases.

Scottish directors can only benefit from an increased salary in this scenario:

- If, and to the extent that, there is spare employment allowance available (or if they are under 21), OR
- The company's CT rate is 26.5% or 25%, AND the director's total income for the year, excluding dividends and interest, does not exceed £75,000.

Self-Employment Income

You may have self-employment income if you have another business that is not a company (i.e. you're a sole trader or belong to a partnership). When we refer to self-employment income, we are talking about the taxable profits of your sole trader business, or your share of the taxable profits of a partnership.

Many entrepreneurs have multiple businesses and it's possible a second or third business will not be a company.

Companies can be wonderful tax shelters but unincorporated businesses have advantages of their own, including lower accountancy fees, more generous treatment of certain expenses, and more generous capital allowances for cars used in the business.

Self-employment income may be difficult to predict, especially close to the beginning of a new tax year, making it difficult to decide how much income to withdraw from the other company business.

Fortunately, as far as your self-employment business is concerned, it may be possible to do some emergency year-end tax planning to reduce your tax bill (for example, by making pension contributions or incurring other tax-deductible expenditure).

Rental Income

When we use the term 'rental income' what we mean is taxable rental *profit*. You may receive rents of £10,000 per year but your taxable rental profit may only be £5,000, after deducting all the expenses property investors can claim.

Unlike interest income and stock market dividends, most rental income cannot be sheltered from Income Tax in an ISA, pension, or other tax shelter. There are, however a couple of exceptions:

- Commercial property held in a pension scheme
- Residential or commercial property held in a company

Some business owners place their business premises inside a self-invested personal pension (SIPP) to avoid Income Tax and CGT (see Chapter 43).

Others put their properties in a separate company. CT is payable on the rental income and capital gains, but the company owner's Income Tax bill will be unaffected, unless the property company's profits are extracted.

Apart from these two exceptions, most landlords own their properties *personally*, which means they are fully exposed to Income Tax on rental profits. These rental profits may then need to be factored into the mix when deciding how much income you withdraw from your other company business.

For example, if you take a salary of £12,570 and expect to have taxable rental profits of £20,000, you can take tax-free dividend income of £500 plus additional dividend income of £17,200 taxed at 10.75%. This takes you up to the £50,270 higher rate threshold. Any additional dividend income you receive will be taxed at a rate of at least 35.75%.

If you take a salary of £12,570 and expect to have taxable rental profits of £50,000 you will pay at least 35.75% tax on any dividend income you receive from your company (apart from the first £500 covered by the dividend allowance).

Mortgage Tax Relief Restrictions

Landlords who own residential property can no longer deduct their mortgage interest from their rental income when calculating their taxable rental profits. Instead, what they receive is a 'tax reduction' equal to the 20% basic rate of Income Tax.

These rules do not apply to commercial properties but do now apply to furnished holiday lets (from 6th April 2025). They do not apply to properties held inside companies.

The reduced tax relief means many landlords have bigger taxable rental profits. In other words, for the purposes of this guide, a landlord's other income from residential rental properties means their rental profits *before interest.*

In many cases, this has pushed more of the dividend income they receive from their company business over the higher rate threshold, where it is taxed at 35.75% instead of 10.75%.

Tax Planning for Landlords

If you are a company owner and separately own mortgaged rental properties personally, you will have to be careful about the amount of dividend income you pay yourself if you want to avoid going over the various tax thresholds.

Example: *Jessie owns a small engineering company and some rental property. Because she earns rental income, she decides to pay herself a salary of £6,708 in 2026/27 (Chapter 31 explains why this might be the best salary for someone with modest income from other sources).*

Her rental property produces income of £20,000 net of all expenses except mortgage interest. Her mortgage interest is £7,500 so her true rental profit is £12,500. However, her taxable rental profit is £20,000 and it is this number she must use when deciding how much dividend income to take.

With a salary of £6,708 and taxable rental profit of £20,000, Jessie can pay herself a dividend of up to £23,562 before she becomes a higher rate taxpayer and has to pay 35.75% tax (£50,270 – £6,708 – £20,000).

Example: *Cillian owns a software company and a portfolio of rental properties. Because he earns significant rental income and has a very profitable company, he decides to pay himself a salary of £12,570 in 2026/27 (Chapter 31 explains why this may be the optimal salary in this case).*

His rental property produces income of £50,000 (net of all expenses except interest). His mortgage interest is £15,000 so his true rental profit is £35,000. However, his taxable rental profit is £50,000.

With a salary of £12,570 and taxable rental profit of £50,000, Cillian is a higher rate taxpayer and will pay 35.75% tax on his dividend income (except the first £500, covered by the dividend allowance).

Cillian can pay himself a dividend of up to £37,430 before he reaches the £100,000 tax threshold where his personal allowance will be gradually withdrawn. He will then pay tax at an effective rate of 55.75% on the next £25,140 of dividend income he receives (see Chapter 23 for an explanation of how the withdrawal of the personal allowance works).

For the rest of this guide, when we refer to 'rental income' received by an individual, unless expressly stated to the contrary, this means their taxable rental profits, after deducting all allowable expenses EXCEPT interest and finance costs relating to residential rental property.

In the case of non-residential property, 'rental income' simply means rental profits.

Rental Losses

If you have rental losses brought forward from previous years you may not have to pay any Income Tax on the rental profit you make during the current tax year (providing the loss brought forward is big enough to offset the current year's profit).

If the rental profit you make during the current tax year is not taxable it does not need to be factored into the mix when deciding how much income you withdraw from your company.

However, because of the restrictions on relief for interest and finance costs discussed above, most residential landlords with rental losses brought forward have seen these effectively eroded away over the last few years and turned into what is officially termed 'unused residential property finance costs', better known as 'unrelieved interest'.

Where you have unrelieved interest brought forward rather than old-style rental losses, it will attract tax relief at the 20% basic rate, the same as your current interest costs, but it will not reduce your taxable rental profit, which will therefore still have to be factored into your decision-making when considering how much income to withdraw from your company.

Note that Income Tax rates on rental income are increasing by 2% across the board from 6th April 2027. For a detailed analysis of the impact on landlords, see the Taxcafe guide *How to Save Property Tax*. We'll deal with the impact on landlords who are also company owners in the next edition of *this* guide.

Pension Income

If you have any pension income, this will usually need to be taken into account when deciding how much income to withdraw from your company. Most pension income is taxable, including:

- Your UK state pension, where applicable
- Occupational pensions
- Private pensions
- Income withdrawn under a drawdown arrangement
- Foreign pensions (subject to the terms of any applicable Double Tax Treaty)

However, there is one key exemption to be aware of, namely the 25% tax-free lump sum available from most private pension schemes.

Subject to this exemption, pension income has the same impact on the optimal salary for a company owner under state pension age as any other form of non-savings income: see Chapters 31 and 32. Yes, bizarrely, pension income is classed as non-savings income for tax purposes (see Chapter 29).

Directors over State Pension Age

Where there is spare employment allowance available, directors over state pension age will benefit from the NI free salaries we looked at in Chapter 16 (up to £40,000 each where the company is run by two directors with no other employees; possibly up to £75,000 for a single director in some cases: see Chapter 14 for details of how to secure entitlement to the employment allowance and calculate how far it might stretch).

In many cases, an NI free salary will be the optimal salary for a director over state pension age to take from their company.

As discussed in Chapter 26, however, (and whether the employment allowance is available or not), it will often be better for directors over state pension age with very profitable companies to use the large salary method where this produces a higher salary.

Alternatively, as with any other director, it may make sense to restrict the amount extracted from the company to avoid exceeding one of the key Income Tax thresholds: £50,270, £60,000, or £100,000. Remember, it is the director's total income from all sources that needs to be considered (including dividends and interest).

Dividends for Pension Recipients

Once a director in receipt of pension income has worked out their optimal salary, the next step is to decide how much dividend income they would like to take. As usual, any amount covered by the dividend allowance will be tax free. Beyond that, we are back into the usual tax planning territory.

Example: *George and Gracie are the owner/directors and only employees of Like Old Times Ltd. In 2026/27, they each receive a state pension of £12,548 and each take a salary of £40,000 out of the company. They have no other income from outside the company.*

They can each take tax free dividends of £500 out of the company, but any further dividends will be taxed at 35.75%. And, if they take any more than £47,452 each in total, they will start to lose their personal allowances, leading to further tax costs.

We've assumed in this example that George and Gracie each own 50% of the shares in their company.

Note that, at company profit levels over £130,000, the large salary method covered in Chapter 26 will often be more beneficial in this scenario.

Example: *Bob is below state pension age, but enters a drawdown arrangement and takes £50,000 out of his pension scheme during 2026/27. However, only £16,000 of this is taxable as the remaining £34,000 represents his 25% tax free lump sum.*

Bob also takes a salary of £12,570 out of his company, but has no other sources of income.

It's still worth Bob taking a dividend of £500 as this is tax free. He can also take up to a further £21,200 in dividends that will only be taxed at 10.75% (£50,270 – £16,000 – £12,570 – £500 = £21,200).

If Bob had taken only his 25% tax free lump sum, it would have had no impact on his company income and he could then have taken a salary of £12,570 plus dividends of up to £37,700 without suffering any tax at 35.75%.

Interest Income

Most personal interest income can be sheltered from tax inside an ISA or SIPP. Other tax-free investments include index-linked savings certificates (when they're available) and offset mortgages (instead of earning interest, your savings are used to reduce the interest on your mortgage). Paying off personal debts is also effectively a way to earn tax-free interest (you pay less interest on your debts and that reduction is not taxed: unless it counts as qualifying loan interest, which we will look at in Chapter 39).

Wealthier individuals, with large cash balances or holdings of corporate and government bonds may, however, have a significant amount of *taxable* interest income and there may also be times in life when less wealthy taxpayers have significant amounts of taxable interest income:

- You sell your home and have a large cash lump sum
- You lend money to a friend or family member
- You receive a big dividend and put the cash in the bank
- You lend money to your company (see Chapter 39)

This income may need to be factored into the equation when you decide how much income to withdraw from your company.

The £5,000 Starting Rate Band

When it comes to interest income, many company owners are in a fortunate position. They can receive up to £5,000 of interest *tax free* each year thanks to the 0% starting-rate band.

The starting rate is supposed to benefit those with low incomes. Hence the £5,000 starting rate band is reduced by any *non-savings* income you have in excess of the personal allowance (see Chapter 29 for the definition of non-savings income).

Hence, if your non-savings income (for example rental income) exceeds £17,570 in total (£12,570 + £5,000), none of your interest income will be covered by the starting rate band.

Of course, most regular salary earners and self-employed business owners will have more than £17,570 of non-savings income. Many *company owners* are in a different position, however. This is because non-savings income does NOT include dividends. Dividends are the top slice of income and do not use up the starting rate band.

Because company owners often pay themselves small salaries and take the rest of their income as dividends, they will often have little or no taxable non-savings income. As a result, many can earn at least £5,000 of tax-free interest.

Example: *Mandy is a company owner with a salary of £12,570, dividend income of £32,700, and interest income of £5,000. Her salary is tax free thanks to her personal allowance and she therefore has no taxable non-savings income that uses up her starting rate band (her dividend income does not count). Her interest income is fully covered by her £5,000 starting rate band and taxed at 0%.*

Many directors will thus pay 0% tax on their interest if they:

- Take a small salary from their company,
- Do not have another source of employment income,
- Do not have a sole trader or partnership business,
- Don't earn much, if any, rental income, and
- Do not receive much, if any, pension income.

It is important to point out that the 0% starting rate band is not given in addition to your basic rate band (currently £37,700). Instead, it is part of your basic rate band.

If you qualify to use the starting rate band, your basic rate band will be reduced, possibly pushing some of your dividend income into a higher tax bracket.

The Personal Savings Allowance

The personal savings allowance exempts the first £1,000 of your interest income from tax if you're a basic rate taxpayer and the first £500 if you're a higher rate taxpayer. Additional rate taxpayers get nothing.

The personal savings allowance operates separately from, and in addition to, the starting rate band. This means some company owners can earn up to £6,000 of tax-free interest every year.

Income covered by the personal savings allowance uses up some of the band it falls into. For example, if you have £49,400 of salary and rental income, and £1,000 of interest income, you will have total income of £50,400.

As a higher rate taxpayer, you will therefore be entitled to a £500 personal savings allowance. Thus £500 of your interest income will be tax free and this will use up £500 of your basic rate band, leaving £370 taxed at 20%. The final £130 will be taxed at 40%. (These are the current rates: Income Tax rates on interest income are increasing by 2% across the board from 6th April 2027.)

The personal savings allowance is helpful to company owners who cannot use the starting rate band because they have too much non-savings income such as rental income. Most can enjoy £1,000 or £500 of tax-free interest. It may also be useful for extracting interest from your own company (see Chapter 39).

Interest Income Examples

The somewhat complex operation of the starting rate band and personal savings allowance is best explained with some examples. These examples are all based on the current, 2026/27 tax year.

Example: *Samantha is a company owner with a salary of £12,570 and interest income of £5,000. She also has £10,000 of rental income.*

Her salary is covered by her personal allowance but thanks to her rental income she has £10,000 of taxable non-savings income. Because her taxable non-savings income exceeds the £5,000 starting rate band, none of her interest income is covered by the 0% starting rate.

However, because she is a basic rate taxpayer (her total income is less than £50,270) she is entitled to a £1,000 personal savings allowance. So, £1,000 of her interest income will be tax free, the remaining £4,000 will be taxed at 20%.

Example: *Elaine is a company owner with a salary of £6,708 (see Chapter 31), rental income of £10,000, interest of £1,500 and dividends of £20,000 (total income £38,208).*

There is no Income Tax on her salary and the first £5,862 of her rental income is covered by her remaining personal allowance. The final £4,138 of her rental income is taxed at 20% and uses up £4,138 of her £5,000 starting rate band. Thus £862 of her interest income is covered by her remaining starting rate band and is tax free.

As a basic rate taxpayer, she is also entitled to a £1,000 personal savings allowance, so the final £638 of her interest is also tax free. The first £500 of her dividend income is covered by the dividend allowance; the remaining £19,500 is taxed at 10.75%.

Example: *Ollie is a company owner with a salary of £12,570 and dividends of £37,700. He also has interest income of £5,500 (total income £55,770).*

There is no Income Tax on his salary and £5,000 of his interest income is tax free thanks to the 0% starting rate band (dividends do not count as non-savings income and do not use up the starting rate band). Because his total income is £55,770, he is a higher rate taxpayer and is entitled to a £500 personal savings allowance, so the final £500 of his interest income will also be tax free.

Turning to his dividend income, Ollie has £32,200 of his basic rate band remaining (£50,270 – £12,570 – £5,500). Of this £500 will be tax free thanks to the dividend allowance and £31,700 will be taxed at 10.75%. The final £5,500 of his dividend income is taxed at 35.75%.

Although all of Ollie's interest is tax free it uses up some of his basic rate band, pushing £5,500 of his dividend income over the higher rate threshold where it is taxed at 35.75%.

Example: *Mark is a company owner with salary and rental income totalling £50,000 (his non-savings income) and dividends of £20,000. He also has interest income of £5,000. Total income: £75,000. Because his taxable non-savings income exceeds the £5,000 starting rate band, none of his interest is covered by the 0% starting rate. However, as a higher rate taxpayer, he is entitled to a £500 personal savings allowance. The final £4,500 of his interest income is taxed at 40%. Turning to his dividend income, the first £500 will be tax free thanks to the dividend allowance and the final £19,500 is taxed at 35.75%.*

As stated above, the Income Tax rates on interest income will all increase by 2% from 6th April 2027. We have, however, stuck with current rates in the above analysis.

Making the Most of Your Personal Allowance

For the last time this year, 2026/27, the personal allowance can be allocated in whatever way is most beneficial for the taxpayer. This will cease to apply next year, when the personal allowance will have to be allocated in a strict order (in other words, the way that is most beneficial for HMRC).

Sticking to this year, though, company owners with interest income may be able to save a little tax by allocating some of their personal allowance to their dividend income instead of their interest income. This is because their interest income will still be tax free thanks to the 0% starting rate.

Example: *In 2026/27, company owner Jameel has salary income of £6,708, interest income of £5,000 and dividend income of £50,000. If most of his £12,570 personal allowance is allocated to his salary and interest, his tax bill will be calculated as follows:*

Salary		**Income Tax**
Personal allowance	£6,708	£0
Interest		
Personal allowance	£5,000	£0
Dividend		
Personal allowance	£862	£0
Dividend allowance	£500	£0
Taxed at 10.75%	£37,200	£3,999
Taxed at 35.75%	£11,438	£4,089
Total tax		£8,088

This is not the optimal outcome. Jameel can reduce his tax bill by reallocating some of his personal allowance from his interest income to his dividend income.

This is because his interest income will still be tax free thanks to the 0% starting rate band:

Salary		Income Tax
Personal allowance	£6,708	£0
Interest		
Starting rate band	£5,000	£0
Dividend		
Personal allowance	£5,862	£0
Dividend allowance	£500	£0
Taxed at 10.75%	£32,200	£3,462
Taxed at 35.75%	£11,438	£4,089
Total tax		£7,551

In this case, Jameel saves £537. This is because an additional £5,000 of his dividend income is tax free, covered by his personal allowance, instead of being taxed at 10.75%. His interest income remains tax free thanks to the 0% starting rate.

Good tax software should perform this calculation automatically, but it's best to check.

Scottish Company Owners with Interest Income

The Scottish Parliament can tax most types of income but not interest and dividends. So Scottish taxpayers will not pay more tax on their interest income than other taxpayers.

This year, it's only when Scottish company owners have salary and other income subject to Scottish tax rates of more than £33,493 that they will pay more tax than other UK taxpayers.

Thus, in all of the above examples the company owners will pay the same tax on their interest and dividend income if they live in Scotland. Samantha and Elaine will, however, pay less tax on their rental income if they live in Scotland, whereas Mark will pay more tax on his salary and rental income.

Note also that, while a Scottish taxpayer with taxable income (excluding dividends and interest) of more than £43,662 becomes a higher rate taxpayer, their personal savings allowance will not be halved from £1,000 to £500 unless their total taxable income exceeds the UK higher-rate tax threshold of £50,270.

Optimal Salaries with Interest Income

Where the company owner's other income includes interest, it behaves a little differently to non-savings income.

Firstly, where the director's income from outside the company includes interest not exceeding £6,000 for a basic rate taxpayer, or £5,500 for a higher rate taxpayer, this does not need to be taken into account in deciding whether a salary of *less than* £12,570 would be optimal. The position differs for those with total income over £100,000, as noted in Chapter 31.

When deciding whether a salary of *more than* £12,570 might be optimal, interest income should generally be included. However, there may be an additional cost of up to £1,225 to be taken into account in 2026/27. We should stress it is only 'up to' £1,225 because the additional cost cannot exceed 45% of the first £500 of interest plus 20% of any excess up to £5,000.

This cost is made up of a maximum of £1,000 because the higher salary uses up the starting rate band, plus an extra £225 if taking the higher salary makes the director an additional rate taxpayer when a lower salary would not: hence it's only a potential additional cost arising in a few rare scenarios.

The maximum additional cost is only £225 if the director's non-savings income from outside the company is at least £17,570 and, being only a rare, potential additional cost, this is not enough to alter any of our conclusions about higher optimal salaries.

From 2027/28, the maximum additional cost will increase to £1,335 (£500 x 47% + £5,000 x 22%), but will be just as rare.

Stock Market Dividends

The big difference between dividends from your own company and stock market companies is that stock market dividends can be completely sheltered from Income Tax in an ISA or SIPP. In practice though, many investors end up with a mixture of shares held inside and outside the tax protection of ISAs and SIPPs. These investors could consider:

- Holding high-income shares inside an ISA (to protect the dividends from Income Tax), and
- Holding growth shares that produce capital gains outside an ISA (because some capital gains will be tax free anyway thanks to the annual CGT exemption: see Chapter 52)

This simplistic strategy will not always produce the biggest tax savings, however. If you bought Apple shares back in 2003 you would be kicking yourself if you didn't stick them in an ISA!

If you have significant dividends from stock market companies, and the shares are not sheltered inside an ISA or SIPP, you may want to reduce the dividends you extract from your own company to avoid going over one of the key Income Tax thresholds.

Remember that you only get one dividend allowance each tax year, so stock market dividends may use up some or all of this allowance.

Stock market dividends can generally be ignored when considering what your optimal salary to take from the company may be: except they must be included in determining whether your total income exceeds any of the key Income Tax thresholds and whether you are a basic, higher, or additional rate taxpayer.

Chapter 34

Tax Planning for Company Owners with Other Income

Short-Term (Emergency) Tax Planning

If your total taxable income is higher than expected, there are some steps you can take to reduce it before the end of the tax year:

Pension Contributions

Everyone under age 75 can make a gross pension contribution of £3,600 per year. The taxpayer personally contributes £2,880 and the taxman tops up the pension plan with £720 of basic rate tax relief. To make bigger pension contributions you require earnings: generally salary income or self-employment profits.

If you have a salary of £12,570, you can make a gross pension contribution of £12,570 (£10,056 from you, £2,514 from the taxman). Your basic rate band will be increased by £12,570, so up to £12,570 of your dividends will escape higher rate tax. The point at which the Child Benefit Charge starts to apply will also increase to £72,570 and the point at which your personal allowance starts to be withdrawn will increase to £112,570.

If you have a modest amount of self-employment income, you can generally make an additional gross pension contribution equivalent to the taxable profits of the business, thereby eliminating any tax problem caused by this type of income. See Chapters 41 and 42 for more on pension contributions.

Tax Deductible Expenditure

Company owners who also have income from self-employment can reduce their taxable income by incurring tax deductible expenditure before the end of that business's accounting period. Possibly the easiest way is to incur expenditure that qualifies for an immediate tax deduction thanks to the annual investment allowance.

Do beware, however, if you don't have a 31st March or 5th April accounting date for your sole trader or partnership business, the way your tax-deductible expenditure reduces your taxable profits will effectively be spread over more than one tax year. For full details see the Taxcafe guide *Small Business Tax Saving Tactics*.

Company owners who also have income from property can reduce their rental profits by spending money on property repairs before the end of the tax year: e.g. replacement kitchens and bathrooms.

Long-Term Tax Planning

Company owners with significant amounts of income from other sources may be able to take the following steps to shift income to another entity or person:

Self-Employment Income

Consider putting the business into a second company (Company 2) so that CT is payable rather than Income Tax and NI.

Dividends can then be extracted from Company 2, taking into account dividends withdrawn from Company 1. This will allow you to control your Income Tax bill from year to year.

Of course, it's not always advantageous to incorporate a second business. Sole traders and partnerships enjoy certain tax benefits, including more generous tax treatment of various expenses (including home office, travel, and car capital allowances).

Incorporation could also cost you a significant amount in professional fees and having a second company will generally lead to an increase in the CT bill for your first company (unless it has profits of less than £25,000, or more than £250,000).

Another possibility for sole traders may be to transfer their sole trade business into their existing company. This may sometimes cost less overall in CT than having two companies; there are also cases where it will make no difference or cost more.

Furthermore, while it is possible for a single company to operate two distinctly separate businesses, there are significant commercial implications to this strategy, which must be considered.

Lastly, remember what we saw in Chapter 28: putting a business into a company will generally lead to bigger tax bills if you need to take all the profits out of the company every year.

Rental Income
Tax can be saved by:

- Transferring properties to your spouse if he/she pays Income Tax at a lower rate.
- Holding commercial properties inside a pension scheme.
- Holding investment properties inside a company, so that CT is payable instead of Income Tax and the extraction of rental profits (as dividends) can be controlled. See the Taxcafe guide *Using a Property Company to Save Tax*.
- Consider alternative investments (e.g. 'blue chip' shares) that can be sheltered from tax in an ISA or pension scheme.

Interest Income
Some company owners can receive up to £6,000 of tax-free interest and most can receive at least £500 (except additional rate taxpayers). Where tax is payable on your interest income, or you fear it will push some of your dividend income into a higher tax bracket, the following strategies can be adopted:

- Transfer savings into an ISA or SIPP
- Use savings to pay off debt or take out an offset mortgage
- Transfer cash to family members who pay tax at a lower rate (but not minor children)
- Invest in assets that produce capital growth rather than interest

Large cash transfers to anyone other than your spouse may have Inheritance Tax implications, although these can be beneficial.

Stock Market Dividends
Tax can be saved by holding shares in an ISA or SIPP, or by transferring holdings to your spouse, or possibly other family members. However, transfers of shareholdings to anyone other than your spouse may have both CGT and Inheritance Tax implications.

Part 5

Splitting Income with Your Family

Chapter 35

Splitting Income with Your Spouse or Partner

In Chapter 19 we saw that couples can double up the tax-free salary and dividend and the amount of dividend income taxed at just 10.75%.

That's all very well if the couple own and run the company together. But what if your spouse/partner isn't involved in the business, for example if the company was started before you met or if they have a separate career and receive salary income from another employer?

In situations like these it may be possible to save Income Tax by gifting shares in the company to your spouse/partner. It may even be possible to save tax by paying them a salary as well.

The amount of tax that can be saved depends on individual circumstances, for example how much profit the company makes and how much taxable income each person has already.

Tax savings are typically achieved where one spouse/partner is a higher rate taxpayer (paying 35.75% tax on their dividend income) and the other spouse/partner has no income at all, has income less than the personal allowance, or is a basic rate taxpayer.

However, it's not just these couples who can save tax. It's possible to pay Income Tax at more than 35.75% on dividend income that falls into any of the following tax brackets:

- £60,000-£80,000 Child Benefit Charge
- £100,000-£125,140 Personal allowance withdrawal
- Over £125,140 Additional rate tax

If your income falls into one of these tax brackets, you may be able to save tax by transferring income to your spouse/partner, even if they are a higher rate taxpayer.

Before we look at some sample tax savings, it is important to point out there are also potential dangers when it comes to splitting dividend income with your spouse/partner. We will return to this important issue later in the chapter.

Capital Gains Tax

If you wish to split your dividend income with your spouse/partner, you generally have to transfer shares in the company to them.

In the case of married couples, a gift of shares would be exempt from CGT. CGT will, however, be payable if the spouse who receives the gift later disposes of the shares. The original base cost of the spouse who made the transfer will be used to perform the CGT calculation.

Gifts between unmarried couples are normally subject to CGT. However, the couple may be able to jointly elect to claim holdover relief.

Holdover relief allows a chargeable gain to be deferred (held over) when gifts of qualifying business assets are made. The person who receives the shares may eventually have to pay CGT on the original owner's held over gain, as well as their own, when the shares are sold.

To qualify for holdover relief, the company must generally be a regular trading company.

Unmarried couples who want to split their income face a further potential danger (see below).

Giving the Business Away

To successfully split your dividend income with your spouse/partner, it is essential that genuine beneficial ownership of shares in the company is handed over. This means your spouse/partner must be able to do what they like with any dividends and any proceeds from a sale of the business.

As we shall see shortly, it is also safer to transfer ordinary shares rather than shares that have fewer voting rights or other rights.

It is probably wise to have any dividends received by your spouse/partner paid into a separate bank account in their name, to show HMRC you have not retained control of the money.

Dividends are generally payable in proportion to shareholdings. So, if you normally take a dividend of £100,000 and want to transfer £40,000 of this income to your spouse/partner, you will generally have to transfer 40% of the business to them or, to be more precise, 40% of your shares in the company.

Because this sort of tax planning, if done correctly, involves effectively giving away ownership and control of part of your business, it is only suitable where there is a significant amount of trust between the parties involved.

How Much of the Business Should Be Transferred?
For many company owners, a 50:50 ownership split with their spouse or partner will prove optimal, but a smaller stake can be transferred if the founder wants to retain more control over the business.

Example: *Steve owns 100% of Steve's Spices Ltd, a small trading company. Steve currently pays himself a salary of £12,570 and dividends of £75,000. He also has £6,000 of rental income from outside the company.*

His total income is £93,570, which means he is getting close to the £100,000 threshold. If his income rises above this threshold, he will start to lose his Income Tax personal allowance.

As things stand, he will pay Income Tax of £18,834 on his dividend income in 2026/27 (see Chapter 6 for how dividends are taxed).

Steve's wife, Lara, does not own any shares in the company, but she does receive rental income of £14,000 from a buy-to-let property. This means she can receive dividends of up to £36,270 this year before she becomes a higher rate taxpayer (£50,270 – £14,000). Of this, £500 will be tax-free and the rest will be taxed at just 10.75%.

Steve therefore transfers 45% of the ordinary shares in the company to Lara. The company continues to pay total dividends of £75,000 but now Steve's dividend is £41,250 and Lara's is £33,750.

Lara's total taxable income is now £47,750 and the tax bill on her dividend income is £3,574. Steve's total taxable income is now £59,820 and the tax bill on his dividend income is £6,768.

The total tax on the dividend income has been reduced by £8,492.

Furthermore, Steve's income is now well below the £100,000 threshold, which means he doesn't have to worry about losing his Income Tax personal allowance.

Additional tax savings may be achieved if the couple are currently receiving child benefit. As we know from Chapter 22, the Child Benefit Charge is payable if the highest earner in the household has income of more than £60,000.

Because Steve's income has fallen from £93,570 to £59,820, he will no longer be subject to the Child Benefit Charge, saving the couple an additional £2,337 if they have two qualifying children.

Potential Tax Savings

The potential tax savings from transferring dividend income to your spouse/partner will vary from case to case. The analysis set out below is based on the current 2026/27 tax year.

Spouse/Partner Has No Income

If you are a basic rate taxpayer (income under £50,270) and your spouse/partner is a 'house-spouse' with no taxable income, they can receive tax-free dividends of up to £13,070 this year (made up of the £12,570 personal allowance and £500 dividend allowance). The potential tax saving is £1,405 (£13,070 x 10.75%).

If you are a higher rate taxpayer and your spouse/partner has no taxable income, they can receive less heavily taxed dividends of up to £50,270 this year. The first £13,070 will be tax free and the remainder will be taxed at 10.75%.

By contrast, you as a higher rate taxpayer could be paying at least 35.75% tax on all of this income.

For example, let's say you gift enough shares in the company so that your spouse/partner receives dividend income of £40,000. Your spouse/partner will pay £2,895 tax (first £13,070 tax free, the remainder taxed at 10.75%).

If we assume you would have paid tax at 35.75% on all of this income, this would have amounted to £14,300, so the net tax saving in this example would be £11,405.

The tax saving may be even greater if you have income of more than £100,000 before you transfer shares. Reducing your income may allow you to claw back some or all of your personal allowance, which will produce an additional tax saving.

Spouse/Partner is Basic-Rate Taxpayer

Even if your spouse/partner works and has taxable income, it may be possible to save tax by gifting shares in the business to them. Again, the tax savings will vary from case to case.

Example: *Rupert is a company owner who expects to have a taxable income of £75,000 this year, made up of a £60,000 dividend and £15,000 of salary and other income. He will pay 35.75% tax on £24,730 of his dividend income (£75,000 – £50,270 higher rate threshold).*

His wife, Wendy, receives taxable income of £30,000 from another source. Thus, she has £20,270 of her basic rate band left and can receive £20,270 of dividends that will be less heavily taxed in her hands.

If Rupert gifts one third of the shares to Wendy and the company normally pays dividends of £60,000, she'll receive £20,000. The first £500 will be tax free thanks to the dividend allowance and tax of £2,096 will be payable on the remaining £19,500 (at 10.75%). Rupert would have paid £7,150 tax on this income so the saving is £5,054.

Spouse/Partner is Higher-Rate Taxpayer

If you and your spouse/partner are both higher rate taxpayers (income over £50,270) it may still be possible to save tax by gifting them shares in the company.

The saving is trivial, however: *unless* your income exceeds £100,000, meaning some or all of your personal allowance will have been withdrawn. In that case, significant savings are possible.

Example: *Saul is a company owner who expects to have taxable income of £130,000 this year, made up of £120,000 of dividend income and £10,000 of salary and other income. With this much income, all his personal allowance will be withdrawn.*

His wife Kylie has income of £60,000 from another source. If Saul transfers 25% of the company to Kylie she will receive dividend income of £30,000. The first £500 will be tax free but she will pay 35.75% tax on the rest (£10,546).

Saul's income will fall from £130,000 to £100,000, which means he will recover all of his personal allowance and his tax bill will fall from £38,096 to £21,777.

All in all, the couple will save £5,773 in tax by transferring the dividend income to Kylie, even though she is also a higher rate taxpayer.

Where you have income significantly over £125,140 and are an *additional rate* taxpayer, it may be possible to save tax by gifting shares to a higher rate taxpayer spouse/partner, but if your income is not reduced below £125,140, the tax savings are not huge: just £36 on every £1,000 of dividend income transferred.

It's also important to be careful that the dividend income transferred to your spouse/partner does not push *their* total taxable income over the £100,000 threshold, so that they begin to lose their personal allowance. In most cases, this would wipe out the saving and turn it into an overall additional tax cost!

Spouse/Partner is Additional-Rate Taxpayer
There is a situation where it may actually be beneficial to transfer dividend income to your spouse/partner, even if they are an additional rate taxpayer with income over £125,140. This arises where your income falls into the £100,000 to £125,140 bracket and you are suffering Income Tax at effective rates of up to 58.25% on some of your dividend income.

Example Revisited: *Let's go back to Saul and Kylie in our last example, but change just one thing: let's say Kylie's income from another source is £150,000 instead of £60,000.*

Saul transfers 25% of the company to Kylie as before and she receives the same £30,000 of dividend income. The first £500 will be tax free and she will pay 39.35% tax on the rest: £11,608.

Saul will recover his personal allowance and his tax bill will fall from £38,096 to £21,777, as before. The couple now save £4,711. It's not quite as good as we saw before, but it's not bad considering Kylie is an additional rate taxpayer.

Will the Tax Savings Last?
There are many reasons why any tax savings that may be achieved in one tax year by splitting income with your spouse/partner may not be achievable in full in future tax years, including:

- Changes to tax rates and thresholds
- Changes to personal circumstances

For example, it's important to remember that the higher rate threshold is to remain frozen at £50,270 until 5th April 2031. As a result, more and more basic rate taxpayers are likely to become higher rate taxpayers. This may make it less attractive for some higher rate taxpayers to shift income to spouses/partners who are currently basic rate taxpayers. If your spouse/partner's income simply increases with inflation, they will have less of their basic rate band left to enjoy dividends taxed at just 10.75%.

Worthwhile Income Tax savings can usually only be achieved if your spouse/partner has a lower tax rate than you. It is possible that, over time, your tax rate will fall or your spouse/partner's tax rate will increase. This could eliminate or even reverse any initial Income Tax saving that is achieved.

Your tax rate could fall if the company's profits fall, resulting in lower dividends. Your spouse/partner's tax rate could rise if their income from other sources increases (for example, if another business they own produces bigger profits).

There are many different permutations. The key point is that couples should look further ahead than just one tax year when deciding what proportion of the company each should own.

HMRC Attacks on Income Shifting

Income splitting arrangements like those described in this chapter have come under attack in the past. The taxman has tried to prevent dividends being paid to non-working spouses/partners, or spouses/partners who do just a small amount of work for the company.

In particular, the taxman's target has been small 'personal service companies' (IT consultants and the like) where most of the work is carried out by one person.

It all came to a head in the notorious 'Arctic Systems' case. HMRC tried to use the so-called settlements legislation to prevent Geoff Jones, a computer consultant, from splitting his dividend income with his wife.

The settlements legislation is designed to prevent income being shifted from one individual to another via a 'settlement', for example by transferring an asset or making some other 'arrangement'.

In the Arctic Systems case Mr Jones did most of the work in the company. Mrs Jones did a few hours admin each week. Because Mr Jones only paid himself a small salary despite all the work he did, more money was left to pay out as dividends to Mrs Jones. HMRC therefore decided a settlement had taken place and tried to have Mrs Jones' dividend income taxed in her husband's hands.

HMRC originally won the case but the decision was overturned by the House of Lords. The judges agreed with HMRC that a settlement had taken place **but** decided that the settlement provisions could not be applied because in this case the couple were protected by the exemption for gifts between spouses. This exemption applies where:

- There is an outright gift of property to a spouse, and
- The property is not wholly or mainly a right to income

On the first point, the judges ruled that, although Mrs Jones had subscribed for her share when the company was set up (i.e. it was not strictly speaking gifted to her by her husband), her share was essentially a gift because it contained an 'element of bounty': the share provided a benefit that Mr Jones would not have given to a complete stranger.

On the second point, the judges also ruled that a gift of *ordinary* shares is not wholly or mainly a right to income because ordinary shares have other rights: voting rights and the right to capital gains if the company is sold or wound up.

Thanks to the courage of Mr and Mrs Jones, who were prepared to fight HMRC all the way to the House of Lords, this exemption should safeguard most types of income splitting arrangements between married couples where ordinary shares are involved.

For this reason, some tax advisers are of the opinion that married couples should make hay while the sun shines, i.e. they should split their dividend income with their spouses while they can.

Preference Shares

The outcome of the Arctic Systems case may have been different if another type of share other than ordinary shares had been involved. In another tax case (*Young v Pearce*), wives were issued with preference shares that paid income but had very few other rights. The shares did not have voting rights and did not entitle the spouses to receive any payout in the event of the company being sold (other than the original £25 payment for the shares).

All the preference shares provided was a right to receive 30% of the company's profits as a dividend. The court therefore decided the preference shares provided wholly or mainly a right to income.

Thus, the exemption for gifts between spouses was not available and the settlement rules applied. The wives' dividends were therefore taxed in the hands of their husbands.

Unmarried Couples & Other Family Members

Although HMRC was defeated in the Arctic Systems case, the judges did agree that a settlement had taken place. The taxpayers only won the case thanks to the exemption for gifts between *spouses*.

There is still uncertainty as to where this leaves income-splitting arrangements between other groups of individuals, in particular, *unmarried* couples.

HMRC may take the view that the settlements legislation applies to unmarried couples and other family members, especially where small personal service companies are involved.

However, to date the taxman has not pursued these individuals aggressively so, again, it may be a case of making hay while the sun shines.

To protect against any potential attack the best defence is probably to have both individuals equally involved in the business (a bit of admin or bookkeeping will not suffice, as Mr and Mrs Jones discovered).

HMRC's main concern seems to be personal service companies (IT consultants and other businesses where the profits are generated from one person's services). Larger businesses that have other employees, premises, equipment, etc, may be safer because the profits come from various sources, not just one person's work.

Future Danger?
In 2007, draft income shifting legislation was published but fortunately never made it onto the statute books after being widely condemned for being completely unworkable.

That draft legislation essentially sought to prevent business owners from receiving dividends unless they effectively earned them! This would have undermined the whole basis of shareholder capitalism: dividends are supposed to be a reward for being an entrepreneur and setting up or investing in a business.

Although income shifting legislation is on the back burner for now, it could be introduced in the future and could upset some income splitting arrangements. This danger has been highlighted by the introduction of new reporting requirements that apply from 2025/26:

- Director/shareholders must report dividends from their own companies separately to stock market dividends (and in the *employment* section of their tax return, what's more!)
- Director/shareholders must also report their percentage shareholdings in their own companies

An additional proposed requirement to report employees' hours worked under PAYE was thankfully shelved.

Maybe we're being paranoid, but we fear these new requirements could be HMRC beginning to gather the data they need to enable them to have another go at income-shifting legislation later this decade. So, like we said, make hay while the sun shines!

Dividend Waivers
Dividend waivers are used by company owners who wish to relinquish their rights to dividends. They can be commercially justifiable, for example if a shareholder waives their dividend to protect the company's cash.

To be effective it is necessary to draw up a formal deed that is executed before the dividend is declared or paid.

Company owners have tried using dividend waivers to avoid tax by diverting income to their spouse/partner: a higher rate taxpayer may try to divert a disproportionate share of the company's profit to their spouse/partner who is a basic rate taxpayer.

HMRC may use the settlements legislation to attack arrangements where shareholders end up with excessive dividends, i.e. more of the company's distributable profit than their shareholding would normally entitle them to. Because dividend waivers involve simply a transfer of income, not assets, they are not protected by the exemption for outright gifts to spouses (see above).

Example: *Mrs M owns 80 ordinary shares in M Limited and also has significant taxable income from other sources. Mr M owns 20 shares and has no other income. The company has retained profits of £50,000. Mrs M waives her right to a dividend and the company then declares a dividend of £2,000 per share. Mr M thus receives a dividend of £40,000, most of which he hopes will be taxed at no more than 10.75%.*

HMRC could apply the settlements legislation in this situation. Clearly a dividend of £2,000 per share could not have been paid on all 100 shares, so the waiver enhanced Mr M's dividend.

This would therefore be seen as a 'bounteous arrangement': it is unlikely Mrs M would have agreed to do the same thing with a third party. £32,000 of the dividend paid to Mr M would therefore be taxed in Mrs M's hands.

Some of the factors HMRC will look for when deciding whether to apply the settlements legislation to dividend waivers include:

- Insufficient retained profits to pay the same rate of dividend on all issued share capital.
- Even if there is sufficient profit to pay the same rate of dividend per share for the year in question, there has been a succession of waivers over several years and, in the absence of the waivers, the total dividends payable exceed the company's retained profits.
- Waiving shareholders wish to benefit non-waiving shareholders.
- Non-waiving shareholders pay tax at a lower rate.

In summary, company owners should be careful of entering into arrangements to waive dividends where there is no commercial reason for the waivers and no evidence the waivers are for non-tax reasons.

Salaries for Spouses/Partners

If your spouse/partner also works for your company they can be paid a salary. Please note, you cannot pay them a salary if they do no work for the company. And you cannot pay them more than is justified for the duties they perform. If you do, the company may be denied tax relief for the expense.

If your spouse/partner is a director, the accompanying legal responsibilities will also justify some remuneration. This factor alone is generally given a lot of weight and will almost always justify a salary up to the personal allowance. However, it remains important for your spouse/partner to be actively carrying out their duties as a director (attending board meetings, reviewing company accounts and other important documents, etc).

Conversely, if your spouse/partner is *not* a director, you must pay them at least the national minimum wage or living wage (Chapter 46). It's probably simpler to make them a director though.

If your spouse/partner has no taxable income from other sources, a small salary will be more tax efficient than simply paying them dividends.

Why? Unlike dividends, which are paid out of the company's after-tax profits, salaries are a tax-deductible expense for the company. In other words, in addition to any *Income Tax* savings enjoyed by the couple, a salary will also save the company *Corporation Tax*.

For example, a salary of £12,570 will save a company at least £1,469 in tax, taking into account the employer's NI usually payable. The savings will be greater for companies with a CT rate of more than 19%.

To minimise NI, salary payments should generally be made monthly instead of as a lump sum. If, however, your spouse/partner is a director, the payment can be made as a lump sum because company directors pay NI on an annual basis.

Second Jobs

What if your spouse or partner already has income from other sources, e.g. a salary from another job? Is it still tax efficient to get your company to pay them a small salary?

Firstly, it's important to point out that if they work for another employer the employment contract may prevent them working for you as well.

If there is no such restriction, paying your spouse or partner a small NI free salary could lead to an overall saving of several hundred pounds in some cases. Why? Because for basic rate taxpayers the combined tax rate (CT and Income Tax) for dividend income is at least 27.7%, compared with 20% for salaries.

Thus, paying your spouse/partner a salary of, say, £5,000 could lead to an overall saving of around £385 (£5,000 x 7.7%), providing there is no NI payable.

Where the company has a marginal CT rate of more than 19%, paying your spouse or partner a salary will be even more attractive because that salary will enjoy more CT relief (up to 26.5%).

If your spouse/partner's other income is not already providing them with a credit for state pension entitlement purposes (e.g. if it is rental income), you may wish to increase their salary to £6,708 (see Chapter 17).

And, if there is spare employment allowance available, a salary of £12,570 could be beneficial, leading to overall savings of between £765 and £1,625 (depending on the company's marginal CT rate).

Chapter 36

Splitting Income with Your Children

It is possible to gift shares in your company to your children. Because they will have their own Income Tax personal allowance and dividend allowance, it may be possible for them to receive tax-free dividends of up to £13,070 each, plus an additional £37,200 taxed at just 10.75%.

However, it is important to point out this type of tax planning generally only works when *adult* children are involved (i.e. children 18 or older).

Transfers of income to minor children are generally ineffective as the income would be taxed in the parent's hands. This section therefore deals exclusively with adult children.

If you gift shares in the company to your adult children there will potentially be CGT payable, as if you had sold the shares to them for their full market value. However, it may be possible for both the parent and child to jointly elect to hold over the capital gain.

To qualify for holdover relief the company must, generally speaking, be a trading company.

The safest route is probably to use ordinary shares, which means your children will obtain full ownership and voting rights in respect of their share of the business, not just a right to receive dividends.

There is a potential tax trap for family members who are gifted shares and are also employees of the company. In certain cases, where shares are obtained because of an individual's employment, a gift of shares can be subject to Income Tax charges.

However, there is an exemption where shares are given in the 'normal course of domestic, family, or personal relationships.'

So, in most family companies, where shares are transferred to a spouse/partner or adult children, the transfer should not give rise to any employment tax charges.

There is nevertheless a danger that, in certain circumstances, HMRC may argue the individuals received shares by virtue of their employment, not because they are family members.

For example, if the individual only receives a small salary from the company (i.e. below market rate) HMRC may have more grounds to argue that the gift was made to increase the individual's remuneration from the company.

If shares are transferred to a family member who is an employee and to other employees who are not family members, this could indicate the gift was made because of the family member's employment.

On the other hand, if shares are gifted to several family members (some of whom are not employees) this may indicate the gift was made solely because of the family relationship.

It may be wise in such circumstances to document the reasons for the gift and (as always) obtain professional advice.

Salaries for Children

It's often worth getting your company to employ your children (including your minor children) at certain points in time. The salary payments will be a tax-deductible expense for the business, providing the payments can be justified by the duties performed. (In one tax case a son's wages were disallowed because there were no time records or other evidence to justify the payments.)

The income will generally be tax free in the hands of the children, if they're at school, college, or university and have no other taxable income.

A tax deduction coupled with a tax-free receipt is the best possible outcome when it comes to extracting money from your company!

Children under 21 can be paid up to £12,570 with no Income Tax or NI consequences for either them or the company (assuming they have no other taxable income).

For those who are 16 and over, employee's NI will be payable on any salary in excess of £12,570 at 8%. To avoid employee's NI on salaries paid to non-directors, it is important to make regular weekly or monthly payments of no more than £242 or £1,048 respectively.

There is no employer's NI on salaries of up to £50,270 paid to employees under 21 and apprentices under 25. The exemption is not lost if the employee earns more than £50,270: employer's NI is only payable on the excess.

It's important to note the restrictions on the hours and work children can do because this affects how much you can pay them.

Restrictions on Work and Hours

Children are of compulsory school age up to the last Friday in June in the academic year of their 16th birthday. After this, they are at the 'mandatory school leaving age' and can apply for an NI number and work full time.

Until that time there are restrictions on the hours and types of work that can be carried out. For starters, children generally have to be at least 14 before they can legally be employed (although regulations may permit 13-year-olds to do some types of work).

Furthermore, children under school leaving age must not work:

- Without an employment permit if local byelaws require it
- In factories or on industrial sites
- During school hours
- Before 7.00 am or after 8.00 pm
- For more than one hour before school (local byelaws permitting)
- For more than four hours without taking a one-hour break
- In occupations prohibited by byelaws/legislation (e.g. pubs)
- If the work will harm their health, wellbeing, or education
- Without having a two-week break during the school holidays in each calendar year

During term time, children under school leaving age can work for no more than 12 hours per week. During school holidays, they can work up to 35 hours per week (25 hours for children under 15). There are also daily limits:

- Two hours on school days
- Eight hours on other days (five hours for children under 15)

There are special rules for certain types of work, such as acting or modelling. This doesn't help many small company owners though.

16- and 17-year-olds over school leaving age can generally work up to 40 hours per week and can do most types of work, although some additional health and safety regulations apply. However, it should be noted that in England children must remain in some form of education or training until they are 18. This could be through part-time education or training while they are working or through an apprenticeship.

National Minimum Wage & Living Wage
If your children are below the compulsory school leaving age, the national minimum wage does not apply. The hourly rates for older children are currently as follows:

- £12.71 Living wage, 21 and over
- £10.85 for those aged 18-20
- £8.00 for those aged 16-17
- £8.00 for apprentices under 19 or in their first year

While there is an exemption from the national minimum wage for members of the employer's household, this exemption cannot apply where the employer is a company. Hence, you must apply the national minimum wage when employing children over school leaving age to work in your company (unless you make them a director).

Part 6

Other Profit Extraction Strategies

Chapter 37

Loans to Directors

It used to be illegal for companies to make loans to directors. This is no longer the case and loans of any size are now permitted. With the exception of loans under £10,000, they generally have to be approved by the company's shareholders. For most small companies this is obviously not a problem because the shareholders and directors are the same people!

You cannot take a loan from your company for an indefinite period without tax consequences. If that was possible most company owners would never pay themselves taxable dividends.

The attractiveness of taking a loan from your company is limited by two potential tax charges:

- A 35.75% tax paid by the *company* (the Section 455 charge)
- A benefit-in-kind charge paid by the *director*

The Section 455 charge was 33.75% for loans made before 6th April 2026.

Fortunately, it is possible to avoid or mitigate the damage caused by these taxes, if you understand the rules.

The Section 455 Charge

Most small family companies are 'close companies'. A close company is one controlled by five or fewer 'participators', or by any number of participators who are also directors. Broadly, a participator is a shareholder.

If a close company lends money to a participator *the company* will have to pay a 35.75% tax charge on the loan. This is known as the Section 455 charge. Failure to pay this charge will result in penalties and interest.

However, there are two reasons why this charge is not as bad as it first appears:

1. Short-Term Loans Escape the Section 455 Charge

The 35.75% tax does not apply if the loan is repaid within nine months of the end of the company's accounting period. This is the normal due date for the company's CT. This means short-term loans to directors do not attract a company tax charge.

Example: *Bill Ltd's accounting period ends on 31st December 2026. The company made a £10,000 loan to Bill, the sole shareholder and director, in July 2026.*

Bill repays the loan before the end of September 2027. The company will not have to pay the 35.75% tax charge because the loan was repaid within nine months of the end of the accounting period in which it was made.

Example: *The facts are the same as before except only £7,000 is repaid before the end of September 2027. The remaining £3,000 is repaid in October 2028. The company will pay a Section 455 tax charge of £1,073 (£3,000 x 35.75%).*

2. The Section 455 Charge is Refundable

Even if the 35.75% tax does end up being paid because the loan is not repaid early enough, the tax will be refunded when the loan is repaid.

That's the good news. The bad news is the company will only be repaid nine months after the end of the accounting period in which the loan is repaid. In Bill Ltd's case this means the £1,073 tax will not be repaid until 1st October 2029.

Exemption for Minority Shareholders

This exemption isn't much use to most small company owners. Nevertheless, it is worth mentioning that there is no 35.75% company tax charge if you own 5% or less of the company's ordinary shares.

There are some qualifying criteria: total loans to the individual cannot exceed £15,000 and the individual must work full time in the company's business. When it comes to the 5% limit you must include shares owned by you, your spouse, and other 'associates' (e.g. close relatives).

Although there is no company tax charge on small loans to minority shareholders, there will still be a potential benefit-in-kind charge for the individual.

The Benefit-in-Kind Charge

If no interest is payable on the loan, or if the interest paid to the company is less than the 'official rate', the director will have to pay Income Tax on the benefit in kind.

The official rate of interest is currently 3.75%. If the interest charged on a loan to a director is less than 3.75%, a benefit-in-kind charge is payable. Employer's NI is also payable, although there is no employee's NI payable by the director.

As far as Income Tax is concerned, most articles state that basic rate taxpayers pay 20% tax and higher rate taxpayers pay 40% tax on benefits in kind.

It's not as simple as that if you're a company owner taking a small tax-free salary and the rest of your income as dividends. The amount of Income Tax payable on the benefit depends on the level of salary and whether the director has income from other sources such as rental income.

Directors who are higher rate taxpayers will effectively suffer between 35.75% and 45% tax on the benefit. The lower 35.75% tax rate is payable to the extent that the taxable benefit is covered by the director's personal allowance. The 45% rate then comes into force and is a combination of the 20% tax suffered on the benefit in kind itself and the 25% increase (from 10.75% to 35.75%) in the tax suffered on an equivalent amount of dividend income.

For example, if the loan is for £20,000 and no interest is charged, the director will potentially face the following benefit-in-kind charge as a higher rate taxpayer in 2026/27:

£20,000 loan x 3.75% interest x 45% tax = £338

The company will also have to pay Class 1A NI:

£20,000 loan x 3.75% interest x 15% = £113

The benefit in kind is reduced if interest is paid to the company. For example, if you pay 2% interest, the benefit in kind will be calculated using an interest rate of 1.75% (3.75% less 2%). If you pay 3.75% interest there will be no benefit in kind charge.

Note that the benefit in kind is only reduced if there is a formal obligation to pay interest to the company. For this reason, it is probably advisable to have a properly drawn up loan agreement.

If you do pay interest on the loan, the good news is you will be paying the money to your own company, not a bank. However, the company will pay CT on the interest it receives.

It must also be remembered that money inside a company is generally less valuable than money outside a company. If you wish to withdraw the interest back out as a dividend, there is likely to be an Income Tax charge.

Should Directors Pay Interest?
Let's compare two scenarios for the current 2026/27 tax year: an interest-free loan, or paying interest at the official rate.

We will assume the loan is for £30,000, the official interest rate is 3.75%, and the director suffers Income Tax at an effective rate of 45% on any benefit in kind. We will also assume, for now, that the company has a marginal CT rate of 26.5%.

With an interest-free loan, the benefit-in-kind charge paid by the director will be £30,000 x 3.75% x 45% = £506. The NI paid by the company will be £30,000 x 3.75% x 15% = £169. The employer's NI is a tax-deductible expense, so the net cost would be £124 (£169 less 26.5% CT relief). Hence, the total cost of the loan is £630 (£506 + £124).

Let's now look what would happen if the director pays interest at the official rate. On a £30,000 loan, the director will currently pay £1,125 interest to the company (£30,000 x 3.75%). The company will pay 26.5% CT on this interest so the cost will be £1,125 x 26.5% CT = £298.

If the after-tax interest is paid out as a dividend, producing an Income Tax charge of £296 for a higher rate taxpayer (£827 x 35.75%), the total tax cost will be £594.

This is a bit less than the cost of an interest-free loan. However, the difference is small, so it may be other factors (such as accountancy fees or simplicity) that determine which route is best.

In the above example, we assumed the company has a marginal CT rate of 26.5%. Paying interest at the official rate becomes more attractive when the company has a lower marginal CT rate.

For example, taking all the same facts as above, but with the lowest CT rate of 19%, the total cost of an interest-free loan would be £643, the cost of paying interest at the official rate would be £540, and the saving generated would increase to £103. Still not much, but better.

The Official Rate of Interest
Back in 2009, the official rate of interest was 6.25%. Despite the phenomenal rise in UK interest rates in 2022 and 2023, the official rate was only increased from 2% to 2.25%. The rate was eventually increased to 3.75% on 6th April 2025. Furthermore, the Government has now given itself the power to change the rate during the tax year and has stated that it will be reviewed on a quarterly basis.

Hence, it remains to be seen if, and by how much, loans to directors might become more or less expensive during the current tax year.

Exemptions from the Benefit in Kind Charge

There are two important exemptions from benefit in kind charges: loans to invest in another company, and loans for no more than £10,000.

Neither exemption makes any difference to the requirement to pay the Section 455 company tax charge. Remember, however, that the company tax charge does not apply to short-term loans (up to 21 months in some cases) and is repayable.

Loans to Invest in Another Company

There is generally no benefit in kind charge on certain *qualifying* loans. A qualifying loan is one where the interest (if interest was charged) would be a tax-deductible expense for the director.

An example of a qualifying loan would be one given to an individual so they can acquire an interest in another close company carrying on qualifying activities: namely either trading or letting property to unconnected third parties.

The person borrowing the money must generally hold more than 5% of the ordinary shares in the company in which the money is being invested.

Whether this is the most tax-efficient way to finance a new business venture is, of course, another question altogether, although we will return to this issue later.

Remember, the Section 455 company tax charge still applies, unless the loan is repaid within nine months of the end of the accounting period in which it is made.

Loans not Exceeding £10,000

There is no benefit-in-kind charge if all loans to the director/shareholder total £10,000 or less throughout the tax year.

It is important to understand that any sum due from the director to the company is counted as a 'loan', including goods or services that have been provided to the director but not paid for.

The Section 455 CT charge still applies if the loan is not repaid on time. Nevertheless, this exemption allows a director/shareholder to take a loan of up to £10,000 for up to 21 months with no adverse tax consequences.

Larger Short-Term Loans

By taking a loan for no more than £10,000 and repaying it on time, both the 35.75% Section 455 tax charge and the benefit-in-kind charge can be avoided. What if you want to borrow more than the tax-free limit for a short period: how does this compare with paying yourself additional taxable dividends?

Example: *Penelope owns Pitstop Hotels Ltd, which has a 31st December accounting date. Penelope normally withdraws a salary of £12,570 and enough dividend income to use up her basic rate band. It's the beginning of January 2027 and Penelope would like to withdraw some additional money from Pitstop Hotels, over and above her usual salary and dividend income. She needs £15,000 for some home improvements.*

If she takes the money as a dividend, she will need to withdraw £23,346. There will be an Income Tax charge of £8,346 payable by 31st January 2028, leaving her with the required £15,000.

Instead, she decides to take an interest-free loan of £15,000 from her company on 6th January 2027. Because it's an interest-free loan and the loan is for more than £10,000, she will be subject to a benefit-in-kind charge (paying interest to her company at the official rate would be more tax efficient, but she decides an interest-free loan will be simpler).

The loan will also be subject to the 35.75% Section 455 tax charge unless it is repaid by the end of September 2028 (nine months after the end of the company's accounting period on 31st December 2027).

She repays the loan on 5th September 2028, after 20 months. The loan falls into the 2026/27 tax year (3 months), the 2027/28 tax year (12 months) and the 2028/29 tax year (5 months). We'll assume the official rate of interest is 3.75% throughout (although it could easily change).

Penny will face the following Income Tax charges:

2026/27: £15,000 x 3.75% x 3/12 x 45%	*£63*
2027/28: £15,000 x 3.75% x 12/12 x 45%	*£253*
2028/29: £15,000 x 3.75% x 5/12 x 45%	*£105*
Total	*£421*

The NI paid by the company will be:

2026/27: £15,000 x 3.75% x 3/12 x 15%	*£21*
2027/28: £15,000 x 3.75% x 12/12 x 15%	*£84*
2028/29: £15,000 x 3.75% x 5/12 x 15%	*£35*
Total	*£140*

This is a tax-deductible expense, so the total net cost to the company may be just £103 (at a marginal CT rate of 26.5%: which is likely if Penelope is extracting income of £50,270 from the company each year). The total cost of the loan is therefore likely to be £524 (£421 + £103).

To repay the £15,000 loan, Penelope withdraws additional dividend income, over and above what she normally takes, of £23,346 during the 2028/29 tax year. The Income Tax on this additional dividend is £8,346, payable by 31st January 2030.

By taking a loan in 2027 instead of a taxable dividend, Penelope has managed to defer paying Income Tax of £8,346 for two years. The total cost is £524 in this scenario, although it could be higher or lower, depending on what happens to the official rate of interest. The point is, she has effectively borrowed £8,346 from HMRC for two years at an annual interest rate of just 3.1%.

Additional points to note:

- If Penelope thinks her marginal Income Tax rate in 2028/29 may be higher than in 2026/27, she may be better off paying herself a dividend in January 2027 instead of taking a loan. In particular she may have to watch out for the £100,000 personal allowance withdrawal threshold.

- If Penelope can repay the loan out of her regular dividend income taxed at just 10.75% (i.e. without having to withdraw an additional dividend taxed at 35.75%) she may be able to *save* £8,346 Income Tax, not just defer paying it.

Longer-Term Loans

Arguably, one could say it's worth every higher rate taxpayer director borrowing £10,000 from their company. There would be no benefit in kind charge but, as we know, a Section 455 charge at 35.75% will arise if the loan is not repaid within nine months of the end of the accounting period in which it is made.

So, if the loan is left outstanding for a longer period, the director has extracted £10,000 from the company at a cost of £3,575.

BUT that's still cheaper than the cost to a higher rate taxpayer of getting a net £10,000 through a dividend. To get £10,000 net of tax at 35.75% means taking a dividend of £15,564 and paying £5,564 Income Tax: £1,989 more than the Section 455 charge.

For an additional rate taxpayer to get a net sum of £10,000 by way of a dividend would mean taking a dividend of £16,488 and paying £6,488 in Income Tax at 39.35%: £2,913 more than the Section 455 charge (the company charge is still at 35.75%, even if the director is an additional rate taxpayer).

Having borrowed £10,000 though, the director needs to be very careful. Even just £1 more borrowed for just one day would lead to a benefit in kind charge for the whole tax year. With an official rate of 3.75%, this could cost a total of up to £214 in combined Income Tax and NI in 2026/27 (net of CT relief).

And remember, borrowing will include any goods or services provided to the director but not *immediately* paid for.

Hence, perhaps, if following this strategy, it may be best to leave a little leeway and only borrow, say £9,000.

Greater borrowings (potentially without limit) will enjoy similar benefits if used to invest in a qualifying close company. As we said above, this may not be the best way to finance, or structure, such an investment, but it could well beat taking a dividend.

Example: *Dick owns Muttley Ltd, a successful trading company with over £200,000 in surplus cash sitting in its bank account. Together with three friends, Dick is planning to set up Pigeon Properties Ltd, a property investment company. Dick and his friends are each going to invest £100,000 in Pigeon Properties Ltd (made up of 25 £1 shares and a loan to the company of £99,975, but it will all qualify).*

Dick has no other resources available, so he will have to obtain the cash he needs from Muttley Ltd. So far this tax year, he has already taken a salary of £12,570 and dividends of £80,000, giving him taxable income of £92,570. He needs that income (£73,449 net of tax) to fund regular living expenses.

To get a further net sum of £100,000 in 2026/27, he will need to take additional dividend income of £172,274, which will suffer Income Tax of £72,274, leaving him with the required sum of £100,000.

On the other hand, if Dick borrows £100,000 from Muttley Ltd, the Section 455 charge will amount to just £35,750, saving £36,524 compared with taking a dividend.

Not only can this strategy lead to a massive, immediate saving, it's worth remembering that tax paid under the Section 455 charge is ultimately repayable, tax paid on dividend income is not.

In fact, so great is this saving it may sometimes be worth contemplating this type of strategy even when the loan does not qualify for the benefit in kind exemption.

Let's say Dick was not going to invest in a qualifying company, but needed the £100,000 for some other type of investment (perhaps residential rental property owned personally). Let's also say his loan is interest free. Let's assume the official rate remains at 3.75%, Muttley Ltd is paying CT at 25%, and Dick takes a salary of £12,570 plus dividends of £80,000 to give him the same total taxable income of £92,570 as at present.

The annual benefit in kind on the loan will therefore be £3,750 (£100,000 @ 3.75%), leading to the following costs:

Income Tax	
Benefit in kind £3,750 x 20%	£750
Dividend pushed into higher rate £3,750 x 25%	£938
Employer's NI £3,750 x 15%	£563
Corporation Tax relief thereon £563 x 25%	(£141)
Total annual cost	£2,110

In this example, it will take eighteen years before the cumulative annual cost of the loan exceeds the initial saving of £36,524.

Furthermore, assuming Dick eventually repays the loan and hence Muttley Ltd recoups the £35,750 Section 455 charge, it will take 35 years before the cumulative annual cost exceeds the tax he would have suffered if he had taken a dividend.

As we have seen, for higher rate taxpayers, taking loans from your company can be a cheaper option than taking dividends. Where money is borrowed to make investments outside the company, and thus can reasonably be expected to ultimately be repaid, such a strategy may make sense.

However, borrowing long term from your own company simply to fund regular living expenses is not generally a good idea, due to the ultimate costs that could arise if the loan eventually has to be written off (see further below). Furthermore, if the company runs into financial difficulty, its creditors will be able to force you to sell personal assets in order to repay your loan.

Large loan balances also carry a risk of legal challenge, as it is questionable whether the director is fulfilling their duty to act in the best interests of the company: unless a market rate of interest is being paid and the company could not have obtained a better return by investing the funds elsewhere.

Loans to Family

You cannot necessarily avoid the Section 455 tax charge and benefit-in-kind charge by making loans to family members. For example, both the Section 455 charge and the benefit-in-kind charge apply to loans to spouses and children of the director/shareholder and other close relatives. The Section 455 charge also applies to loans to business partners. The charges do not apply to loans to friends and some more distant relatives BUT you will incur the taxman's wrath if the benefit of the loan passes back to you or a close relative.

Loans Written Off

If the loan is formally released or written off by the company, the amount of the loan will be treated as a deemed dividend for Income Tax purposes. In most instances, the amount released will also be subject to employer's NI, like a benefit in kind.

This treatment was confirmed in the case of Stewart Fraser Ltd, which involved a write off of loans by a close company to an employee shareholder. The loan write offs were treated as distributions taxable on the employee and HMRC successfully argued that NI was also payable by the company.

Because of this NI cost, you may wish to consider declaring a dividend to settle the debt, providing the company has sufficient distributable reserves. One drawback of this is a dividend would have to be paid to all shareholders pro rata.

A loan written off in these circumstances will not be deductible for CT purposes. Any Section 455 tax charge paid is, however, refunded to the company if the loan is released or written off. The safest course of action may be to ensure that any loan is always repaid, wherever possible, rather than written off.

In the recent case of HMRC v Gary Quillan, it was held that, when a company is liquidated with a director's loan balance still outstanding, this should be treated the same as if the loan had been formally written off for the above purposes.

Paperwork

Although it's simple in small companies to obtain shareholder approval for loans, it's important to get the paperwork right. There should be a proper loan agreement outlining the nature of the loan, the company's liability and the amount and purpose of the loan. The shareholders should grant approval at a meeting or by written resolution with appropriate documentation. Shareholder approval is not required for loans of up to £10,000, although it is good practice to produce the same paperwork as this may provide more certainty as to the tax treatment of the borrowed money.

Financial Reporting Standard 102 (FRS 102)

A recent financial reporting standard (FRS 102) may affect the accounting treatment of directors' loans in certain circumstances.

Where interest is not charged at a market rate, the loan may have to be discounted in the company's accounts. For example, if the market interest rate is 5%, and an interest-free loan of £100,000 is made to a director repayable after three years, the present value of the loan is £100,000/(1.05 x 1.05 x 1.05) = £86,384.

The initial shortfall of £13,616 would be treated as a 'distribution' for accounts purposes.

The tax treatment does not, however, follow the accounting treatment. The Section 455 charge is still based on the total amount of the loan and the director's taxable benefit will be calculated in the way described earlier in this chapter.

To avoid the complexities of FRS 102, tax commentators suggest it should be specifically recorded that directors' loan accounts are repayable on demand, or to charge a market rate of interest.

Of course, it's only an accounting adjustment, and there's no tax cost involved, but it is a nuisance. And one indirect consequence is that the deemed distribution (e.g. £13,616 in our example) reduces the company's distributable profits available for paying dividends.

Loan Recycling
To prevent directors simply repaying loans before the Section 455 charge is payable, and then taking a new loan out straight away (known as 'bed and breakfasting'), there are some additional rules:

The 30 Day Rule
Relief from the Section 455 charge is denied if:

- A shareholder makes repayments totalling £5,000 or more to the company and within 30 days...
- new loans totalling £5,000 or more are made to the same person or their associates

For this rule to apply, the original loan and repayment can take place in the same or different accounting periods. The new loan must be in a subsequent accounting period to the original loan.

It's important to point out that the 30-day rule does not apply where the loan is repaid using amounts that give rise to an Income Tax charge, for example where a taxable dividend is declared and credited to the director's loan account.

Example 1: *During accounting period 1 there is a loan outstanding of £6,000. Two days before the end of the accounting period £6,000 is repaid. Three days into accounting period 2 a new £6,000 loan is taken. The repayment will be matched with the new loan, not the old loan. The loan from accounting period 1 is treated as still outstanding and will be subject to the Section 455 tax charge if not repaid.*

Example 2: *C Ltd is a close company in which Jim is a shareholder. C Ltd's accounting period ends on 31st March 2027. On 25th March 2027, Jim borrows £15,000 from C Ltd. If the loan is not repaid within nine months of the end of the accounting period, C Ltd must pay a 35.75% Section 455 tax charge (£5,363).*

On 1st December 2027, a dividend of £9,000, which is chargeable to Income Tax, is declared by C Ltd and credited to Jim's loan account. On the same day, Jim repays the remaining £6,000 of his loan. On 10th December 2027, Jim borrows £3,500 from the company. On 15th December 2027, Jim borrows a further £2,000.

The Section 455 tax charge is calculated as follows:

- £9,000 was repaid by applying a chargeable dividend towards the loan. This is ignored when it comes to applying the 30-day rule. The remaining £6,000 that Jim repays exceeds the £5,000 minimum repayment under the 30-day rule.

- Nine and fourteen days later respectively (i.e. within 30 days) Jim withdraws a further £5,500 (£3,500 + £2,000), which is also in excess of the £5,000 limit for new loans.

- The new loans (£5,500) are less than the repayments (£6,000). Relief from the Section 455 tax charge is denied on the lesser amount of £5,500, resulting in a tax charge of £1,966. Only the net repayment of £500 is recognised.

The Arrangements Rule

This rule applies even if the new borrowing takes place after 30 days. Relief from the Section 455 charge will be denied if:

- Prior to repaying the loan, the total amount owed by the shareholder to the company is £15,000 or more, and
- At the time of the repayment, arrangements had been made for new loans of £5,000 or more to replace the amounts repaid.

The relief denied is the lower of the amount repaid and the new loan. 'Arrangements' are not defined and HMRC will give the term a wide meaning.

Once again, the arrangements rule does not apply if the loan is repaid with a taxable dividend or bonus. In other words, if a loan account is credited with a taxable dividend this will be treated as a valid loan repayment.

Example: *Brigitte owes her company £25,000, which she borrowed on 1st June 2026 during the accounting period ended 30th June 2026. After the end of the accounting period, Brigitte takes a 45-day loan from the bank for £25,000 and uses it to repay the loan to her company. 40 days after repaying her company, Brigitte takes a new loan of £30,000 from her company and uses it to repay the bank.*

There is a significant risk HMRC will argue that, at the time she repaid her company, Brigitte had made arrangements to withdraw a new amount from her company (to repay the bank), so the original loan will be treated as not repaid. Thus, the Section 455 charge will be payable on the initial £25,000 loan, unless a further repayment is made.

What is a Valid Income Tax Charge?

As mentioned above, the anti-avoidance rules do not apply if the amount repaid gives rise to an Income Tax charge in the hands of the director-shareholder. This will be the case if a loan is repaid by means of a dividend credited to the director's loan account that is included as income on the director's tax return (or where a bonus is paid subject to PAYE before being credited to the director's loan account). According to HMRC, if a dividend is first paid out in cash and the money is then paid back into the company and credited to the director's loan account, the exemption does not apply. HMRC also contends that, if the director owns the business premises and the company pays them rent, the exemption does not apply to rent credited to the director's loan account.

The Repayment Tool

We all know HMRC don't like coughing up when it's time for them to repay tax, and this is especially true of Section 455 tax. They have recently introduced an online tool for directors or their agents to use when responding to queries related to Section 455 repayments. That means they'll be able to process a lot more queries and that means they'll be able to ask a lot more questions, especially about things like the 30-day rule.

So you'll need to know all the rules and make sure you obey them before you'll get your money back.

Chapter 38

Rental Income: Better than Dividends

Many company owners own their business premises *personally* and the company pays them rent.

Paying yourself rent is often more tax efficient than paying yourself a higher salary. Like salaries, rental payments are a tax-deductible expense (providing the rent does not exceed a market rent). But, unlike salaries, there is no NI cost.

Rental income is also more tax efficient than dividend income and has become even more attractive for those whose companies face higher CT rates (Chapter 1).

There are also non-tax reasons why you may wish to pay yourself rental income instead of withdrawing dividends from your company. For starters, to pay dividends the company must have sufficient distributable profits. There is no such requirement when it comes to paying rent.

Secondly, with rental income it is relatively straightforward to pay yourself a fixed monthly amount throughout the year, for example by setting up a standing order from your company bank account to your personal bank account. This could be helpful if you have to personally pay various costs associated with the property, especially mortgage interest.

With rental income there is no requirement to continually do all the paperwork that often accompanies dividends, for example holding directors' board meetings and shareholder meetings.

How much better off could you be by paying yourself rental income instead of dividends? It all depends on your personal circumstances, for example how much taxable income you have and the amount of tax-deductible mortgage interest you have.

Example 1: Basic Rate Taxpayer
Warren is a company owner and a basic rate taxpayer. He personally owns the property out of which the company operates but the company currently doesn't pay him any rent. He does not have any tax-deductible mortgage interest to offset.

During the current 2026/27 tax year, he pays himself a salary of £12,570 and withdraws the rest of the company's profits as dividends.

Let's say he gets the company to pay him rental income of £10,000 per year. After paying Income Tax at 20% he will be left with £8,000 this year.

If the company had not paid him rent it would have had an extra £8,100 at most to pay dividends (£10,000 profit less at least 19% CT). Warren would have been left with £7,229 at most after paying 10.75% Income Tax.

By getting the company to pay him rent Warren is better off by at least £771 this year. This is because, for basic rate taxpayers, the combined tax rate on dividends is around 27.7% (at least), compared with 20% for rental income.

From 6th April 2027, basic rate tax on rental income will increase to 22%. That will still leave Warren at least £571 better off next year.

Example 2: Higher Rate Taxpayer
The facts are exactly the same except Warren is a higher rate taxpayer. If he gets the company to pay him rental income of £10,000, after paying Income Tax at 20% he will be left with £8,000.

However, his rental income will use up £10,000 of his basic rate band, which means £10,000 of his dividend income will be taxed at 35.75% instead of 10.75%, resulting in additional tax of £2,500. Overall, Warren will be left with £5,500 (£8,000 – £2,500).

Since Warren is a higher rate taxpayer, it is likely that his company will have annual profits in excess of £50,000, so we will now assume it has a marginal CT rate of 26.5%. If the company had not paid him any rental income, it would have been left with an extra £7,350 to pay out as dividends and Warren would have been left with £4,722 after paying Income Tax at 35.75%.

Rental income is again more tax efficient than dividends for a higher rate taxpayer, with a saving of up to £778 on £10,000 of rental income. If the company has a lower marginal CT rate, however, the saving will be less: £681 at a CT rate of 25%, or just £296 if the CT rate is 19%.

These savings will reduce next year when basic rate Income Tax on rental income increases to 22%. However Warren will still enjoy savings of up to £578, and at least £96 in any case.

Example 3: Higher Rate Taxpayer
This time we'll assume Warren's premises are more substantial and he gets the company to pay him rental income of £37,700. Along with his salary this will take him up to the £50,270 higher rate threshold. After paying 20% tax on his rental income he will be left with £30,160 of this income.

His rental income will use up his entire £37,700 basic rate band, which means £37,200 of his dividend income will be taxed at 35.75% instead of 10.75%, resulting in additional tax of £9,300 (it's £37,200 and not £37,700 because of the £500 dividend allowance).

Overall, Warren will be left with £20,860 (£30,160 – £9,300) from his rental income of £37,700.

If the company had not paid him £37,700 of rental income, it would have been left with an extra £27,710 of after-tax profit to pay out as dividends (again assuming a marginal CT rate of 26.5%). Warren would then have been left with £17,804 after paying Income Tax at 35.75%.

In this example, Warren is £3,056 better off by paying himself rental income. If the company's CT rate were 25%, he would be £2,693 better off and, even at the lowest possible CT rate of 19% (which is unlikely), he would still be £1,240 better off.

Next year, when the tax rates on rental income all go up by 2%, Warren would be left with £20,106 of his £37,700 rental income. That will still leave him up to £2,302 better off (£1,939 better off if the company is paying CT at 25%; £486 better off if it has a CT rate of just 19%).

Mortgage Interest and Other Property Expenses

Many company owners who personally own their business premises will also have a mortgage over those premises on which they personally pay the interest. These interest payments can be offset against your rental income, effectively making some or all of it 'tax free'.

Note that, although tax relief on mortgage interest for residential property has been reduced (see Chapter 33), mortgages used to buy commercial properties are unaffected.

Most company owners will instinctively realise it would be foolish not to receive rental income if they also have mortgage interest to set off (or other tax-deductible property expenses). Tax-free rental income has to be better than a taxable dividend!

Example 4: Higher Rate Taxpayer

Warren has a salary and other income of £12,570, is a higher rate taxpayer and has tax deductible mortgage interest of £5,000. If he gets the company to pay him rental income of £10,000, he'll have a taxable rental profit of £5,000. After paying Income Tax at 20% he will be left with £4,000 (£10,000 – £5,000 interest – £1,000 tax).

His taxable rental income will use up £5,000 of his basic rate band, which means £5,000 of his dividend income will be taxed at 35.75% instead of 10.75%, resulting in additional tax of £1,250. Overall, Warren will be left with £2,750 (£4,000 – £1,250).

If the company had not paid him any rental income, it would have been left with an extra £7,350 to pay out as dividends (again assuming a marginal CT rate of 26.5%) and Warren would have been left with £4,722 after paying Income Tax at 35.75%. After paying his interest costs Warren would be £278 out of pocket.

Overall, Warren is £3,028 better off paying himself rental income.

At lower CT rates, Warren might not be quite as badly off under the dividend route, but taking £10,000 of rental income from the company will always leave him at least £2,546 better off.

Next year, Warren will pay Income Tax at 22% on his rental profit, leaving him with £3,900 (£10,000 – £5,000 interest – £1,100 tax). He will be between £2,446 and £2,928 better off than if he had not pad himself rent, depending on the company's marginal CT rate.

Summary

The above examples illustrate it is often more tax efficient to get your company to pay you rent instead of dividends. Rental income is most tax efficient to the extent you have tax deductible costs to offset, such as mortgage interest. The savings vary from case to case, so it is essential to do your own number crunching.

While the savings will be reduced next year, when there is a 2% increase in Income Tax rates on rental income, they will still be well worthwhile.

Business Asset Disposal Relief (BADR)

Although you may save Income Tax by paying yourself as much rental income as possible, there is one reason why you may prefer to get your company to pay you a below-market rent. If you sell your company, you may be able to claim BADR, which means you could pay CGT at a reduced rate of 18%.

Trading premises can also qualify for BADR, even if you own them personally. But you cannot claim the relief if your company has paid you a full market rent (although rent paid for periods before 6th April 2008 is ignored). If your company pays you a rent that is lower than the market rent, or if you owned the property before April 2008, a partial claim can usually be made.

If BADR is not available when you dispose of your premises, you will be subject to CGT at 24% if you're a higher rate taxpayer or 18% to the extent your basic rate band is not used up by your income.

So, it's possible that, even without BADR, company owners will be able to benefit from an 18% tax rate on at least some of their capital gains by making sure they don't have much taxable income in the year they sell their trading premises.

Furthermore, since the lifetime maximum cumulative claim for BADR by any individual is just £1m, many company owners will exhaust their potential relief on the sale of the company itself, so that there is none remaining for the gain on their business premises: in which case, there is no disadvantage in paying yourself a full market rent.

Capital Allowances

Company owners who also own the company's business premises personally may be entitled to claim capital allowances on part of the cost of the property. However, where less than full market rent is charged, the company owner can only claim a suitable proportion of the available capital allowances. For example, if the rent charged equates to 75% of a full market rent, 75% of the available allowances may be claimed.

This means the Income Tax advantages of paying yourself full market rent may be even greater than we have seen so far: and this may be enough to outweigh any potential loss of business asset disposal relief.

For further details of the capital allowances available on business property, see the Taxcafe guide *How to Save Property Tax*.

Chapter 39

Pay Yourself Tax-Free Interest Income

If your company owes you money you can make it pay you interest. In some cases, the interest will be both a tax-deductible expense for the company and tax free in your hands: the best-case scenario when it comes to extracting money from your company.

In this situation, extracting interest income may be more tax efficient than other types of income, including dividends.

How can interest income be tax free? For starters, interest is not subject to NI. As for Income Tax, there is the 0% starting rate band for up to £5,000 of savings income.

There's also the personal savings allowance which shelters up to £1,000 of interest income from tax if you're a basic rate taxpayer or £500 if you're a higher rate taxpayer (additional rate taxpayers do not benefit).

In Part 4, we looked at company owners with income from *other sources*, including interest from investments. In this chapter, we're looking at a different type of interest income: interest that comes out of your own company.

The £5,000 Starting Rate Band

Not everyone can benefit from the 0% starting rate. It's designed to benefit those with very low income. Hence the £5,000 starting rate band is reduced if you have any *taxable non-savings income.*

Non-savings income includes income from employment, self-employment, pensions, and rental properties. Crucially, it does not include dividend income.

Furthermore, thanks to the personal allowance, the first £12,570 of non-savings income you receive is effectively not taxable and thus cannot reduce the £5,000 starting rate band (unless your total income exceeds £100,000).

For example, if you have a salary of £12,570 this year and no other income apart from dividends, you won't have any taxable non-savings income and can receive £5,000 of tax-free interest.

You may also be able to receive up to £1,000 of additional tax-free interest thanks to the personal savings allowance.

But if you have a salary of £12,570 and rental income of £5,000 or more, your rental income will eat up your entire starting rate band, so none of your interest income will be tax-free under the 0% starting rate. You may, however, still be able to receive up to £1,000 of tax-free interest thanks to the personal savings allowance.

The £5,000 starting rate band is not given in addition to the basic rate band: it is part of the basic rate band. In other words, if you have £5,000 of interest income your basic rate band will be reduced by £5,000.

This means some of your dividend income may be pushed into the higher rate tax bracket. This may reduce the attractiveness of extracting interest income from your company, but will not usually eliminate the benefit altogether.

The Personal Savings Allowance

The personal savings allowance operates separately from, and in addition to, the starting rate band. This means some company owners will be able to pay themselves up to £6,000 of tax-free interest per year.

The personal savings allowance is especially useful to company owners who cannot use the starting rate band because they have too much non-savings income, e.g. rental income.

They can typically extract £1,000 (basic rate taxpayers) or £500 (higher rate taxpayers) of tax-free interest from their companies.

Lending to Your Company

There are lots of circumstances in which company owners may lend money to their companies. For example, it may be a new company that needs some cash to get started or a well-established company that needs money to buy some new equipment.

In some cases, company owners lend money to their companies indirectly, for example when a dividend is declared but the cash is not withdrawn immediately, perhaps because the company owner wants to reinvest it to help the business grow.

The Mechanics of Extracting Interest Income

There is no requirement for a director to charge interest on a loan account with their own company but, if they do, it must not exceed a reasonable commercial rate.

If the company pays more than a commercial rate, the excess payment could be treated as salary income and subject to Income Tax and NI.

Interest paid to a director on their loan account will usually be an allowable expense for the company, providing the money is used for business purposes. The interest will therefore provide CT relief.

Although your interest income may ultimately be tax free, the company will have to deduct Income Tax at 20% (22% from 6th April 2027) and pay this to HMRC quarterly, using form CT61 (which can be requested online). If this results in a tax overpayment, you can reclaim the excess through your self-assessment tax return. The company should also issue you an annual interest certificate.

While interest can be a very tax efficient way to extract money from your company, the additional reporting duties and payments may put some company owners off. However, both the negative cashflow impact and admin burden can be mitigated by paying interest annually, during the quarter to 31st March.

Another way to improve cashflow is to have the company pay you interest up to twelve months in arrears, after the end of its accounting period.

For example, let's say your company owes you £5,000 in interest for the accounting period ending 31st March 2026. Provided the company pays this interest by 31st March 2027, it will still be able to claim tax relief, saving it between £950 and £1,325 in CT on 1st January 2027.

Let's say the company pays you during the quarter ending 31st March 2027. The £1,000 (20%) tax charge it needs to deduct and pay over to HMRC is only due by 14th April 2027 and you will only need to pay any further Income Tax due by 31st January 2028. That's good, generally positive, cashflow!

While this is good for cashflow purposes, however, one thing to watch is that this income now falls into a later tax year for Income Tax purposes, so you will need to factor this into your planning: especially if you're looking to maximise the benefit of your starting rate band and/or personal savings allowance.

It may also be unwise to delay taking interest payments out of your company until after 5th April 2027, as the Income Tax rate applying will then increase by 2%. If this is only a case of paying at 22% via the CT61 and getting the tax back later when you submit your tax return, this probably doesn't matter too much, but if you're stuck with the higher tax charge in the long run, you've cost yourself an extra 2% unnecessarily.

How Much Tax Can You Save?
This will depend on *how much* and what *type* of income you earn. The examples that follow are all based on current tax rates applying for 2026/27.

Example 1 Basic-Rate Taxpayer, No Taxable Non-Savings Income: *Gillian is a company director with a salary and other non-savings income (e.g. rental income) of £12,570. She has £30,000 of dividend income. She charges her company £5,000 interest for a substantial loan she made to help it buy new equipment. Interest is at a commercial rate.*

The interest will be a tax-deductible business expense, saving the company at least £950 CT (£5,000 x 19%). Gillian has no taxable non-savings income, so all of her interest income will be tax free, being covered by the £5,000 starting rate band (although the company will initially have to withhold 20% tax and pay this to HMRC).

If instead Gillian decided to NOT pay herself interest, the company would have an extra £5,000 of taxable profit. After paying at least £950 CT there would be an extra £4,050 at most that could be paid out as dividends taxed at 10.75%, leaving Gillian with £3,615.

The potential tax saving is at least £1,385.

Example 2 Higher-Rate Taxpayer, No Taxable Non-Savings Income: *As before Gillian has £12,570 of salary and other non-savings income and £5,000 of interest from her company. However, this time she has dividend income of £50,000, which means she pays some tax at 35.75%.*

Gillian can enjoy £5,000 of tax-free interest income but because the starting rate band is part of the basic rate band an additional £5,000 of her dividends will be taxed at 35.75% instead of 10.75%, resulting in additional tax of £1,250. So, effectively Gillian receives £3,750 after tax.

If she did not pay herself interest, the company would have an extra £5,000 profit. As the company is already paying dividends of £50,000, it is reasonable to assume it will have a marginal CT rate of 26.5%. Hence, after CT, there will only be £3,675 of the extra profit remaining to pay out as further dividends. This would leave Gillian with just £2,361 after tax.

Hence, for a higher rate taxpayer with no taxable non-savings income the maximum potential saving is £1,389 (£3,750 – £2,361).

The saving will be less where the company has a lower marginal CT rate. However, even at the lowest possible CT rate of 19%, there would be a saving of £1,148 in this scenario.

Example 3 Basic-Rate Taxpayer, No Starting Rate Band Available: *This time Gillian has £17,570 of salary and rental income, £5,000 of interest income and £25,000 of dividend income.*

Because she has £5,000 of taxable non-savings income (£17,570 – £12,570 personal allowance) she will have no starting rate band available. However, thanks to the personal savings allowance, £1,000 of her interest income will be tax free and the rest will be taxed at 20%, leaving her with £4,200.

If Gillian did not pay herself interest, the company would have an extra £5,000 of taxable profit. After paying at least £950 CT there would be an extra £4,050 at most that could be paid out as dividends taxed at 10.75%, leaving her with £3,615.

So, in this case, Gillian is at least £585 better off paying herself interest. Not only is £1,000 of her interest Income Tax free, the remaining £4,000 is taxed at just 20% (remember the total combined tax rate on dividend income is at least 27.7% for a basic rate taxpayer).

Next year, 2027/28, Gillian will still be at least £505 better off, even factoring in the increased Income Tax rates on interest income.

Example 4 Higher-Rate Taxpayer, No Starting Rate Band Available: *This time Gillian has £17,570 of salary and rental income, £5,000 of interest income, and £50,000 of dividend income. Once again, she will have no starting rate band available. However, thanks to the personal savings allowance, £500 of her interest income will be tax free and the rest will be taxed at 20%, leaving her with £4,100.*

An additional £5,000 of her dividend income will be taxed at 35.75% instead of 10.75%, resulting in an additional Income Tax charge of £1,250. So effectively Gillian ends up with £2,850 after tax.

If instead she had decided to not pay herself interest, the company would have an extra £5,000 of taxable profit. As the company is already paying dividends of £50,000, it is reasonable to assume it will have a marginal CT rate of 26.5%. Hence, after CT, there will only be £3,675 of the extra profit remaining to pay out as further dividends. This would leave Gillian with just £2,297 after tax.

So, in this case Gillian is £553 better off paying herself interest.

The tax saving will be less if the company has a lower marginal CT rate, but it would still be £441 if the company is paying tax at 25% and, in the unlikely event that the company's CT rate is only 19%, there remains a saving of £248.

Gillian's savings will reduce by £90 next year when the Income Tax rates on interest income increase by 2%, but will still be between £158 and £463.

Making the Most of Your Personal Allowance

If you pay yourself a salary of, say, £6,708 and do not have any other non-savings income, you will have spare personal allowance of £5,862 (£12,570 – £6,708) to set against your interest or dividends. In Chapter 33, we saw how you can save tax this year by allocating your spare personal allowance to your dividend income rather than your interest income (if your interest is tax free anyway). This opportunity will cease to be available after the current, 2026/27 tax year.

In that chapter, we were focusing on interest income from investments but the same principle applies when you extract interest income from your own company.

Example 5 Higher-Rate Taxpayer, Spare Personal Allowance:
Roisin's company pays her a salary of £6,708 and she extracts the remaining profits as dividends totalling £50,000. She has no other income and therefore has spare personal allowance of £5,862 to use against her dividends. She ends up with after-tax income of £50,407.

Let's now assume Roisin receives £5,000 of interest from her company. This also reduces the amount of profit that can be distributed as dividends. At a marginal CT rate of 26.5%, this reduces her dividends by £3,675, but the reduction will be more where the company has a lower marginal CT rate.

If £5,000 of her £5,862 spare personal allowance is set against her interest income (and the remaining £862 against her dividends), she will end up with after-tax income of £51,259, or £852 more than before.

But if her spare personal allowance is set against her ***dividends****, she will end up with £51,796, an additional £537.*

Overall, Roisin ends up £1,389 better off by extracting £5,000 of interest from her company but the maximum saving is only achieved if she allocates her personal allowance correctly. If the company has a lower marginal CT rate, the overall saving will be less, but it will always be at least £1,148, of which £537 comes from allocating the personal allowance correctly.

Next year, Roisin will not be able to allocate her personal allowance in this way, but she will still enjoy a saving of between £610 and £852 by paying herself interest of £5,000.

Tax-Free Loan Repayments

Apart from the beneficial tax treatment of interest income, it's worth pointing out that some or all of the outstanding balance on a director's loan account can be paid out tax free at any time.

Having such an amount 'banked' inside your company that can be withdrawn tax free at any time could prove useful, for example if the director unexpectedly requires additional money that would be taxed heavily as a salary or dividend.

The only potential cost of making loan repayments is where the director is claiming qualifying loan interest on amounts borrowed to invest in the company. Let's say, for example, a director borrowed £100,000 and then loaned that sum to their own company. Provided the company was carrying on a qualifying business (trading or letting property to unconnected third parties will qualify), the director can claim the interest paid on their personal borrowing for Income Tax purposes (it can be set against any personal income, not just against interest income).

As long as the company continues to owe the director at least £100,000, they may claim full Income Tax relief for their personal interest cost. However, if the company repays part of the director's loan so the balance falls below £100,000, the director's qualifying loan interest claim must be restricted accordingly.

Having said that, losing some of the tax relief for the director's personal interest costs will almost certainly be a lot cheaper than the Income Tax suffered on additional dividends taken out of the company instead of a loan repayment.

Note that qualifying loan interest is subject to an annual cap, which is generally the greater of £50,000 or 25% of the director's total income for the year. That's usually enough for most people though.

Summary

Some company owners may be able to save over £1,000 by getting their companies to pay them interest.

The potential tax saving is smaller if there is no starting rate band available, for example if the taxpayer has a significant amount of salary or rental income.

While the savings will be a little less next year when Income Tax rates on interest income are increased, they will still be worthwhile.

There is additional tax paperwork to contend with, but this burden can be reduced by making a single, annual interest payment.

Finally, it's important to remember the interest you charge your company must be at no more than a commercial rate. However, in most cases, your loan to the company will be unsecured and for no fixed term. Hence, it will be more akin to an overdraft than a mortgage or personal loan, and the question of what constitutes a commercial rate can be judged in that context.

Chapter 40

Charitable Donations: You or the Company?

Who should donate to charity: you or your company?

In this chapter we'll focus on the tax benefits and drawbacks of both types of donation, although *non-tax* factors may be more important.

For example, charitable donations by your company could enhance its reputation and good standing in the community, which in turn could help its business.

Donations by Your Company

Charitable donations are a tax-deductible expense for CT purposes. So, if your company donates £1,000, its taxable profits will be reduced by £1,000, saving between £190 and £265 in CT.

The company can also enjoy tax relief when it gives money to community amateur sports clubs, a list of which can be obtained by entering 'community amateur sports clubs registered with HMRC' into a search engine like Google.

No gift aid declaration is necessary for company donations (see below for more on gift aid declarations).

Nevertheless, you should still obtain documentation from the charity to support the donation, just as you would for any other business expense.

Charitable donations cannot create or increase a trading loss for tax purposes. If the donation exceeds the company's taxable profit, the excess will not enjoy any CT relief and cannot be carried forward to the next year.

Donations do not enjoy automatic CT relief if there are strings attached, for example a condition that the charity will buy goods from the company (or anyone connected with the company). However, where the donation was clearly intended to benefit the company's business, the cost may still be allowable as a regular business expense, like advertising.

For more information on charitable donations by companies, as well as other tax-deductible donations, such as to community amateur sports clubs, or in aid of grassroots sports, see the Taxcafe guide *Putting it Through the Company*.

Donations by You Personally

If you make a charitable donation of, say, £80 the charity can claim £20 gift aid. Essentially what the charity is doing is reclaiming from HMRC the 20% basic rate tax you will typically have paid on £80 of after-tax income.

The charity will require you to make a gift aid declaration. This entails stating you have paid sufficient tax to cover the basic rate tax the charity reclaims.

It is important that you are actually liable for the tax the charity reclaims. The tax can be either Income Tax or CGT (but not NI).

For example, a company owner with a salary of £12,570 and dividend income of £20,000 will face an Income Tax bill of £2,096 in 2026/27.

If that company owner makes a £12,500 charitable donation, the gift aid rules require that the donor has paid tax of £2,500. The company owner will therefore have to make up the shortfall of £404.

Higher Rate Taxpayers

Higher rate taxpayers who make charitable donations can claim higher rate tax relief when they submit their tax returns.

Example: *Melinda, a company owner who takes most of her income as dividends, donates £80 to a charity. The gift aid on the donation is £20, resulting in a gross donation of £100.*

Melinda's basic rate band is extended by £100, which means she will pay 10.75% tax instead of 35.75% tax on an additional £100 of dividend income. This will save her £25 Income Tax.

In summary, Melinda has effectively made a £100 donation with a net cost to her of £55. The basic rate tax relief goes to the charity, the higher rate tax relief goes to the person making the donation.

Protecting Child Benefit & Personal Allowance

Your family's child benefit is gradually taken away when the highest earner in the household has adjusted net income of more than £60,000. All the child benefit will be withdrawn when that person's income exceeds £80,000.

Your personal allowance is also gradually taken away when your adjusted net income exceeds £100,000. All of your personal allowance is withdrawn when your income exceeds £125,140.

Like pension contributions, gift aid donations reduce your adjusted net income and can therefore be used to increase your personal allowance or protect your family's child benefit payments, in addition to enjoying higher rate tax relief.

Example: *Hassan is a company owner with salary and dividend income of £120,000. He donates £4,000 to his favourite charity. The gift aid on the donation is £1,000, resulting in a gross donation of £5,000. As a result, his adjusted net income is reduced by £5,000 from £120,000 to £115,000. This in turn increases his personal allowance by £2,500.*

If Hassan has taken a salary of £12,570 and the rest of his income as dividends, his £4,000 donation will save him £2,375 in Income Tax, meaning the net cost to him is only £1,625: that's more than £3 for the charity for every £1 it costs Hassan.

Carrying Back Donations to the Previous Tax Year

You can claim tax relief on donations a year early if you like. For example, you can claim tax relief for donations you have made during the current 2026/27 tax year when you submit your tax return for 2025/26.

Understandably, you can only claim tax relief for donations made between 6th April 2026 and the date you file your 2025/26 tax return, and the return must be filed on time (i.e. by 31st January 2027 if filed online).

This option to carry back donations is attractive if you want the tax relief sooner, or if you were a higher rate taxpayer during the previous tax year but you are not certain whether you will be a higher rate taxpayer this year.

When you come to submit your 2025/26 tax return, you will know for certain your taxable income for that year and thus how much tax relief you will obtain.

Similarly, carrying back donations may be attractive if your income in the previous 2025/26 tax year was in the £100,000 to £125,140 bracket (personal allowance withdrawal). You may enjoy extra tax relief on your charitable donations if you do not expect your income to fall into this tax bracket this year.

Only specific donations may be carried back and not an arbitrary sum: for example, if you made a single net donation of £800 (£1,000 gross), you can either carry it back or not, you cannot carry back, say, £400.

By contrast, if you had made four separate donations of £200 each (even if to the same charity) you could carry back any combination of those donations totalling £200, £400, £600, or £800, thus giving you far greater flexibility.

For this reason, regular, small donations will offer more opportunities to optimise your tax position. Alternatively, if you want to make a large donation, break it up. For example, let's say you want to donate £8,000. Instead of a single, large donation, you could make payments of £4,000, £2,000, £1,000, £500, and two of £250. You could then carry back any combination of these donations totalling between £250 and £8,000.

Company versus Personal Donations

Let's now compare the tax relief enjoyed by companies on charitable donations with the tax relief enjoyed by individuals.

Example: Basic Rate Taxpayer
Beric's company has £1,000 in its bank account, which he would like to give to charity. If the company makes the donation, it will enjoy CT relief, so the whole £1,000 can be paid directly to the charity with no further tax consequences.

If instead Beric decides to make the donation personally, the company will pay at least 19% CT, leaving £810 at most to pay out as additional dividend income.

Let's say Beric holds onto £10 and gives £800 to the charity. The taxman will add £200 of gift aid, leaving the charity with the same amount: £1,000. But that's not the end of the matter: Beric will still have to pay 10.75% tax on his £810 dividend: £87. Beric is worse off by £77 (£87 less the £10 of dividend income he held onto).

Thus, if you're a basic rate taxpayer, for every £1,000 that ends up with the charity you will have to pay at least 7.7% in additional tax, and it will be more if your company's CT rate is more than 19%.

In this case, a company donation is clearly more tax efficient than a donation made personally by the company owner.

Example: Higher Rate Taxpayer

This time we'll assume Beric is a higher rate taxpayer. If the company makes the donation, it can pay £1,000 directly to the charity. Alternatively, Beric can pay himself additional dividend income. However, since he is a higher rate taxpayer, his company may have a marginal CT rate of up to 26.5%, meaning his additional dividend could be as little as £735.

Beric may therefore have to add up to £65 out of his own pocket so he can give £800 to the charity. The taxman will add £200 of gift aid, resulting in the same donation of £1,000.

Again, that's not the end of the matter. Beric still has to pay Income Tax on the additional dividend. With a gross donation of £1,000, his basic rate band will be increased by £1,000. This means the £735 dividend will be taxed at just 10.75%, not 35.75%, so the tax will be £79. Furthermore, an additional £265 of his other dividend income will also be taxed at 10.75% instead of 35.75%, saving him an extra £66.

All in all, a £1,000 donation made by the company owner is up to £78 more expensive than a donation made by the company (£65 + £79 – £66). That extra cost could be as little as £30 in some cases (depending on the company's CT rate), but the company donation will always be better overall.

Example: Additional Rate Taxpayer

Sophie is a company owner with a salary of £12,570 and dividend income of £150,000. If she makes a net charitable donation of £4,000, this will reduce her Income Tax bill by £1,430, and the charity will receive a total of £5,000 under gift aid.

Alternatively, if Sophie's company makes a gross contribution of £5,000, it will enjoy CT relief on this sum, leaving between £3,675 and £4,050 less available to pay out as a dividend. After accounting for Income Tax at 39.35%, Sophie's after-tax income will reduce by between £2,229 and £2,456. But, since she is no longer paying £4,000 to the charity, she is somewhere between £1,544 and £1,771 better off overall.

It's pretty clear that additional rate taxpayers should get their company to make charitable donations wherever possible.

UK Charities Only

Note that only donations to UK-registered charities enjoy relief under gift aid, or automatic relief for CT purposes if paid by a company.

Chapter 41

Pension Contributions: Better than Dividends

Following increases in dividend tax rates and CT in recent years, some company owners may be thinking about paying themselves smaller dividends and getting their companies to make bigger pension contributions instead.

The CT increase means many companies will enjoy more tax relief on pension contributions they make for their directors and employees, whereas profits used to pay dividends will have been more heavily taxed.

There are several reasons why pension contributions are an attractive alternative to dividends:

- Like salaries, company pension contributions enjoy CT relief. In other words, they're a tax-deductible expense.
- Unlike salaries, there is no NI on the income you eventually withdraw from your pension.
- When you eventually withdraw money from your pension, up to 25% can be taken tax free.
- Pension income is taxed at the 'regular' Income Tax rates, typically 20% or 40%. By contrast, the combined tax rate on dividends (Income Tax and CT) is now at least 27.7% for basic rate taxpayers and between 48.0% and 52.8% for higher rate taxpayers.
- When you start withdrawing income from your pension, you could find yourself in a lower tax bracket than you are now (many retirees are basic rate taxpayers). This means you could end up paying Income Tax at just 20%.

Putting all this together, it's possible you could ultimately pay Income Tax on your pension withdrawals at an overall effective rate of just 15%.

By contrast, you may face a combined tax rate that is possibly two, three, or even more, times higher if the same money is paid out as dividend income.

There is, of course, a major drawback with pensions: your money is locked away until you are 55 (rising to 57 in 2028). Nevertheless, when you do reach the minimum retirement age, you can make unlimited withdrawals.

Another drawback with pensions is you are potentially exposed to any future increase in Income Tax rates. Essentially your savings are at the mercy of future governments.

Having said this, we do believe pension contributions are still worth making in many cases.

Example: Higher Rate Taxpayer

Lesleyanne is a company owner and a higher rate taxpayer (i.e. her taxable income is more than £50,270).

Let's say she is trying to choose between taking an additional £1,000 of the company's profit as a dividend and getting the company to invest £1,000 in her self-invested personal pension (SIPP).

Let's also say (as will often be the case) her company has a marginal CT rate of 26.5%. Hence, with a dividend the company will first pay CT of £265, leaving £735 to distribute. Lesleyanne will then pay Income Tax at 35.75%: £263. The total combined tax rate on the dividend is 52.8%.

By contrast, a company pension contribution will enjoy CT relief, so the whole £1,000 will go straight into Lesleyanne's SIPP. Ignoring investment growth (it doesn't affect the outcome), when she eventually withdraws the money from her pension, the first £250 will be tax free and the remaining £750 will be subject to Income Tax.

If Lesleyanne is a basic rate taxpayer when she retires in the future, she will pay 20% Income Tax (£150), leaving her with £850 overall. Thus, her effective overall tax rate will be 15%.

If Lesleyanne is a higher rate taxpayer when she retires (for example, if she ends up with a significant amount of rental income from buy-to-let properties) she will effectively pay 40% tax on her taxable pension income (£300), leaving her with £700 overall. Thus, the effective tax rate on her pension withdrawals will be 30%.

In summary, Lesleyanne's choice is between paying tax at 52.8% on her additional dividend income and paying tax at 15% or possibly 30% on her pension withdrawals.

What this example shows is that, for company owners who have not yet built up significant pension savings, a company pension contribution is an extremely attractive alternative to additional dividend income.

Of course, we must never lose sight of the fact your pension savings are placed in a locked box until you are at least 55 (soon to be 57).

So, a company pension contribution is only an attractive alternative to a dividend if you have already withdrawn enough money from your company to cover your living costs.

Example: Basic Rate Taxpayer
Poppy is a company owner and a basic rate taxpayer. She too is trying to choose between taking £1,000 of the company's profit as a dividend and a £1,000 company pension contribution. As she is a basic rate taxpayer, we will assume her company pays CT at 19%.

With a dividend the company will pay £190 CT, leaving £810 to distribute. Poppy will pay Income Tax at 10.75%: £87. The total combined tax rate on the dividend is 27.7%. (Note, if the company has profits over £50,000 the combined tax rate could be 34.4%.)

With a company pension contribution, the whole £1,000 will go straight into Poppy's SIPP. As with Lesleyanne, the effective tax rate on her pension withdrawals will be either 15% if she is a basic rate taxpayer when she retires or 30% if she is a higher rate taxpayer.

In summary, Poppy's choice is between paying tax at between 27.7% and 34.4% on her additional dividend income and paying tax at 15% or possibly 30% on her pension withdrawals.

A company pension contribution is a reasonably attractive alternative to dividend income. However, pension contributions may not be very attractive if Poppy is a higher rate taxpayer when she retires (for example, if she accumulates a significant amount of assets and the income takes her over the higher rate threshold before she starts withdrawing money from her pension).

Chapter 42

Pension Contributions: You or the Company?

In the previous chapter we showed that company pension contributions can be an attractive alternative to dividends. However, company directors can also make pension contributions *personally*, so a key question is: *"Who should make the contributions: the director or the company?"*

When you make pension contributions *personally* (as opposed to getting your company to make them) the taxman will top up your savings by paying cash directly into your pension. For every £80 you invest, the taxman will put in an extra £20.

Why £20? Your contributions are treated as having been paid out of income that has already been taxed at 20%, the basic rate of Income Tax.

The company that manages your pension plan, usually an insurance company or SIPP provider, will claim this money for you from the taxman and credit it to your account.

So, whatever contribution you make personally, divide it by 0.80 and you'll get the total amount that is invested in your pension pot (your gross pension contribution).

Example: *Peter is a company owner who takes most of his income as dividends. He invests £800 in a self-invested personal pension (SIPP). The taxman will top up his pension with £200 of basic rate tax relief, which means he'll have £1,000 in his pension pot: £800/0.80 = £1,000.*

If Peter is a higher rate taxpayer, he can also claim higher rate tax relief when he completes his tax return. This is given by increasing his basic rate band by the amount of his gross pension contribution.

Example continued: *Peter's gross pension contribution is £1,000 so his basic rate band will be increased by £1,000. This means £1,000 of his dividend income will be taxed at 10.75% instead of 35.75%, i.e. a 25% saving. Thus, Peter's higher rate tax relief is: £1,000 x 25% = £250.*

In total Peter will enjoy £450 of tax relief (£200 basic rate relief plus £250 higher rate tax relief). Peter's total tax relief is 45% of his £1,000 gross pension contribution and the overall cost of his £800 net contribution is just £550.

Directors with Small Salaries

To obtain tax relief on your pension contributions they have to stay within certain limits:

- **Earnings:** Contributions made by you *personally* must generally not exceed your 'relevant UK earnings'. Earnings include your salary, bonus and taxable benefits in kind but do NOT include your dividends.

- **The Annual Allowance:** Total pension contributions by you and your company must not exceed £60,000 per year, although it is possible to carry forward any unused annual allowance from the three previous tax years. The annual allowance may be reduced if your 'adjusted income' exceeds £260,000 (see Chapter 27).

For a company director taking a salary of £12,570 (see Chapter 12), the maximum personal pension contribution that can be made with tax relief is therefore £12,570.

This is the maximum *gross* contribution. The director would personally invest £10,056 (£12,570 x 80%) and the taxman will top this up with £2,514 of basic rate tax relief for a total gross contribution of £12,570.

Directors who want to make bigger pension contributions personally have to pay themselves bigger salaries. However, this may not be an attractive option because a bigger salary may be subject to employer's NI at 15%, employee's NI at 8%, or both.

Company Pension Contributions

As a company owner, you can also get your company (your employer) to make pension contributions on your behalf. Company pension contributions are always paid *gross* (there is no top up from the taxman), but the company will normally enjoy CT relief on the payment. For example, a company with a marginal CT rate of 26.5% can make a pension contribution of £10,000 and enjoy £2,650 of tax relief.

You do not need a dedicated company pension scheme to make company pension contributions. Most firms that offer SIPPs allow your company to pay directly into your pension (these plans may not be qualifying schemes for auto-enrolment purposes).

In the November 2025 Budget, it was announced that, from 6th April 2029, employer's NI will apply to employer pension contributions in excess of £2,000 under salary sacrifice schemes. Fortunately, this is unlikely to affect many small company owners, and rumours that employer's NI would apply more widely to company pension contributions have thankfully proved unfounded.

Hence, company pension contributions made on behalf of director/shareholders continue to be exempt from both employer's and employee's NI.

How much can your company contribute? Unlike the contributions you make personally, the company's contributions are NOT restricted by the size of your salary. In other words, the company can make a pension contribution that is bigger than your salary. However, there are other restrictions:

- Total pension contributions by you and your company must not exceed the annual allowance (typically £60,000) although you can carry forward unused allowance from the previous three tax years.

- The company may be denied CT relief on any pension contributions made on behalf of directors, if the taxman views them as 'excessive'.

Corporation Tax Relief on Pension Contributions

Unlike the pension contributions that you make personally, tax relief for company pension contributions is not automatic. Company contributions will only be a tax-deductible expense for CT purposes if they are incurred wholly and exclusively for the purposes of the business. There is a danger HMRC could deny CT relief for 'excessive' pension contributions although, in practice, this is relatively rare.

When determining whether company pension contributions qualify for CT relief, HMRC will look at the director's total remuneration package. The total package (including salary, pension contributions, and other benefits in kind) must not be excessive relative to the work the individual carries out and his or her responsibilities.

Relevant factors may include:

- The number of hours you work, your experience, and your level of responsibility in the company.
- The pay of unconnected employees who perform duties of similar value in your company, or in other companies.
- The pay required to recruit someone to take over your duties.
- The company's financial performance.

Extra care may be necessary in the event of a large one-off company pension contribution.

It may be sensible to document the commercial justification (for example, strong recent financial performance of the company) in the minutes of a directors' board meeting and hold a shareholders' meeting to approve the contribution.

In some cases, when a company is making pension contributions on behalf of all employees, including directors, of more than £500,000 in total, it may be necessary to spread tax relief for the excess over a number of years. These spreading rules will obviously not affect most small companies.

Although the risk that your company will be denied CT relief may be small, it is important to stress that, when it comes to company pension contributions, unlike contributions made by individuals, there is no cast-iron guarantee the company will enjoy tax relief. That's why we would recommend speaking to a tax adviser before your company starts making significant contributions.

Pension Contributions: You or the Company?

Using some case studies, we will now compare company pension contributions with pension contributions made personally by company owners to see which is most tax efficient.

Case Study 1: Basic Rate Taxpayer

Eva owns Cassidy Ltd. She is a basic rate taxpayer and pays herself a salary of £12,570 this year (2026/27). She takes the rest of her income as dividends. She also decides to use £1,000 of the company's pre-tax profit to fund a pension contribution. If Cassidy Ltd makes the contribution it can pay £1,000 directly into Eva's SIPP and the amount will be a tax-deductible expense.

Alternatively, Eva can pay herself a dividend to fund a pension contribution she makes personally. We'll assume the company pays 19% CT on the £1,000 profit, leaving Eva with £810 to take as dividend income.

Eva holds onto £10 and invests £800 in her SIPP. The taxman will add £200 of basic rate tax relief, leaving her with the same amount in her pension: £1,000.

But that's not the end of the matter: Eva will still have to pay 10.75% tax on her £810 dividend, £87.

Eva is worse off by £77: £87 less the £10 of dividend income she held onto. And she would be even worse off if her company pays CT at more than 19%.

Thus, if you're a basic rate taxpayer, for every £1,000 that ends up in your pension, you will have to pay at least 7.7% in additional tax. In this case, a company pension contribution is clearly more tax efficient than a contribution made personally by the director.

Other Important Points

If Eva wants more than £12,570 invested in her pension, making the contribution personally will be even more expensive. She would have to pay herself a bigger salary and this could result in a significant amount of NI becoming payable. This is because, to enjoy tax relief, any pension contribution you make personally cannot exceed your earnings (i.e. salary). The additional salary would typically attract 8% employee's NI plus 15% employer's NI, unless the company has spare employment allowance.

Case Study 2: Higher Rate Taxpayer

This time we'll assume Eva is a *higher rate taxpayer* and again wants to make a £1,000 pension contribution.

If Cassidy Ltd makes the contribution, it can pay £1,000 directly into Eva's SIPP. Alternatively, Eva can pay herself an extra dividend. We'll assume the company pays 26.5% CT on the £1,000 profit, leaving Eva with £735 to take as dividend income.

Thus, Eva may have to contribute up to £65 out of her own pocket to invest £800 in her SIPP. The taxman will add £200 of basic rate tax relief, resulting in the same gross pension contribution of £1,000.

Again, that's not the end of the matter. Eva still has to pay Income Tax on the additional dividend.

With a gross pension contribution of £1,000, Eva's basic rate band will be increased by £1,000. This means the extra dividend of £735 will be taxed at just 10.75%, not 35.75%, so the tax is £79.

Furthermore, an additional £265 of her other dividend income will also be taxed at 10.75% instead of 35.75%, saving her a further £66.

All in all, a £1,000 pension contribution made by the director is £78 more expensive than a contribution made by the company: £79 Income Tax + £65 (cash added) – £66 extra relief = £78.

A company pension contribution is again more tax efficient than a contribution made personally by the director, producing an overall saving of 7.8%. If the company has a lower marginal CT rate, the saving will be smaller: e.g. just 3.0% if the company has a marginal CT rate of 19% (i.e. profits less than £50,000).

Other Important Points

If Eva wants to enjoy full higher rate tax relief on a gross pension contribution of £12,570 (i.e. equal to her salary), she must have at least £12,570 of dividend income above the higher rate threshold (total income of at least £62,840 in 2026/27). If Eva wants to make a pension contribution bigger than £12,570 personally, she will have to take a bigger salary and this may result in a significant amount of NI becoming payable.

Case Study 3: Personal Allowance Withdrawal

Katie owns Melua Ltd, which has a marginal CT rate of 26.5%. She takes a salary of £12,570 plus dividends of £107,430 to give her total income of £120,000.

Katie wants to make a £12,570 pension contribution. If Melua Ltd makes the contribution, it can pay £12,570 directly into Katie's SIPP. Alternatively, Katie can pay herself an extra dividend. However, with a marginal CT rate of 26.5%, that £12,570 will only fund a dividend of £9,239.

Katie will have to contribute £817 out of her own pocket to invest £10,056 in her SIPP. The taxman will add £2,514 of basic rate tax relief, resulting in the same gross pension contribution of £12,570.

As usual, that's not the end of the matter. Katie will pay 58.25% Income Tax on the £9,239 dividend: £5,382 (see Chapter 23 which explains why the effective tax rate is 58.25%).

However, Katie's pension contribution will increase her basic rate band by £12,570, meaning £12,570 more of her dividends are taxed at 10.75% instead of 35.75%, producing a saving of £3,143 (£12,570 x 25%). It also means she regains £6,285 of her personal allowance, saving a further £2,828 (£6,285 of her salary becomes tax free instead of taxed at 20% and £6,285 more dividend is taxed at 10.75% instead of 35.75%). Total tax relief: £5,971.

All in all, Katie's Income Tax bill is reduced by £589 if she makes the contribution personally. However, she had to pay £817 from her own pocket to top up her pension contribution so, in the end, the company contribution would leave her £228 better off overall.

If the company was paying CT at 25%, Katie would end up £149 better off overall. If it was paying CT at just 19%, a pension contribution made personally would become more attractive than a company contribution, saving Katie £166 overall. However, it is highly unlikely that someone with this much income would own a company paying CT at just 19%.

All in all, the position is pretty marginal, with a difference of no more than 1.8% of the gross pension contribution at most. Thus, in this scenario, it doesn't matter much whether pension contributions are made by the company or the director personally.

However, the most important point to make is that, if Katie wanted to put more than £12,570 into her pension, she would have to increase her salary (and possibly reduce her dividend income). Employer's NI at 15% may be payable on any additional salary she pays herself, and employee's NI at 8% will also be payable. These additional tax costs can be avoided by getting her company to make the contribution.

Case Study 4: Additional Rate Taxpayer

Let's take the same facts as Case Study 3 above, except that Katie takes dividends of £135,000 out of her company, giving her total income of £147,570 and making her an additional rate taxpayer.

A further dividend of £9,239 (as before) would now lead to additional Income Tax of £3,636 (£9,239 x 39.35%). However, Katie's gross pension contribution of £12,570 would mean £12,570 more dividends were taxed at 10.75% instead of 39.35%. The saving, at an effective rate of 28.6%, would be £3,595.

Overall, Katie's Income Tax bill is increased by £41. Additionally, as before, she will have had to pay £817 from her own pocket to top up her pension contribution so, in the end, the *company* contribution would leave her £858 better off.

This saving reduces if the company has a lower marginal CT rate. Nonetheless, the conclusion here is that additional rate taxpayers will be better off getting their company to make pension contributions on their behalf.

And, in any case, the important point, once again, is that, if Katie wants to put more than £12,570 into her pension and makes the contribution *personally*, she would have to increase her salary and this may result in a significant amount of NI becoming payable.

Lifetime ISAs

Under the current rules, those aged 18 to 39 can open a Lifetime ISA, which can be used to save for a first home or for retirement.

Up to £4,000 per year can be invested and receives a 25% Government bonus. So, if you put in £4,000, the Government will add £1,000. This is the same as the basic rate tax relief enjoyed on pension contributions.

It is possible to continue making contributions up to age 50. This means you can invest a total of up to £128,000 between age 18 and 50, with a Government bonus of up to £32,000.

Unlike a pension, your savings are not locked up inside a Lifetime ISA. However, if you withdraw money before reaching age 60, for any reason other than to buy your first home, there will be a 25% early withdrawal charge. This will claw back all the Government bonus, plus an additional 6.25% of the amount you invested.

Lifetime ISA versus Company Pension Contribution

The Lifetime ISA is an attractive alternative to saving in a pension if you are a basic rate taxpayer. Like pensions, they attract a top up from the Government but, unlike pensions, ALL the money you take out will be tax free.

Let's say a company owner who is a basic rate taxpayer is trying to decide between a £1,000 company pension contribution and using a dividend to fund a Lifetime ISA contribution.

A £1,000 pension contribution will attract CT relief so the whole £1,000 will go directly into the company owner's pension.

If the same money is used to pay a dividend to fund a Lifetime ISA contribution, and assuming the company pays 19% CT, £810 will be left to pay out. After paying 10.75% Income Tax, the company owner will be left with £723 to invest in a Lifetime ISA. Adding the Government bonus, the company owner will end up with £904 in the Lifetime ISA.

When the company owner reaches age 60, all withdrawals from the Lifetime ISA will be tax free, whereas only 25% of the money withdrawn from the pension will be tax free (although they can get it slightly earlier). The rest will possibly be taxed at just 20% if they are a basic rate taxpayer.

If we ignore investment growth to keep the example simple (it doesn't affect the outcome), with a Lifetime ISA the company owner will end up with £904; with a pension they will end up with just £850 after tax.

Thus, if you're a basic rate taxpayer, your retirement income could be up to 6.4% higher with a Lifetime ISA

If you're a higher rate taxpayer when you retire, you might enjoy up to 29% more income with a Lifetime ISA!

On the other hand, if your company is paying CT at more than 19%, the advantage of a Lifetime ISA will be reduced, or could even be eliminated.

For example, at the highest marginal CT rate of 26.5%, £1,000 of pre-tax profit will only fund a dividend of £735. After Income Tax at 10.75%, a basic rate taxpayer will be left with £656. If they put that in a Lifetime ISA, the Government will add £164 for a total investment of £820. In the end, if they're a basic rate taxpayer when they retire, a company pension contribution could have left them with £850, i.e. £30 more.

The difference is fairly marginal, however, and it's important to remember, if you're a higher rate taxpayer when you draw your pension, you might end up with only £700 after tax.

So, basic rate taxpayers who own a company making profits between £50,000 and £250,000 face a choice between a certain £820, or a possible £850 that might, in fact, only be £700.

We think you'd need to be pretty certain you were going to be a basic rate taxpayer in retirement before you went for the pension contribution, but it's up to you!

Higher Rate Taxpayers

What about higher rate taxpayers? Once again, a £1,000 pension contribution will attract CT relief, so the whole £1,000 will go directly into the company owner's pension.

If the same money is used to pay a dividend to fund a Lifetime ISA contribution, the amount received by the director will vary depending on the company's marginal CT rate. If we assume it's 26.5%, the amount left to pay a dividend will be £735. After paying 35.75% Income Tax, the company owner will be left with £472 to invest in their Lifetime ISA. Adding the Government bonus, the company owner will end up with £590 in their Lifetime ISA.

When the company owner reaches age 60, all withdrawals from the Lifetime ISA will be tax free, whereas only 25% of the money withdrawn from the pension will be tax free. The rest could be taxed at just 20% if they are a basic rate taxpayer at that point.

Ignoring investment growth again, with a Lifetime ISA the company owner will end up with £590, with a pension they will end up with £850 after tax.

Thus, your retirement income could be up to 44% higher with a pension.

If the company owner is a higher rate taxpayer when they retire (e.g. if they have a lot of income from other sources, such as rental property) they will end up with £700 from a pension, compared with £590 from a Lifetime ISA. So, again, a company pension contribution will generally be better.

Finally, it's also important to remember you can only invest £4,000 per year in a Lifetime ISA (with an additional £1,000 bonus from the Government), compared with the maximum gross pension contribution of £60,000 per year. Furthermore, you can only open a Lifetime ISA if you're under 40, and it's only possible to make contributions up to age 50.

Changes Ahead

Under current Government proposals, it will not be possible to open a new Lifetime ISA after 5th April 2028, as Lifetime ISAs are to be replaced with a new 'First-Time Buyer ISA', which cannot be used to save for retirement, but only to buy your first home.

However, it will remain possible to continue contributing to a Lifetime ISA opened before 6th April 2028 until you reach age 50. If you are currently under 40, it may therefore be worth opening a Lifetime ISA now (even just £1 will do), so you will have the opportunity to invest in the future.

Summary

Company pension contributions are generally more tax efficient than contributions made personally by directors. There are a few rare exceptions and some other cases where the position is fairly marginal. Frankly though, if you go on the basis that company pension contributions are always best, you will usually be right and, even if you're not, you won't lose out by much.

Furthermore, making large pension contributions personally may mean taking a bigger salary, often leading to significant NI costs.

Tax relief for company pension contributions is not automatic, however, and could be denied if the contributions are viewed as excessive, although this is rare in practice.

A Lifetime ISA may be an attractive alternative to a company pension contribution for basic rate taxpayers. Company pension contributions generally remain better for higher rate taxpayers, however.

Opening a Lifetime ISA now (if you're eligible) will mean you have the opportunity to contribute to it until you reach age 50.

Chapter 43

Putting Property into a Pension

In Chapter 38, we explained that company owners who own their business premises personally can get the company to pay them rent and this may be an attractive alternative to dividends.

Some company owners also use a specialist SIPP or other pension plan to hold their business premises and, in this chapter, we'll take a look at the benefits and drawbacks of this alternative. Note that, while you can put *commercial property* into a pension, you cannot do this with residential property.

Holding business property in a pension has some key benefits:

- **Tax-free rent**. There is no Income Tax payable by you on the rent your business pays to your pension. These rent payments will be a tax-deductible expense for the business.

- **No Capital Gains Tax**. When a property held inside a pension is sold, there is no CGT payable.

Although the ability to roll up rental income tax free inside a pension is enticing, you must never lose sight of the fact that all the money you eventually withdraw from your pension over and above your tax-free lump sum will be subject to Income Tax, typically at 20% or 40%.

If you are a higher-rate taxpayer at present but expect to be a basic-rate taxpayer when you retire, it's possible the rental income will ultimately be less heavily taxed by going the pension route.

Similarly, although property held in a pension can be sold without incurring CGT, when you eventually withdraw the capital gain most of it (at least 75%) will be subject to Income Tax, again typically at 20% or 40%.

Alternatively, if you sell commercial property that you own personally you will be subject to CGT at 24%, although it's possible some of the gain will be taxed at just 18%.

In some cases, a sale of business premises that you own personally will qualify for business asset disposal relief. If so, a tax rate of 18% now applies. The relief is restricted if your company has paid you rent at any time since 6th April 2008.

Business premises held inside your pension do not have to be sold when you retire. If your own business ceases to occupy the property, it can remain in your pension and be rented out to someone else and the rent will roll up tax free in your pension.

When comparing pension ownership with personal ownership, it's important to remember that you cannot withdraw any money from your pension until you are at least 55 (rising to 57 in 2028).

There are benefits and drawbacks to holding business property inside a pension. Each case would have to be decided on its merits with help from a professional.

Inheritance Tax

From 6th April 2027, pensions will become subject to Inheritance Tax (IHT). The value of any business premises (or other commercial property) held inside a pension will be fully subject to IHT and will not be eligible for business property relief.

By contrast, if you hold your company's business premises personally, it generally qualifies for 50% relief from IHT under business property relief (providing it is used in a qualifying trading business).

There are also serious concerns surrounding payment of IHT. If your pension holds a highly illiquid asset such as a commercial property, a significant challenge could be faced raising the cash to settle any IHT bill. Unlike property held personally, there will not be an option to pay the tax in ten yearly instalments.

For further details of both business property relief and the instalment option available in respect of property held personally, see the Taxcafe guide *How to Save Inheritance Tax*.

Funding the Property Purchase

The purchase of a business property by a pension can be funded in several ways. Typically, you will use your existing pension savings, topped up with fresh contributions (including company pension contributions if you run a company).

It is also possible for your pension fund to borrow money: but only up to 50% of its net assets. For example, if you have pension savings of £100,000, an additional £50,000 can be borrowed.

Some pension providers allow a part share in a property to be acquired by the pension plan, with the balance owned outside the pension. Alternatively, several individuals could pool their pension savings to collectively buy a property.

Transferring Existing Property

If you already own the property, you may be able to sell it to your SIPP and release a sizeable amount of cash from your pension savings.

Transferring an existing property into a pension is likely to result in CGT becoming payable (typically at 24%) if the property has risen in value since you bought it. It is unlikely business asset disposal relief would be available in such cases.

A sizeable CGT bill may put off many existing property owners going down the pension route, but others may still be tempted by the prospect of receiving a large cash payment out of their pension savings.

The transfer may also result in a Stamp Duty Land tax bill, and VAT may also be payable in certain circumstances, although it may be possible to claim a VAT refund.

In Specie Contributions

Properties have in the past been transferred into pensions as *in specie* pension contributions, with the member claiming Income Tax relief. However, in specie contributions are no longer permitted following a clamp down by HMRC due to perceived abuse.

Costs and other Formalities

Not all pension providers deal with property purchases, so you may need to transfer your existing pension savings to a specialist provider.

When your property is held inside a pension, your business will have to be treated just like any other tenant, with no special favours, which means rent will have to be paid at a full market rate come hell or high water.

If rent is not paid this will be treated as an unauthorised payment by your pension and HMRC may levy a charge of 40% on you personally and a charge of up to 40% on the pension itself.

Property SIPPs are also much more expensive to run than those that only allow you to invest in traditional 'stocks and shares'. Initial set up costs include legal fees, surveyor fees, lenders fees and fees to the pension company managing your SIPP. Fees will have to be paid for regular rent revaluations, and a third party property manager may have to be appointed to collect the rent from you.

Chapter 44

Selling Your Business

One of the most tax-efficient ways to grow your wealth is to build up a successful company and then sell it. This allows you to convert heavily taxed income into a less heavily taxed capital gain.

Many company owners who receive dividends have a marginal Income Tax rate of 35.75%. Those with income over £125,140 have a marginal rate of 39.35%, and those with income between £100,000 and £125,140 often face a marginal tax rate of 58.25%.

But when you sell a company and receive a cash lump sum, which replaces all of this heavily taxed income, you could end up paying CGT at a reduced rate of 18%, thanks to business asset disposal relief.

The 18% rate is, of course, the same rate as applies to gains falling within your basic rate band, when this is not all used up by income. However, business asset disposal relief applies this rate to gains of up to £1 million, whereas the basic rate band is only £37,700 and is not always available.

The lifetime limit for business asset disposal relief used to be £10 million of capital gains per person, but in 2020 this was slashed to just £1 million. Nonetheless, because it applies on a per person basis, couples can enjoy up to £2 million of capital gains taxed at a reduced rate.

Business asset disposal relief is, however, no longer very attractive to serial entrepreneurs, who build up and sell many businesses during their careers. Many will have already exhausted their £1 million allowance.

If you are denied the relief, all is not lost. You could end up paying 24% CGT – still a lot more attractive than the top tax rates for dividends.

Qualifying for Business Asset Disposal Relief

Company owners are entitled to business asset disposal relief when they sell their shares or wind up the company. To qualify:

- The company must be your 'personal company' which, generally speaking, means you must own at least 5% of it (but matters can get more complicated: see below)
- You must be an officer or employee of the company
- The company must be a trading company

Each of these rules must be satisfied for at least ***two years*** before the company is sold or wound up.

Where the company has ceased trading, each of the rules must be satisfied for at least two years before it ceases trading. The disposal of the company must then take place within three years after trading has stopped.

Selling a Recently Incorporated Business

If you have only recently transferred an unincorporated business (a sole trade or partnership) into your company wholly or partly in exchange for shares, you don't have to own the shares of the newly formed company for two years. The period you owned the unincorporated business is added to the period you own the company shares in this situation.

Transferring Shares to Your Spouse/Partner Etc

You do, however, have to be wary of transferring shares to your spouse within the two years before selling the company. Transfers to spouses are exempt from CGT and your spouse can then claim business asset disposal relief when the business is sold, but they personally must satisfy the necessary conditions outlined above in their own right. This generally means the transfer must have taken place at least two years before selling the company for the spouse to qualify for business asset disposal relief.

Spouse transfers weren't always necessary when the lifetime limit for the relief was £10 million, but are probably more important now it is just £1 million. As we saw in Chapter 35, many company owners also transfer shares to their spouse to reduce the Income Tax payable on dividends.

Similar principles apply to transfers to an unmarried partner or other adult family member; although a holdover relief claim will be necessary (see Chapter 35).

What is a Personal Company?

As stated above to qualify for business asset disposal relief the company must be your personal company. This means you must own at least 5% of the ordinary share capital and have at least 5% of the voting rights.

HMRC was concerned that ordinary shares encompass a very broad range of share arrangements, including those where the shareholders have restricted rights to dividends and company assets. As a result, you must now also meet at least one of the following two conditions:

- You must be entitled to at least 5% of the profits available for distribution and at least 5% of the assets available for distribution if the company is wound up, or
- In the event of a disposal of all the ordinary share capital of the company, you would be entitled to at least 5% of the disposal proceeds

Initially the Government introduced just one additional condition (the first bullet point above). However, several expert tax commentators pointed out this would have prevented owners of alphabet shares (common in many small family companies) from claiming the relief.

For example, where a company has A and B shares and a different rate of dividend can be declared on each type, it could be argued that neither type of shareholder is entitled to at least 5% of the profits available for distribution: because there is no dividend entitlement until the dividends are declared.

As a result, the second condition was tagged on. This allows the company owner to instead enjoy business asset disposal relief if they are entitled to at least 5% of the proceeds when the company is sold.

What is an Officer?

Company officers include non-executive directors and company secretaries, so you don't have to work full-time at the company to qualify for business asset disposal relief.

What is a Trading Company?

To qualify for business asset disposal relief, the company must be a trading company. HMRC regards the following as non-trading activities:

- Holding investment property, including property for letting
- Holding shares or securities
- Holding surplus cash

If there is substantial non-trading activity, you could be denied business asset disposal relief. HMRC generally regards non-trading activities to be substantial where either non-trading income or non-trading assets exceed 20% of the totals for the company as a whole. However, this test is only a rule of thumb and does not have any statutory basis. It must be remembered that, in cases of dispute, it is for the courts to decide the matter, not HMRC. For further analysis of this issue and the current legal position established in court, see Chapter 1.

Nonetheless, it remains the fact that if just 20% of the assets or income of the company are not trading assets or income, you may be denied business asset disposal relief when you sell your shares.

In this context, it is worth pointing out that business goodwill is a trading asset and should be taken into account, even if its value is not reflected on the company's balance sheet.

If your company doesn't own investment property or invest in other companies, the most serious danger is holding too much cash. In the early days of what was then called entrepreneurs' relief, many people were concerned that excessive amounts of cash could result in the company losing its trading status, and hence the relief (now called business asset disposal relief) could be taken away.

However, more recent case law has placed far less emphasis on surplus holdings of cash than HMRC seemed to think was appropriate. After all, the legislation only talks about substantial non-trading ***activity:*** and there is not much activity involved in simply holding cash!

Remember, case law now tells us non-trading activities will only be regarded as substantial if they are of material or real importance in the context of the company's activities as a whole (see Chapter 1).

So, if, for example, a company has a trading business, whose total net assets are worth £700,000, plus surplus cash of £300,000, which is simply being held in a bank account and not actively invested then, while that cash amounts to 30% of the company's assets, it is clearly not a substantial activity and the company remains a trading company.

Nevertheless, while the 20% used as a benchmark by HMRC has no legal substance, and were it to relate purely to a holding of cash, they would be laughed out of court, there *would* still come a point when the cash held by a company came to be so significant that it threatened the company's trading status.

So, this brings us to the question of when is cash surplus? Let's say a company has £500,000 in its bank account. That's a lot of cash. But if that company buys £1 million of trading stock every month, the cash is only covering two weeks' supplies. It is therefore simply working capital, it is not surplus cash, and is part of the assets of the trade.

But larger holdings of cash proportionate to the size of the company's trading activities will eventually become surplus to the requirements of the company's business.

Eventually, a large enough cash holding will begin to pose a risk. However, even such large holdings should not be a problem if you can prove the cash was required for business purposes, for example as part of a well-documented expansion plan.

Like many aspects of tax law, this issue is something of a grey area and, in cases of doubt, professional advice is recommended. (And, despite all we have said, any holding that represents more than 20% of the company's assets will always cast a degree of doubt.)

If the company really does have a substantial amount of surplus cash that cannot be justified for business reasons, it may be necessary to extract it at least two years in advance to prevent the company's trading status being challenged on a sale of the company's shares.

You then have to weigh up the potential costs and benefits: the benefit being a CGT rate of 18% instead of 24% on a gain of up to £1 million (per person); the cost being the Income Tax on any additional dividends.

Associated Disposals of Business Premises

Many business owners purchase business premises *personally* and rent them to their company. The good news is business asset disposal relief is available when 'associated' assets like these are sold. The bad news is many company owners will not qualify!

The asset will only qualify for business asset disposal relief if you also make a 'material disposal' of shares in your company. The stake being disposed of must generally be at least 5%.

It is possible to claim business asset disposal relief on an associated disposal even if the stake in the business is sold or gifted to a family member, for example an adult child.

However, there must also be no 'share purchase arrangements' in place at the time of disposal. This rule is designed to prevent you from taking back your stake in the business after the property has been sold and business asset disposal relief has been claimed.

To qualify for business asset disposal relief the 'associated' asset must have been in use in the business for at least two years. The asset must also have been held for at least three years to qualify.

The relief is also restricted if you've received any payment for the use of the property since 5th April 2008 (e.g. if your company has paid you rent).

Where the property was acquired after 5th April 2008 and a full market rent was received throughout the period of its use in the company's trade, no business asset disposal relief is available. Where the property was acquired at an earlier date, or rent was charged at a lower rate, there will be a partial restriction in relief.

As we saw in Chapter 38, getting your company to pay you rent is an attractive alternative to dividends, especially when the company owner (who owns the property) has expenses such as mortgage interest that can be deducted for tax purposes.

Another advantage of charging your company rent is so that capital allowances can be claimed on the qualifying fixtures in the property. If a market rent is not charged, the property owner will not be treated as having a proper 'property business', which is necessary for them to make a full capital allowances claim (although a partial claim is possible where a lower level of rent is charged).

For properties built after October 2018, or that have undergone conversions or improvements since then, the owner may also be able to claim the structures and buildings allowance (see the Taxcafe guide *How to Save Property Tax* for details). This claim may be denied altogether if the owner charges less than a full market rent.

In summary, company owners who own their business premises personally have to weigh the benefits of business asset disposal relief against the benefits of paying themselves rental income. The reduction in the relief's lifetime limit from £10 million to £1 million has made paying rent considerably more attractive.

Winding Up Your Company

It is not always possible to sell your company shares to a third party. Buyers are often fearful of acquiring companies outright for fear of taking on any unknown liabilities. Instead, they often prefer to buy the assets (e.g. premises, goodwill, stock, and customer lists).

The disadvantage of an asset sale such as this is the double tax charge: the company will pay CT on the sale, and you will pay Income Tax or CGT when you extract the after-tax proceeds.

Providing you meet the qualifying criteria though, business asset disposal relief is still available if you wind up your company following an asset sale and extract the cash as a capital distribution.

There are generally two ways to wind up a company:

- Dissolution under the Companies Act
- Voluntary liquidation under the Insolvency Act

With a *dissolution* CGT treatment is only possible if the total distributions are no more than £25,000. Where the total distributions exceed £25,000, they are taxed as dividends, possibly at 35.75% or 39.35%.

A *voluntary liquidation* ensures payments to shareholders are treated as capital distributions for CGT purposes. However, voluntary liquidation requires the appointment of a licensed insolvency practitioner with fees running to many thousands of pounds in some cases (the fees may be less if the company's affairs are simple and its main asset is cash).

To qualify for business asset disposal relief, the capital distribution must be made within three years of the cessation of trading.

The following criteria must be met for the two years before cessation of trading:

- The company must be your 'personal company' (see above)
- You must be an officer or employee of the company
- The company must be a 'trading' company (see above)

As discussed above, in some cases a large surplus cash balance (a non-trading asset) already held in the company before the sale, or cessation, of the business, may throw into doubt the ability to claim business asset disposal relief.

It goes without saying that in all cases where a winding up of the company is to be carried out, professional advice should be obtained to ensure the desired tax treatment of the distributions.

The Anti-Phoenixing Rule

The anti-phoenixing rule means a distribution made when winding up a company will sometimes be taxed as a dividend. This is to prevent company owners continually winding up companies and starting new ones to enjoy the lower CGT rates.

The rule applies where ***all*** of the following conditions are met:

- **Condition A & B:** The individual holds at least 5% of the ordinary share capital and voting rights immediately before the winding up and the company is a close company at some point in the two years before the winding up

- **Condition C:** Within two years after the distribution, the company owner carries on the same or a similar trade or activity to the company being wound up

- **Condition D:** It is reasonable to assume the main purpose or one of the main purposes of the winding up is to avoid Income Tax

With regards to Condition C, it makes no difference whether you operate as a sole trader, through a partnership, a new company in which you have at least a 5% interest, or a connected person (e.g. your spouse or another close relative).

The test is clearly very subjective and it is feared it could catch many innocent situations, for example where a company owner retires, winds up their company, and a year later decides to take on a few clients or do some work for a family member involved in the same trade.

It is also feared Condition D could be applied broadly. For example, HMRC could argue that if a company owner decides not to pay surplus funds out as dividends prior to the winding up, there is as an 'arrangement' to reduce Income Tax.

HMRC has provided the following examples, which are intended to allay these fears and explain when the rules apply:

Example 1: *Mr A has been the sole shareholder of a company which carries on the trade of landscape gardening for 10 years. Mr A decides to wind up the business and retire. Because he no longer needs a company, he liquidates the company and receives a distribution in a winding up. To subsidise his pension, Mr A continues to do a small amount of gardening in his local village.*

Conditions A to C are met, because gardening is a similar trade or activity to landscape gardening. However, when viewed as a whole, these arrangements do not appear to have tax as a main purpose. It is natural for Mr A to have wound up his company because it is no longer needed once the trade has ceased.

Although Mr A continues to do some gardening, there is no reason why he would need a company for this, and it does not seem that he set the company up, wound it up, and then continued a trade, all with a view to receive the profits as capital rather than income.

In these circumstances, Mr A's distribution in the winding up will continue to be treated as capital.

Example 2: *Mrs B is an IT contractor. Whenever she receives a new contract, she sets up a limited company to carry out that contract. When the work is completed and the client has paid, Mrs B winds up the company and receives the profits as capital.*

Again, conditions A to C are met because Mrs B has a new company which carries on the same or a similar trade to the previously wound up company. Here, though, it looks like there is a main purpose of obtaining a tax advantage. All the contracts could have been operated through the same company, and apart from the tax savings, it would seem that would have been the most sensible option for Mrs B.

Where the distribution from the winding up is made in these circumstances, the distribution will be treated as a dividend subject to Income Tax.

Example 3: *Mrs C is an accountant who has operated through a limited company for three years. She now feels the risk involved in running her own business is not worth the effort, and so decides to accept a job at her brother's accountancy firm as an employee. Her brother's firm has been operating for eight years. Mrs C winds up her company and begins life as an employee.*

Conditions A to C are met because Mrs C is continuing a similar activity to the trade that was carried on by the company. She is continuing it as an employee of a connected party, triggering Condition C.

But looking at the arrangements as a whole, it is not reasonable to assume they have tax advantage as a main purpose, so Condition D will not be met. Mrs C's company was incorporated and wound up for commercial, not tax, reasons; although she works for a connected party, it is clear that other business was not set up to facilitate a tax advantage because it has been operating for some time.

In these circumstances, the distribution from the winding up will continue to be treated as capital, absent any other considerations.

Transaction in Securities

HMRC can also use the so-called 'transaction in securities' rules to attack distributions when a company is wound up if it thinks the main reason for the liquidation is to save Income Tax.

The transaction in securities rules are contained in vague legislation that can be used to convert capital gains into income subject to the dividend tax rates if HMRC takes the view that income has been incorrectly extracted as a capital gain.

This introduces a second obstacle for business owners who wish to liquidate their companies. Hence, given the wide-ranging nature of the transaction in securities legislation, most tax advisers recommend obtaining pre-transaction clearance from HMRC. While the liquidation of a long-standing company after it has ceased trading, or sold its business assets to a third party, will seldom be challenged, it is better to be safe than sorry.

The transaction in securities rules cannot apply if there is a simple, straightforward, genuine third-party sale of company shares, even if one of the main reasons for the sale is to save tax.

Overdrawn Directors Loan Accounts

When a director owes their company money, the overdrawn loan account is an *asset* of the company. When there is a members' voluntary liquidation, it is common practice to distribute this asset to the shareholders *in specie* (i.e. not as a cash payment).

In other words, instead of the director repaying the company and receiving the cash back as a liquidation distribution in their capacity as a shareholder, the distribution is handled as a paper transaction.

In the past, the distribution of the director's loan account during a liquidation was treated as a capital distribution and taxed at a reduced rate if the company owner was entitled to business asset disposal relief.

Apparently, however, HMRC is now taking the approach that such distributions are subject to Income Tax at the dividend tax rates (i.e. at up to 39.35%).

For this reason, several expert tax commentators recommend that directors with overdrawn loan accounts should pay back their loans to the company before the company enters liquidation.

Conclusion

There is some uncertainty among tax professionals as to how the various anti-avoidance measures will be applied in practice when a company is liquidated.

Where capital gains treatment is in doubt, it may make sense to pay actual dividends over several tax years, rather than making a single large distribution when you wind up the company.

Adopting a phased approach to the withdrawal of profits from your company may allow you to enjoy the 10.75% tax rate that applies to basic rate taxpayers, rather than the 35.75% or 39.35% tax rates that apply to higher and additional rate taxpayers.

Adopting this strategy over several tax years could allow a significant amount of cash to be extracted from the company, especially when the amounts taxed at 10.75% can be doubled up in the case of a company owned by a couple.

A Final Note on Business Asset Disposal Relief

Business asset disposal relief is complicated and constantly changing. This chapter is by no means a definitive guide.

There are various quirks in the legislation that we have deliberately ignored for simplicity's sake, but which could see the relief denied in certain circumstances. For this reason, anyone who wants to benefit from business asset disposal relief should seek advice from a tax professional with experience in this area.

And finally, please note that, although business asset disposal relief is currently available, its value has been eroded significantly in recent years, and we would not be surprised to see it scrapped altogether at some point in the foreseeable future. In other words, it may be unwise to make plans under the assumption the relief will still be available when you sell or wind up your company.

Chapter 45

Employee Ownership Trusts

In the previous chapter, we saw how, thanks to business asset disposal relief, company owners may be able to pay CGT at a reduced rate when they sell their businesses.

Another alternative in some cases may be to sell your company to something called an employee ownership trust. Before 26th November 2025, qualifying sales to such a trust were completely tax free. Sadly, this complete exemption no longer applies, but half of the gain arsing on a qualifying sale still enjoys exemption, giving rise to an effective CGT rate of just 12% (24%/2).

With an employee ownership trust, the company ends up being owned by a trust for the benefit of employees generally (shares are not earmarked for individual employees).

Note, employee ownership trusts are not to be confused with the much-discredited use of employee benefit trusts to give employees interest-free loans that were supposedly tax free. The CGT relief for the sale of company shares to employee ownership trusts was introduced in the 2014 Finance Act and therefore has the Government's blessing.

A typical business sale would take place as follows:

- An employee ownership trust is established.
- Shares in the company are sold to the trustees of the employee ownership trust. An independent valuation will be required so the correct market value is used.
- The trust does not need to have any money to buy the company. The purchase consideration will typically take the form of a debt owed to the original shareholders.
- The company will contribute its earnings to the employee ownership trust to pay off the original owners over a number of years. These gifts of earnings are not an allowable expense for CT purposes, so money will need to be retained by the company to settle its CT bills.
- The employees will only be indirect owners of the company and will therefore not receive dividends. Instead, the trustees of the employee ownership trust can arrange for bonuses to be paid by the company. Annual cash bonuses of up to £3,600 per employee are allowed free from Income Tax (but not NI).

Qualifying Requirements

Various conditions have to be met to qualify for the tax benefits:

- The company must be a trading company or the holding company of a trading group
- The trustees of the employee ownership trust must provide benefits to all eligible employees on the same terms. It is, however, possible to distinguish between employees based on their levels of pay, length of service, and hours worked.
- The trustees of the employee ownership trust must acquire at least 51% of the company and thus have a controlling interest. Up to 49% of the shares can, however, remain in direct ownership.
- The directors can remain at the company following the sale. However, the number of continuing shareholders (and any other 5% participators) who are directors or employees (or persons connected to them, such as close relatives) must not exceed 40% of the total number of employees. So, if a company has five employees only two of them can be the original shareholders. This is to show there has been a genuine change of ownership in the business.

Business asset disposal relief cannot be claimed on a qualifying sale to an employee ownership trust. The annual exemption and reduced 18% rate for gains falling into the basic rate band continue to apply, however.

The CGT relief can be clawed back if a disqualifying event occurs before the end of the *fourth* tax year after the tax year of disposal.

The former owners of the company (and people connected to them) are prevented from retaining control of the company by controlling the employee ownership trust itself.

Employee ownership trusts are supposed to be long-term ownership vehicles, but it is possible that the 51% controlling interest requirement could be breached if, for example, the trustees decide to sell shares in the company to a third party on the basis that this is in the interest of the beneficiaries of the trust.

Of course, selling to an employee ownership trust will not appeal to all company owners. The upfront costs could be high and some owners may be put off by the potentially long delay in receiving payment for the sale of the business. If the company starts making losses, the employee ownership trust may be unable to pay the original owners.

Furthermore, now that the relief only covers half the gain, there is the problem of funding a CGT bill long before receiving the sale proceeds.

Nonetheless, selling to an employee ownership trust has other benefits besides the 50% tax exemption. It can be a good way to solve succession issues, where there are no family members willing to carry on with the business and the owners are unwilling to sell to a competitor or third party with all the hassle this may involve.

Part 7

Salary & Dividends: Practical Issues & Dangers

Chapter 46

How to Avoid the Minimum Wage Rules

If you take a small salary from your company (for example, £12,570 or less) there may be a danger of falling foul of the national living wage rules.

Where wages are too low and the rules apply, HMRC will force the company to make up the shortfall. Bigger wage payments may result in bigger NI bills for both the company and the director.

There is also a penalty equivalent to 200% of the unpaid wages with a maximum penalty of £20,000 per worker. Those found guilty will also be considered for disqualification from being a company director for up to 15 years.

However, the key point to note about the national living wage is that it only applies to directors if they have a contract of employment.

Due to the informal set up in many small companies, there may be some uncertainty as to whether an employment contract exists between the director and the company (employment contracts do not need to be in writing).

However, it is generally accepted among the tax profession that if you do not issue yourself with an explicit contract of employment, the minimum and living wage regulations do not apply.

This means you should be able to continue paying yourself a small salary, even if it is less than the national living wage.

However, risk-averse company owners (those worried about potential penalties) might consider paying themselves enough salary to satisfy the minimum wage regulations.

National Living Wage Rates
The national living wage (NLW) now applies to those aged 21 and over. The rate is £12.71 per hour from 1st April 2026.

If you spend, say, 35 hours per week actively managing your business, the total salary due for 2026/27 will be: 35 x 52 weeks x £12.71 = £23,132.

Such a salary could result in unwelcome NI charges. The NI payable by the director would be £845 and £2,720 would be payable by the company (unless it has spare employment allowance available).

Of course, every case is different and some directors will be able to argue they spend fewer hours actively managing the business.

Although it may seem the best strategy is to simply not have a contract of employment, there may be other reasons why having such a contract is important.

Note that directors are exempt from the national living wage with respect to hours spent performing their duties as directors: as distinct from hours spent managing the business. In a small company, this can often be a difficult distinction to draw. But if, for example, the company owner appointed their spouse/partner as a director, but that spouse/partner did no other work for the company apart from fulfilling their duties as director, then the national living wage would not apply in their case.

Family Members Who Aren't Directors
It is possible some family members will be employees of the company but not directors. These individuals are subject to the national minimum wage or living wage for all hours spent working in the business. The exemption for members of your own household does not apply where the employer is a company.

However, it is possible that, if they only work part time, the salary that must be paid to them will still be within the typical optimal salary for 2026/27 of £12,570.

Chapter 47

Is My Salary Tax Deductible?

One of the benefits of getting your company to pay you a salary is that the amount will normally be a tax-deductible expense and reduce the company's CT bill. However, there is no automatic right to CT relief. The amount paid has to be justified by the work carried out for the business and the individual's level of responsibility.

While this may not be an important issue for company owners who work full time in the business and pay themselves a small salary, it may be important if you start paying salaries to other family members, in particular those who only work part time.

The question of whether your employment income will attract CT relief may also become an issue if you decide to pay yourself a large one-off bonus, if you take a higher salary to utilise the company's spare employment allowance, or if you are following the large salary method we looked at in Chapter 26. Factors that may determine whether a salary or bonus payment is tax deductible include:

- The number of hours worked in the business
- The individual's legal obligations and responsibilities
- The pay received by the company's other employees
- The pay received by employees at other companies performing similar roles
- The company's performance and ability to pay salaries/bonuses.

In the case of large one-off bonus payments made only to the company's director/shareholders it may be necessary to document the commercial rationale for the payment to show it is justifiable. This can be done in the minutes of a directors' board meeting. It may also be advisable to record the approval of any bonus in the minutes of a shareholders' meeting.

Finally, remember it is the director's whole remuneration package that must be justified in order to obtain CT relief: including pension contributions and other benefits provided.

Chapter 48

Salary vs Dividends: Non-Tax Factors

Most of this guide focuses on choosing the most tax efficient *level* of income and the most tax efficient *mix* of income (i.e. salary versus dividends).

However, when it comes to withdrawing money from your company there are lots of other non-tax factors that may need to be considered. This chapter provides a short overview of some of the issues but is not definitive.

Cashflow and Working Capital Needs

When deciding how much income you withdraw from your company you must consider the cashflow and working capital requirements of the business. It would naturally be irresponsible to pay yourself a large bonus or dividend if this affects the company's ability to carry on its business.

If you prefer to retain the cash in your company, it may be possible for a dividend to be declared but not paid out. The dividend can simply be credited to the director's loan account and withdrawn at a later date when it is more convenient. Income Tax will still be payable on any dividends declared but not paid.

Dividends & Company Insolvency

Dividends should not be declared when the company is insolvent or if the payment of those dividends will render the company insolvent. Dividends that are deemed illegal may have to be repaid, even if this results in the director being made bankrupt or being forced into an individual voluntary arrangement (IVA).

Director's Ability to Borrow

If you take a small salary and the rest of your income as dividends there is a possibility this will affect your ability to borrow money personally.

Some lenders may only be interested in the level of your salary and ignore your dividends, being unfamiliar with this sort of pay structuring. Others, on the other hand, will look at the complete picture and will look at your recent tax returns and the company's most recent accounts when assessing your ability to repay a loan.

Effect on Share Value

The value of a company is usually based on a multiple of its after-tax profits. A small minority shareholder's stake, however, is often valued according to the dividend history of the company. A consistent or steadily increasing annual dividend may enhance the value of the shares.

Company's Profitability

The payment of a large salary or bonus will depress the company's profits. This may affect the company's ability to borrow.

It could also affect the amount received in the event of a sale of the company or its underlying business: although more sophisticated buyers will generally discount actual payments to directors and substitute a market rate when valuing the company's shares or business goodwill.

Government Support

It's worth remembering that during the covid pandemic, one of the groups that received very little support from the government was small company directors paying themselves a small salary.

While sole traders and business partners were able to claim grants and regular employees could get most of their pay, all a small company director could claim was a proportion of their salary and then *only if* they stopped work in their business. Those following the small salary/large dividend route received very little support. Perhaps this was the Government's revenge for years of tax savings.

There is always the risk of something similar happening again one day, so it's worth remembering what happened last time!

Chapter 49

Paying Salaries & Dividends: Profits & Paperwork

Real Time Information

Employers have to report salary payments to HMRC under the Real Time Information (RTI) regime. Under real time information, employers are required to submit a Full Payment Submission (FPS) to HMRC at the same time or before each payment is made to a director or employee.

The idea is to make sure the right amount of tax is paid at the right time. Under the previous system, employers generally only had to report payroll information to HMRC at the end of the year.

Under RTI, the directors' own salaries could result in additional payroll costs (for example, in small 'husband and wife' companies or 'one man band' companies, where the only salaries paid are those of the directors themselves).

Where the directors receive small salaries, it may be cheaper and easier to register with HMRC as an annual scheme and pay salaries as a single annual lump sum (for example, in March just before the end of the tax year). With annual schemes an FPS is only expected in the month of payment and HMRC only has to be paid once a year. However, it is only possible to register as an annual scheme if all employees are paid annually at the same time.

Once a business is registered as an annual scheme, an Employer Payment Summary (EPS) is not required for the 11 months of the tax year where no payments are made to the directors. Schemes not registered as annual schemes have to make monthly submissions, even if no salaries are paid.

Overdrawn Loan Accounts

An additional problem may arise where directors withdraw cash from their companies and only later decide how these payments are to be treated (for example, as salaries or dividends).

Where the director's loan account is overdrawn, an amount withdrawn and subsequently designated as salary could result in a late filing penalty under RTI.

When directors withdraw money from their companies, it is essential to decide up front the nature of the payment (salary, loan, dividend, reimbursement of expenses, etc) and to have evidence supporting that decision. For example, where a director borrows money from the company, the terms of the loan should be set out in writing. Withdrawals by directors that cannot be categorised might be treated as earnings by HMRC unless the company can prove otherwise.

Loan Accounts in Credit

The exception to these stringent requirements is where the director is simply drawing from a director's loan account that is in credit (the company owes them money). In these cases, withdrawals can usually be safely debited to the loan account (provided it does not then become overdrawn) and then a salary, dividend, etc, might later be declared and credited to the loan account to re-establish the balance. The supporting evidence still has to be there, but there is a little more time to sort things out.

Dividends

Distributable Profits

Under the Companies Act, a company cannot legally pay a dividend unless it has sufficient distributable profits to cover it.

A company's distributable profits are its accumulated realised profits, less accumulated realised losses. This information can generally be found in the company's most recent annual accounts. It is critical to understand that distributable profits are based on the company's accumulated after-tax *accounting* profits, subject to a deduction for any profits not yet realised (e.g. on revaluation of an investment property still held by the company).

Accounting profits differ from taxable profits in many ways. The two key areas are that fixed assets (buildings, vehicles, equipment, etc) are treated completely differently for accounting and tax purposes, and other expenditure that is disallowed for tax purposes (e.g. business entertaining) must still be deducted from accounting profits.

The company's accounts must also be prepared under statutory accounting standards and generally accepted accounting practice (GAAP), and this leads to many notional adjustments that make little or no sense to the layperson, such as depreciation, a weird thing called deferred tax (don't worry, you don't actually have to pay it), and the adjustment to the value of a loan to a director discussed in Chapter 37.

Despite the rather hypothetical nature of these adjustments, they all reduce the company's distributable profits available to pay out as dividends.

The good news on the other hand, though, is that one major set of tax deductions, which reduce the company's taxable profits, are not deducted from its distributable profits: capital allowances.

Let's look at a brief example: not to explain all the strange nuances of accounting practice, but just to give you some idea of the difference between taxable profits and distributable profits.

Example: *In its first year of trading, Newco Ltd makes a profit of £200,000 before accounting for two last items: £5,000 spent on business entertaining and £80,000 spent on new commercial vehicles and equipment. For tax purposes, the entertaining cannot be claimed, but a deduction of £80,000 can be claimed for the asset purchases (under the annual investment allowance). This results in a taxable profit of £120,000 and a tax charge of £28,050.*

Now, along comes the company's accountant, Suzie Strict. She insists on applying a depreciation charge of £20,000 to the equipment (£80,000 x 25%). This, together, with the entertaining expenditure, reduces the company's accounting profit before tax to £175,000 (£200,000 – £5,000 – £20,000). Then, in addition to the actual CT bill, Suzie also includes a deferred tax charge of £15,000 (I could explain why, but does anyone really care?)

As a result, the company's profit after tax per its accounts is £131,950 (£175,000 less £28,050 of actual tax and £15,000 of pretend, hypothetical tax).

In this case, the company's distributable profits are £131,950, and that's how much dividend it can pay (subject to any other practical or legal restrictions).

Most accounting adjustments (e.g. accruals or stock valuation) affect the company's tax bill, but some, such as depreciation, do not. Nonetheless, with a few exceptions (e.g. investment property revaluations), they nearly all affect the company's ability to pay dividends.

Note that the 25% depreciation charge used in the example is purely an illustration. The charge will vary from case to case.

It is not necessary for the company to actually make a profit in the year the dividend is paid, as long as there are sufficient accumulated distributable profits (after tax) from previous years.

So, all is not necessarily lost if your company has been experiencing difficult trading conditions in recent times. As long as there are sufficient distributable profits from previous years, it may be possible to continue paying dividends.

Where the most recent annual accounts do not show sufficient profits, interim or management accounts can be prepared with more up to date information. This may be useful if business conditions have improved since the last accounts were prepared.

It's also important to remember directors have a duty to promote the company's success, protect its assets, and take reasonable action to ensure the company can pay its debts. If future trading losses are expected, this is a factor that should be taken into account when considering the cashflow implications of any proposed dividend.

Thus, even if the most recent set of accounts show there are sufficient distributable profits, the directors must take account of any change in the company's financial position since the accounts date and consider whether the company will remain solvent after any proposed dividend is paid. The key point is that directors must act honestly and reasonably at all times.

Before paying any dividends, it is probably wise to speak to your accountant to check whether the company does indeed have sufficient distributable profits.

If the company does not have sufficient distributable profits to cover its dividend payments, the dividends will be illegal and the shareholder will be liable to repay the company. While this is seldom enforced unless the company becomes insolvent, it is important to be aware of the legal position and wise to 'play it safe' by avoiding any illegal dividends.

For details of some recent, and rather bizarre, changes to the accounting standards for small companies that affect both taxable profits and accounting profits (and hence also distributable profits), see the Taxcafe guide *Putting it Through the Company*.

Dividend Formalities & Paperwork

If the proper formalities are not observed, it is possible HMRC will try to tax dividends as employment income. To help avoid any such challenge it is essential to ensure dividends are properly declared and you have the supporting paperwork to prove it. This includes:

- Holding a directors' board meeting to recommend the dividend payment (with written minutes to prove the meeting took place).
- Holding a general meeting of the company's members (i.e. shareholders) to approve the dividend payment (with written minutes to prove the meeting took place).
- Issuing a dividend confirmation to each shareholder.

See Appendix A for sample documentation.

Some commentators also argue it is not advisable to declare dividends monthly because this will look more like salary income, especially if the above formalities are neglected.

A better alternative would be an infrequent dividend credited to the director's loan account which can then be drawn down throughout the year.

Paying a dividend towards the end of the tax year, when it may be easier to work out how much Income Tax will be payable, is possibly best in timing terms. If a dividend is paid at the beginning of the year and income from other sources (for example, rental income) turns out to be higher than expected, the company owner could end up paying tax at a higher rate on their dividend income.

Interim versus Final Dividends

A final dividend must be recommended by the directors and endorsed by a shareholders' meeting. For tax purposes, the dividend is treated as paid on that date (unless a later date is specified). Interim dividends can be authorised at the discretion of directors and are recognised for tax purposes only when they are paid, for example by crediting the director's loan account.

Chapter 50

Reporting Requirements

From 2025/26 onwards, most small company directors are required to report dividends received from their own company separately to other dividends on their tax return. Ominously, the dividends from their own company now have to be included in the employment section of the tax return.

This new requirement applies to director/shareholders of 'close companies'. Broadly speaking, a company is a close company if it is under the control of five people or less. Control is generally deemed to exist where more than 50% of the company's shares are held. For this purpose, shares held by an individual's connected persons (Appendix B) must be treated as if held by the individual themselves. A company where all the shareholders are directors is also a close company.

As well as the amount of dividends received from the company during the tax year, the director must also report:

- The name of the company
- Its company registration number
- The percentage of the share capital that they own in the company

HMRC has also recently consulted on proposals to introduce further reporting requirements for transactions between close companies and their directors.

This may result in companies having to report the date, amount, and recipient of each individual transaction with directors, as well as identifying the recipient with their NI number and unique taxpayer reference: that's the ten digit code you will see on your tax return, often referred to as your UTR.

Big Brother is not only watching, he's getting ready to put small company directors under the microscope.

Chapter 51

Dividends Taxed as Earnings and Other Potential Dangers

Back in 2013, HMRC managed to get something called the general anti-abuse rule (GAAR) onto the statute books. As the name implies, the rule is aimed at blocking abusive tax arrangements. An arrangement is considered abusive if it cannot reasonably be regarded as a reasonable course of action: commonly referred to as the double reasonableness test.

Clearly this is very subjective, but HMRC has sought to reassure us there is a high threshold for showing that tax arrangements are abusive:

"In respect of any particular arrangement there might be a range of views as to whether it was a reasonable course of action: it is possible that there could be a reasonably held view that the tax arrangements were a reasonable course of action, and also a reasonably held view that the arrangement is not a reasonable course of action. In such circumstances the tax arrangements will not be abusive for the purposes of the GAAR."

An indicator that tax arrangements are not abusive is if they were established practice when entered into and HMRC indicated its acceptance of that practice at the time.

On the other hand, tax arrangements may be abusive if, for example, the tax result is different to the real economic result, such as tax deductions or tax losses significantly greater than actual expenses or real economic losses.

If you think all of the above is a bit vague, you are not alone. Even the best tax brains in the land don't know what this test means in practice. When legislation contains words like 'reasonable' and 'abusive' you know you have to be on your guard!

The question for us in this guide is: could the anti-abuse rule ever be used to attack 'normal' or 'mainstream' tax planning carried out by small company owners, such as taking small salaries and large dividends? Thankfully, most tax experts are confident that well-established, conventional tax planning will not be attacked by HMRC using the GAAR. Instead, the focus is on 'aggressive' or 'artificial' tax avoidance schemes.

This view is backed up by HMRC guidance, which says the following about small company dividends:

"Just as it is essential to understand what the GAAR is targeted at, so it is equally essential to understand what it is not targeted at. To take an obvious example, a taxpayer deciding to carry on a trade can do so either as a sole trader or through a limited company whose shares he or she owns and where he or she works as an employee. Such a choice is completely outside the target area of the GAAR, and once such a company starts to earn profits a decision to accumulate most of the profits to be paid out in the future by way of dividend, rather than immediately paying a larger salary, is again something that should in any normal trading circumstances be outside the target area of the GAAR."

Phew! So, routine tax planning carried out by small company owners extracting money from their company as tax efficiently as possible is safe from the GAAR... but what about case law?

There have been some tax cases which demonstrate there is a potential danger that dividends paid to a director/shareholder could, in some circumstances, be vulnerable to an NI liability and possibly a full PAYE charge.

It is unlikely these decisions will ever affect small family companies with simple share structures, but it's worth us taking a look at them as they illustrate the courts' attitude to this area of tax planning.

P A Holdings: PA Holdings switched from a conventional bonus arrangement to a more intricate structure whereby an employee benefit trust was funded by the company, which in turn awarded preference shares to employees. These preference shares duly paid a dividend after which they were redeemed.

The company and its employees argued the dividends should be taxed as dividends using dividend tax rates and without any PAYE or NI implications. By contrast, HMRC took the view that the dividends were simply earnings and the normal PAYE and NI payments should have been deducted from them.

The Court of Appeal decided the dividends were indeed earnings for employment and should therefore suffer deductions of Income Tax at source through PAYE. Both employers' and employees' NI should also have been paid. PA Holdings initially decided to appeal to the Supreme Court but later threw in the towel.

Uniplex (UK) Ltd: Uniplex was sold a scheme aimed at giving employees dividend income instead of remuneration, issuing different classes of share to each employee. This type of arrangement is generally known as alphabet shares.

The scheme failed as it was not implemented as planned. However, the First Tier Tribunal judge added that the scheme, even if implemented correctly, might still have failed.

Practical Implications

The practical implications of these cases relate to the boundary between normal dividend payments and those which, under the PA Holdings/Uniplex principles, would be treated as employment earnings and hence attract Income Tax and NI deductions through PAYE. For instance, in PA Holdings the First Tier Tribunal said:

"if something is paid out as a distribution by a company to an investing shareholder then the issue of derivation may arise if the shareholder is also an employee. The facts may show that the derivation of a dividend from a share may not be related to earnings because the acquisition and ownership of the share was not related to earnings or more generally to the status of the individual as an employee of the company"

In Uniplex, the First Tier Tribunal said: *"The PA Holdings case is authority for the proposition that payments from a party other than the employer can be from an employee's employment"* and *"It may well have still been the case that the full amount would have been taxable because employees had given no consideration for the payment other than their services"*

What all this demonstrates is there can come a point where dividends paid to an employee-shareholder could be vulnerable to an NI liability, and possibly a full PAYE charge.

However, both these cases involved complex tax avoidance schemes: a million miles from the normal, routine tax planning whereby a small company owner structures the payments they take from their company in the most tax efficient way.

Most tax advisers would argue the aggressive tax planning undertaken by PA Holdings (trying to change bonuses into dividends for a large number of employees) is entirely different to the profit extraction model of most small companies.

As yet, the simple salary versus dividend planning we have examined throughout most of this guide, where we are concerned only with payments to one or more director/shareholders, each of whom holds a sizeable stake in a company with only one class of share capital, would not appear to be threatened by the decisions in the more complex cases examined above.

Nonetheless, there is a fear among some more cautious advisers that cases like these might one day be seized upon by HMRC as having created a wider precedent they can apply to any employer that pays dividends to its staff.

The most vulnerable are those who use tax planning HMRC may view as aggressive. We already know some of their main targets. Those we would class as ***'Close to Extinction'*** include:

- Large scale contrived arrangements where dividends are created for tax avoidance purposes (as in *PA Holdings*).
- 'Alphabet' share arrangements, where different classes of shares (A, B, C, etc) have no substantive rights other than to dividends and are used to share profits in a way that relates to the amount of work carried out in the business (by substituting dividends for salaries or bonuses).

These contrived arrangements have probably had their day and there is a strong risk that dividends paid under these circumstances will be taxed as employment income. In short, we wouldn't touch these types of schemes with a bargepole.

Beyond these, there are other arrangements that we would view as being on the ***'Endangered Species'*** list, including:

- Alphabet share arrangements or other shares that have no capital or voting rights, used to divert income to spouses/partners or other family members with lower Income Tax rates. These arrangements are highly likely to fall foul of the settlements legislation.
- Directors' loans written off and taxed as dividends.
- Dividend waivers used to divert income to other shareholders, for example where a director waives their own dividends so that their spouse/partner can receive more income. HMRC succeeded in challenging dividend waivers in the case of *Donovan & McLaren v HMRC.*
- Situations where previous salaries paid to minority shareholders have been reduced in favour of dividends.

While these arrangements might still work in some cases, we would urge anyone considering using them to proceed with extreme caution and to seek independent professional advice (independent of whoever is recommending them to you).

Back to Normal

The sixty-four-thousand-dollar question is: where does all this leave the average small company owner taking a small salary and the rest of their income as dividends?

At the time of writing, it would appear the vast majority of small companies are not under any threat of attack, but this state of affairs could change in the future. The small salary/big dividend tax planning technique may not continue to produce the same savings company owners are currently able to enjoy indefinitely. There is a danger, no matter how small, that HMRC may try to tax your dividends as earnings at some point in the future.

Some tax advisers recommend taking a salary slightly larger than the 'optimal' amounts, so that at least some Income Tax and NI is paid by the director. Some even argue that if you are currently taking a salary larger than the usual 'baseline' salary of £12,570, you should not reduce it.

However, there are still many tax advisers who are content to continue with the current, long-standing tax planning technique, where the most optimal salary is taken each year, until such time as there is an actual change in the law that puts a stop to it.

Remember, HMRC do not make tax law, they only administer it. It's only judges and politicians who can change the law: now isn't that comforting!

Part 8

More Tax Planning Ideas

Chapter 52

How to Pay Less CGT by Postponing Dividends

The main Capital Gains Tax (CGT) rates applying to disposals made after 29th October 2024 are:

- 18% for basic rate taxpayers
- 24% for higher or additional rate taxpayers

Where the individual is entitled to business asset disposal relief, the whole gain (subject to the lifetime limit of £1 million: see Chapter 44) is taxed at 18%. This relief is generally only available when you sell or wind up a trading business. When business asset disposal relief is not available, the CGT rate depends on how much income you've earned during the tax year.

The basic-rate band is £37,700, which means you can have up to £37,700 of capital gains taxed at the lower rate this year. The maximum CGT saving that can be achieved by reducing your income and freeing up your basic-rate band is as follows:

£37,700 x 6% = £2,262 (18% instead of 24%)

Postponing Dividends

If you expect to realise a large capital gain, for example by disposing of a buy-to-let property, you may be able to save some tax by making sure the disposal takes place during a tax year in which your taxable income is quite low.

In this respect, company owners can control their incomes more easily than regular employees, sole traders, or business partners.

The company itself can keep trading and generating profits, but the company owner can make sure very little of these profits are extracted and taxed in his or her hands.

Example: *Richard, a company owner, sells his second home in March 2027, realising a gain of £40,700 after deducting all buying and selling costs. Deducting his annual CGT exemption of £3,000 leaves a taxable gain of £37,700.*

Richard hasn't paid himself any dividends during the current tax year and decides to postpone paying any so that his £37,700 capital gain is taxed at 18% instead of 24%. This simple piece of planning saves Richard £2,262 in CGT.

Richard can still pay himself a tax-free salary of £12,570 to utilise his Income Tax personal allowance. Utilising the Income Tax personal allowance does not interfere with the CGT calculation.

Limitations

Although postponing dividends could help you pay less CGT, it's probably not worth doing this unless you can withdraw the postponed dividends in a future tax year and pay no more than 10.75% tax. If you take a bigger dividend in a later tax year, and end up paying 35.75% Income Tax, you may end up worse off overall.

Example continued: *In the above example Richard postponed taking a dividend of £37,700 to free up his basic rate band and pay 18% CGT.*

If during 2027/28 he takes an additional dividend of £37,700, on top of his usual salary and maximum dividend taxed at 10.75%, he will pay additional Income Tax of £13,478 (£37,700 x 35.75%). If he had taken that income in 2026/27, however, he would have paid Income Tax of £3,999: so he ends up paying £9,479 more Income Tax.

He saved £2,262 in CGT in 2026/27, but pays an additional £9,479 in Income Tax in 2027/28. Overall, Richard is £7,217 worse off.

Postponing dividends from 2026/27 to 2027/28 may also be a bad idea from a cashflow point of view: see Chapter 8.